Titles From GICPress

ORGANIZATIONAL CONSULTING: A GESTALT APPROACH
Edwin C. Nevis

GESTALT RECONSIDERED: A NEW APPROACH TO CONTACT AND RESISTANCE
Gordon Wheeler

THE NEUROTIC BEHAVIOR OF ORGANIZATIONS
Uri Merry and George I. Brown

GESTALT THERAPY: PERSPECTIVES AND APPLICATIONS
Edwin C. Nevis

THE COLLECTIVE SILENCE: GERMAN IDENTITY AND THE LEGACY OF SHAME
Barbara Heimannsberg and Christopher J. Schmidt

COMMUNITY AND CONFLUENCE: UNDOING THE CLINCH OF OPPRESSION
Philip Lichtenberg

BECOMING A STEPFAMILY
Patricia Papernow

ON INTIMATE GROUND: A GESTALT APPROACH TO WORKING WITH COUPLES
Gordon Wheeler and Stephanie Backman

BODY PROCESS: WORKING WITH THE BODY IN PSYCHOTHERAPY
James I. Kepner

HERE, NOW, NEXT: PAUL GOODMAN AND THE ORIGINS OF GESTALT THERAPY
Taylor Stoehr

CRAZY HOPE & FINITE EXPERIENCE
Paul Goodman and Taylor Stoehr

IN SEARCH OF GOOD FORM: GESTALT THERAPY WITH COUPLES AND FAMILIES
Joseph C. Zinker

THE VOICE OF SHAME: SILENCE AND CONNECTION IN PSYCHOTHERAPY
Robert G. Lee and Gordon Wheeler

HEALING TASKS: PSYCHOTHERAPY WITH ADULT SURIVIVORS OF CHILDHOOD ABUSE
James I. Kepner

ADOLESCENCE: PSYCHOTHERAPY AND THE EMERGENT SELF
Mark McConville

GETTING BEYOND SOBRIETY: CLINICAL APPROACHES TO LONG- TERM RECOVERY
Michael Craig Clemmens

INTENTIONAL REVOLUTIONS: A SEVEN- POINT STRATEGY FOR TRANSFORMING ORGANIZATIONS
Edwin C. Nevis, Joan Lancourt and Helen G. Vassallo

IN SEARCH OF SELF: BEYOND INDIVIDUALISM IN WORKING WITH PEOPLE
Gordon Wheeler

THE HEART OF DEVELOPMENT: GESTALT APPROACHES TO WORKING WITH CHILDREN, ADOLESCENTS, AND THEIR WORLDS (2 Volumes)
Mark McConville and Gordon Wheeler

BACK TO THE BEANSTALK: ENCHANTMENT & REALITY FOR COUPLES
Judith R. Brown

THE DREAMER AND THE DREAM: ESSAYS AND REFLECTIONS ON GESTALT THERAPY
Rainette Eden Fantz and Arthur Roberts

GESTALT THERAPY—A NEW PARADIGM: ESSAYS IN GESTALT THEORY AND METHOD
Sylvia Fleming Crocker

THE UNFOLDING SELF
Jean-Marie Robine

In Search of Good Form

Joseph C. Zinker

Foreword by Gordon Wheeler

In Search of Good Form

Gestalt Therapy with Couples and Families

GICPress

Published by GICPress, Cambridge, Massachusetts
Gestalt Institute of Cleveland: 1517 Hazel Drive,
Cleveland, Ohio, 44106

Distributed by The Analytic Press, Inc., Hillsdale, NJ.

Library of Congress Card No. 94-29710
ISBN 0–88163-293-7
Credits on page 320

Second Printing

A Gestalt Institute
of Cleveland
publication

Contents

Foreword

To all those familiar with the Gestalt model and its many extensions and applications, the name Joseph C. Zinker needs no introduction. As a founder and leader of the Gestalt Institute of Cleveland for over three decades, he has been active in the training of thousands of clinicians and others in teaching and training programs, both in Cleveland and around the world, making him certainly one of the best-known and most widely revered teachers of the Gestalt model active today. For most of the past two decades, together with Sonia Nevis, he has co-led the Center for the Study of Intimate Systems, which has taken a leading role in pioneering the application of the Gestalt model to work with couples and families. Moreover, his popular and groundbreaking 1976 book, *Creative Process in Gestalt Therapy,* remains a best-seller and a classic in the articulation of a humanistic and holistic approach to psychotherapy and human development, with an impact far beyond the bounds of clinicians who already identify themselves with a specifically Gestalt approach.

In a very real sense, the book you are about to read is the long-awaited sequel to that pioneering and influential first volume. *In Search of Good Form* builds on the same basic Gestalt precepts that have guided and informed Zinker's work over the years—experiment and creativity, reliance on the natural human drive for growth and integration, the validation of emotion and passionate commitment as the keys to satisfaction, and a conception of the self as the artist of life. But Zinker moves beyond the individual to explore and articulate the dynamics and play of all these issues in those most challenging and deeply felt arenas of living (and of psychotherapeutic work): our intimate couple and family relationships themselves. Throughout this book, he emphasizes *seeing* and *being with* as the keys to a couple and family therapy that is truly phenomenological in its spirit, in the sense that the therapist stands with the patients in their co-creation and mutual articulation of their own experience, their own meaning. This contrasts with the approach of many schools, both newer and older, that would prefer (in the words of Erving Polster, another revered member of the pioneering generation of Gestalt teachers and therapists) to "reintroduce the couch"—that is, to interpose some fixed technique or analytical tool for viewing clients "objectively," from outside their experience, in order to make judgments about that experience and at the same time ensure a safe distance (for the therapist!) between "doctor" and "patient." There is no "couch" here, no procrustean rule for the grading and diagnosis of the construction of the client's experience, but rather a wise and humane method for searching together for the places where that experience may be blocked, or distorted, or impoverished, or lacking in passion, as well as for the concrete interpersonal gestures in couples and families that may support or diminish that self- and other-creating process. Therapy here is an art, a discipline—a *ritual,* to use Zinker's word—a particular kind of deep personal contact and not a substitute for it, not an "objectification" in which the subject or person is ultimately suppressed and lost, in the way of many other schools and approaches.

Which is not to say there is no methodology, no intellectual framework grounding and informing the work. There very much is, and Zinker devotes Part One of the book to the articulation and careful building up of that framework, with a theoretical richness that is completely without pedantry and never far from the actual lives and phenomenological reality of both clients and therapist. In Chapter One, he begins laying the groundwork in narrative form for the theoretical tools and concepts of the next six chapters. With his deft painter's hand and eye (Zinker is a successful professional artist in visual media), he sketches Fritz and Laura Perls as "improvizational artists," perceived by the staid psychoanalytic establishment of the post-war period "at best as renegades and at worst as quacks"—but then takes this life sketch one step further into theory by articulating the Perlsian distinction between "acting out" and "acting through," which is the crucial clinical/experiential distinction between action with and action without grounded awareness. In a sense, this is the hinge on which all of Zinker's work and indeed all of the Gestalt model swings. The sequence here is pure Zinker (and a pure example of what makes him such a successful and influential teacher and writer): first the concrete, the visual, the particular—and only then the theoretical elaboration or remark. Always first and foremost the inductive, the phenomenological, the experientially real; never the deductive, the rigidly procrustean, the abstract dictating the individual case.

Zinker then takes the same approach with other major influences on his work and on the Gestalt model for couple and family work in general: Whitaker, Satir, Minuchin, Bowen, and others—as well as a number of other figures and schools with which he differs sharply. At the same time, he begins here with the theme that will be the leitmotiv and open subtext of the book, which is the meaning of *aesthetics* and *form,* when applied to clinical work with couples and families, and to our experience of living. Typically, in Zinker's hands these terms do not remain abstractions, much less avoidances of the clinically real, but rather are built up carefully and eloquently as concrete descriptors of experience and as the building blocks of a model—the Interactive Cycle of Experience—for analyzing and intervening in the processes and quality of living itself.

Since the author himself gives his own "walking tour" of the remaining chapters at the end of Chapter One, I do not need to repeat that synopsis here. Rather, I will discuss each of the following eleven chapters briefly in terms of some of the major practical insights and applications offered to the reader, clinical or nonclinical, Gestalt oriented or otherwise.

Chapter Two introduces the reader to the underlying values and working assumptions of the Gestalt approach elaborated by Zinker and Nevis over the years. This in itself is striking: How long has it been since you picked up a clinical book that opened with an exposition of the author's *values*—and then went on to build the theoretical links between values and method, personal stance and clinical tools, that are the core of the Gestalt approach? At the heart of those values and assumptions is a proposition similar to one articulated by the distinguished art historian E. H. Gombrich, who based a lifetime of art criticism and aesthetic theory on the idea that certain visual forms, certain formal creations, are inherently more satisfying, more aesthetically pleasing than others—and that these "process" distinctions will hold across differences in medium, content, even culture. Likewise, Zinker begins the argument here for an *aesthetics of process,* which can then become a diagnostic tool, without reliance on cumbersome and arbitrary systems of behavioral rules and historical interpretations—which in any case make a poor guide to actual clinical intervention, as couple and family therapists know all too well. (It is worth noting here that Gombrich himself was very familiar with the Gestalt model, through the work of his lifelong friend, the eminent Gestalt psychologist James J. Gibson.)

Chapter Three takes up the issues involved with systems and boundaries, grounding these concepts in a new way, with particular attention to the Gestalt field theory of Kurt Lewin. What emerges for the clinician from this discussion is a new way of *seeing,* which comes out of Zinker's fertile union of the systemic and the aesthetic. Seeing, after all, is a constructivist activity, and not merely a matter of passive reception of what "is there." This is the core of the entire legacy of Gestalt psychology from the early decades of this century, which in turn transformed perceptual and cognitive psychology to such a degree that there really is no psychology today that is not fundamentally Gestalt in nature. And the whole point of a theory and method is to provide a guide for that construction—to tell us what to look at and what to look for. In the well-known dictum of Kurt Lewin that serves as an epigraph to Chapter Four, there is nothing so practical as a good theory. Zinker shows us the validity of that proposition directly, by encouraging the reader to take up a new stance and see the "whole picture" of the couple or family process, as well as the parts of which it is made up.

Zinker credits Nevis with development of the Gestalt Interactive cycle, which is taken up in Chapter Four. This tool or "lens" for viewing process is based in turn on the Gestalt Experience Cycle. The Gestalt Experience Cycle has grown out of the work of Perls and Goodman and forms the basis of much writing and development by members of the "Cleveland School" of Gestalt therapy and its many extensions and applications, ranging from individual and group therapy all the way to organizational development and political intervention. Here the key concepts are the familiar Gestalt ones of contact and awareness, which take on new directness and clarity for the clinician in Zinker's presentation, richly illustrated with clinical material.

The Gestalt concept of awareness is further developed in Chapter Five, which emphasizes the processes of change itself. Change, after all, is what psychotherapy is all about, yet many models of couple and family work do not directly address the question of what change is and how it comes about. The relationship of awareness to behavior and behavioral change goes right to the heart of the phenomenological approach advocated by Zinker and constitutes the central and organizing precept of the Gestalt model (as well as amounting to a complete paradigm shift, from the perspective of other models). We organize our own behavior, after all, in terms of our own *organized awareness,* about ourselves and our feelings and desires, our world and its perceived possibilities, and the relationships between and among these things (which constitute our goals and aims, toward which we move). Thus to change behavior, in any lasting and organized way, we have to change our awareness—of what the possibilities of satisfaction are in the world, and what the possible and permissible goals and feelings are for ourselves. To work "behaviorally," against the grain of our own perception of the dangers and possibilities for us in the world, is to create "resistance," which to Zinker simply means asking people to do things they are not supported to do, in their own view of the world and of themselves. Zinker's answer to this most frustrating and familiar of clinical dilemmas is first and always to *support the resistance.* The clinical mileage he gets out of this stance, again illustrated here with clinical vignettes, can serve as an inspiration and a model for all of us who struggle to help couples and families through the many difficult tasks and passages of life.

Chapter Six takes up the topic of resistance in more detail, building on Zinker's and others' previous work under the Gestalt model. Again, from the phenomenological perspective, resistance is understood in terms of what the person is trying to manage, or achieve, or keep at bay. And again, Zinker's clinical faith lies in the power of awareness—not to remove resistance necessarily (since that is not seen here as possible or even desirable), but to lift it to the level of choice, which is to say of greater integration into the couple's and family's goals, style of contact, and processes of living.

With Chapter Seven, we come to the end of the theoretical part of the book—though in the best Gestalt tradition, theory and application are interwoven throughout the book, each giving rise to the other, each enriching the other, each serving (in the familiar Gestalt terminology) as figure against the other's ground. *Boundary* is of course a key concept in couple and family therapy in general, much used but seldom defined. The Gestalt model offers a clarifying perspective here on the implications of the term *boundary* and on its role in the construction of meaning and the supporting of *energy* (another crucial and usually ill-defined term). Zinker shows that the quality and amount of energy available in a system to do the work of living together are directly dependent on the condition of the boundaries in the system—boundaries within people, boundaries between people, and boundaries between and among the various overlapping subsystems that may be important in the family at various times.

Chapter Eight begins the examination of practice. What is new here, in addition to the ongoing development of themes of theory and application that run through the book, is that Zinker, in contrast to so many writers in the field, tells us exactly how he goes about conducting a session: how he sets it up, what he says, what he looks for, follows, and supports—and why. This demystifies the process and leaves the reader in a position of enlightened autonomy, well placed to evaluate means in relation to outcomes, and thus to make choices supported by awareness—again, in the best Gestalt tradition.

Chapter Nine pursues similar issues, but now in the more complex field of the larger family system. Here, as elsewhere, Zinker's practice of making his "basic assumptions," "orienting principles," and underlying values obvious clarifies and grounds the work, orienting us (and no doubt the clients) as well as the author, and making the relationship between theory and action accessible to the reader. As in Chapter Eight on couples (and indeed, throughout the book), his insistence on viewing dynamics dialectically, in terms of the polar issues of life (self and other, individual and group, fusion and autonomy), avoids oversimplification of the organic processes and choices of living, and yields a theoretical system and methodological approach with a level of complexity commensurate with that of life itself.

Chapter Ten takes up one of these fundamental relational polarities—privacy versus sharing—and explores it with simple and stunning philosophical depth. Here the reader will find no easy answers or clinical/moral prescriptions, but rather a carefully nuanced exploration of the relationship between truth and intimacy—and between truth and injury as well. As always in Zinker's work, in place of judgments we find great concern for the issue of *support*. If people act destructively, or self-destructively, in this view the question is always why they are not supported to act better—by the people around them (including first and foremost the therapist), by their view of themselves, by their world as they know it. It is not that Zinker shrinks from identifying behavior as healthy or unhealthy (though he might prefer the terms *aesthetic* or *unaesthetic*), even right or wrong. Rather, he knows as a clinician and as a person that these categories are not helpful—that is, they do not lead to change, to better living. And maintaining the focus on better living (and the identity of "clinician" and "person") is another way of saying what this book is all about.

Nowhere is that point clearer than in Chapter Eleven. Again, Zinker moves straight to the real issues of living (and dying) that are crucial to the quality of family life, yet never adequately discussed in clinical literature. And again the emphasis is on contact, awareness, support—in a context of faith in the inherent human and relational drive for cohesion, integration, creativity, and meaning.

In Chapter Twelve—a concluding chapter—Zinker offers a "meditation" on the aesthetics of process, or what he has called *good form* all through this book. In a sense, he ends where he began, with an articulation of the values that guide and inform his work—values of grace, movement, belongingness, relationship, "isness," the validity of experience, wholeness of form, commitment, growth, particularity, and aesthetics.

And what, finally, does he mean by the term *aesthetics,* in the context of a work on couples and families? Let me try to answer that question here, in good Zinker fashion, with a particular vignette, a memory from some years ago, from a time of preparation for a mutual friend's wedding. I remember asking Zinker on that occasion what marriage itself means. "Marriage?", he "squinted" into the distance, just the way he describes doing in Chapter One. "Marriage . . . " (long pause here, for reflection or possibly for effect) "means something *you can't just walk away from.*" Then another long pause. "Well," he added, "I suppose you *could* . . . but it wouldn't be *aesthetic.*"

Being "aesthetic" has to do with integrity, connectedness, wholeness, commitment to form. In his moving prologue to this volume, Zinker speaks of the integrity of his colleague Sonia Nevis, whom he credits with a central role in the creation of the ideas in this book. Such is Nevis's respect for the validity and integrity of each person's experience, Zinker says, that in all the years of their collaboration he has never once heard her speak ill of a couple or a family, out of their hearing. Such integrity, he concludes, is hard to come by in this world.

The same can be said of Zinker's commitment to aesthetic form and the related commitments to hanging in, "hanging out," seeing, appreciating, and respecting that permeate the pages of this book. Such integrity of intentionality is likewise hard to come by in this world, in this day of magic bullets and bottom lines, or in any day. And the irony, of course, is that by privileging *being with* over *doing to,* Zinker gets to the heart of the matter and gets results more effectively and efficiently than other, more "scientific" approaches can hope to do.

There is a tide and a pendulum in the affairs of psychotherapy, as in all human affairs. Two generations ago, Gordon Allport called for putting the "person back in psychology." Today, with the family under siege and the couple seemingly in full retreat, the voices calling for quick solutions and lowered expectations of living are more clamorous than ever. Yet it is just when those calls are at their loudest that we should be listening for the buried voices underneath, the voices reminding us that each person, each family, each relationship after all is a uniquely important ongoing creation, with its own aesthetic form and its own potential for grace and beauty in living. When the pendulum swings back—as it is already starting to do—in the direction of humanism and human creativity, Joseph C. Zinker will be there, as he has been for a generation now, eloquent, witty, impassioned, charming, wise, and ever aesthetic: the artist as therapist, and the person as the artist of life.

Cambridge, Massachusetts Gordon Wheeler
July 1994

Acknowledgments

From the beginning of this project in the early 1980s, Edwin Nevis coaxed and prodded me to write and provided funds in partial support toward that end. Before I acquired computer equipment, editorial comments and revisions of the manuscripts were patiently typed and retyped by Myrna Freedman and later by Marlene Eisman, my secretary. Major editorial shaping of the material in its early form was done by Shirley Loffer, who also edited *Creative Process in Gestalt Therapy*.

Sonia Nevis always helped. She provided material for the Gestalt theory of intervening with couples and families, principles and assumptions of family therapy, the notion of "acting with regret," and ideas about lying as a major obstacle to intimacy. These subjects were discussed in interviews with Eleanor Warner, Sonia, and myself for our *Newsletter* of the Center for the Study of Intimate Systems at the Gestalt Institute of Cleveland during the 1980s.

Reviews of early versions of the book and much-needed moral support came from various members of Gestalt Institutes in Cleveland, Phoenix, Calgary, Chicago, New England, Richmond, and New Orleans; from my therapy groups in Bloomington, Indiana, and Dallas, Texas; and from colleagues in Great Britain, Canada, Mexico, France, Germany, and Israel.

Many talks and years of working with my close friend and colleague Donna Rumenik have enriched my understanding of the following: how secrets and having a "secret life" profoundly shape couple and family relationships; that there are lone victimizers in families independent of the system involved; that Gestalt values must include the therapist's responsibility for the client; how couple intimacy involves curiosity and the repeated asking of questions and answering them; and that the therapist's "presence" is as important as her technique.

Friends who constantly reminded me that I *do* write well included Gordon Wheeler, Wendell Price, Philip Rosenthal, Thomas Reif, Anne Teachworth, Penny Backman, Joseph and Gloria Melnick, Richard Borofsky, Florence Zinker, Robert Barcus, Janine Corbeil, Barbara Fields, Judith Geer, Ed Harris, Edith Ott, Ira Rosenbaum, Claire Stratford, Robert Weiskopf, Erving and Miriam Polster, and many others.

The emphasis on *values* in this book, especially as related to aesthetics, came from Sonia Nevis, from Donna Rumenik, and from papers I delivered before the *Gestalt Journal* Conference in 1986 and at the British Gestalt conference at Cambridge, England, in 1993. The person who pushed me to highlight these values as being both unique and essential for this writing was Paul Shane. Paul, who is a brilliant writer, editor, and perpetual doctoral student of existential phenomenology at Saybrook Institute, came to my aid at the nadir of my hopes for this book. He added necessary crisp thinking and youthful energy to the production of the final manuscript. The finished book came to life in the "dialogic space" between Paul and myself.

Toward the end of the project Tony Skinner, a talented graphic artist, was brought into our fold to transform my rough sketches into line drawings.

Personal crises in my life repeatedly sideswiped my creative energy. These included my divorce and the deaths of my parents, brother, and uncle. The departure of these senior members of the Zinker family left me devastated. There was no wall behind me. I became the wall. But, as I discovered, every wall has an opening, and so, finally, I want to thank two great young women who have given me the will to create and to *live:* my daughters, Judith and Karen Zinker.

Cleveland Heights, Ohio Joseph C. Zinker
July 1994

For Sonia M. Nevis
and Edwin C. Nevis,
loyal colleagues and dearest friends

The Author

Joseph C. Zinker was born in Luck, Poland, in 1934. He lost all his extended family to the Nazis during World War II, while he and his parents and brother were scattered as refugees, eventually finding haven in Uzbekistan. After the war, he and his family spent four years in various displaced persons camps in Poland and Germany.

Zinker emigrated to New York City in 1949; although multilingual, he did not learn English until after his arrival in the United States. Throughout his childhood and adolescence, Zinker demonstrated artistic talent. He studied art in New York and later graduated from New York University in 1957 with an undergraduate degree in psychology and literature. He became interested in existentialism and phenomenology and attended graduate school at Western Reserve University in Cleveland, concentrating on learning theory and clinical psychology. He received his doctorate from there in 1963 after researching personality growth in terminal illness. His doctoral dissertation later led to his first publication, *Rosa Lee: Motivation and the Crisis of Dying* (1966).

In 1958, while he was in graduate school, Zinker entered a circle of early Gestalt therapists in Cleveland and began studying with Fritz and Laura Perls, Paul Goodman, and Isidore From. From this group developed the Gestalt Institute of Cleveland, where Zinker has served on the staff as well as head of the postgraduate faculty.

Combining his interests in art, creative experiment, and human movement, Zinker published *Creative Process in Gestalt Therapy* in 1976, which remains to this day a classic work in psychotherapy as an art form. It was judged "Book of the Year" by *Psychology Today* in 1977 and has been translated into three languages.

In the Gestalt professional community, Zinker is known for refining the clinical concepts of complementarity and middle ground in couples work and for the creative application of Gestalt experiment in individual, couple, family, and group settings. Since 1980 he has been active in the study of couples and families at the Center for Intimate Systems at the Gestalt Institute of Cleveland.

Artist, author, poet, and Gestalt therapist, Zinker has been in private practice since 1962. A popular lecturer and workshop leader, Zinker spends much of his time traveling in the United States, Canada, South America, Europe, and the Middle East. His current clinical interests are in the aesthetics and polemics of human interaction. He is the father of two daughters, both of whom are artists. He resides in Cleveland Heights, Ohio.

Prologue

More than a decade ago, Sonia Nevis invited me to join her as a faculty member in the Center for the Study of Intimate Systems at the Gestalt Institute of Cleveland. Our beloved colleague William Warner had recently died, leaving a hole in our programs. He had been an excellent Gestalt therapist, especially with children, couples, and families. Stepping into Bill's shoes felt like a bird taking the place of a beautiful horse.

I had little idea about therapy with couples or families. As a World War II refugee, I came from a tiny family: no aunts, cousins, sisters, nieces, nephews, grandparents. My parents, my brother, and I were not a cohesive family; today one would say that I came from a "dysfunctional family."

The family I created with my spouse was a bit healthier, but not much more so. Although I had written about couples, conflict, and love, I had no "blood knowledge" of the sanctity and beauty of couples, families, and how children belong and function in families.

Sonia ordered a pile of books for me and proceeded to teach me and feed me outlines of her lectures.

With each lecture and with each session supervising students, she taught me fundamental values not only of couple and family therapy but of being a healer in general:

- Respect people's experience *as it is.*
- Show regard for every "symptom" as people's creative effort to make life better for themselves.
- Every disagreement or lack of confluence with the therapist is "good" and an affirmation of patients' strength and ability to learn for themselves.
- Support a couple's or a family's resistance.
- Establish clear boundaries between your private sentiments and the patient's phenomenological world.
- Support competence.
- Provide an environment and a presence in which the worst offender can contact his or her pain and vulnerability.
- We are all capable of terrible actions—the therapist must have compassion for both victim and victimizer.
- The therapist protects or creates protective boundaries between persons in families—each person's experience is *real* and must be taken into account.
- The therapist's presence and affirmation of a family allows everyone to grow.
- Take a clear stand on disallowing abusive behavior between family members—set clear limits.
- The therapist models a good patient-leader and teacher.
- The therapist is supportive without being sentimental, long-winded, or self-indulgent.
- Each family has its own ethnic origins, its own textured culture. Do not force-feed a given family with your social or ethnic values: they may not apply anyway.

Working together for years as co-therapists, we developed a particular style. First, one of us introduces the other and (assuming this is the first session) asks the couple or family to tell us anything they want us to know "up front." Every member of the family is addressed. No one speaks for anyone else and no one is permitted to interrupt another. Sonia might gently say, "Excuse me, but let John finish, and we promise you that you'll have a chance to speak up." We meticulously follow up on our promises.

The next step is to have the family talk to each other, promising them that they can turn to us for help or that we will (respectfully) interrupt them to tell them our observations of their process.

After taking time to observe the family, we stop them and ask them to listen to our talk about their theme in that session. Turning to each other, we then compare themes and quickly choose one that makes sense to both of us. One of us then presents the theme to the family and asks if it makes sense to them and if that happens at home as well.

Typically, we hit the bull's-eye with our mutual observation. For example, we might say, "You are so good at telling each other your true feelings no matter how much it hurts you inside." This is presented as a strength of the family. As we work together, a second step emerges and the following intervention is made, often by Sonia, in which she explains the weak side of the family's strength. She might say, "Did you notice that when you say your true feelings, some other member of the family might cringe or shed a tear because it is so painful? What you may need to learn is how to check something out with another member of the family before telling the rest of the family a personal matter that is too difficult to take. Are we making sense by observing that?" We both then sit back and let the family talk about how indeed they have repeatedly hurt each other while observing a truth-telling principle and "telling all" in good faith. Members of the family might then complain to each other about being openly criticized and hurt in the service of telling truths and expressing true feelings.

At the right moment, Sonia and I excuse ourselves again,

interrupting the family and asking them to listen to our next consultation. The following generally happens: Sonia turns to me and says, "You know, Joseph, can you come up with an experiment that would help them practice expressing their feelings without hurting each other so much?"

And I might reply, "Well, one way to practice would be for each person to think about an idea or a feeling that they want to say to another person in the family and then tell that person how they imagine that person will respond without revealing the content of the feeling. For example, Joey would say to Marlene, 'If I told you what I am thinking about how you act with your boyfriend, I am afraid that you'll cry.' And then Marlene could say to Joey, 'I'm in no place to get criticized by you about this and I'm not ready to hear about it.' In this way, the experiment would teach the family how to gradually express feelings and at the same time to protect each other from unnecessary hurt."

Next, I might offer another experiment, possibly a third, and Sonia almost always chooses the one that is simplest and easiest to execute. Then one of us turns back to the family to slowly and carefully explain the purpose of the experiment, making sure that everyone understands what we are driving at.

If we are lucky, the family follows through and, with a little coaxing and support, experiences a degree of success in learning how to regulate expression of feelings so that each member's vulnerability is respected. Afterward, one of us gives feedback as to how well they did practicing the experiment. By now, the session is coming to an end, and one of us encourages the family to practice their new skill at home with each other. Sonia is gifted at making the full completion of the session with grace, charm, and good sense. She might say, "Look, it's snowing outside even harder than it was when you came in. How far are you driving on your way home?" or "Do you want to know a place to have a nice lunch?" The session is then over.

Sonia and I began to notice in the course of working with one another that we had developed and meticulously followed an aesthetic process—a process we have divided into the following steps:

1. Making small talk (initial "precontact")
2. Introducing and welcoming the family into the environment
3. Asking each individual to tell us how he or she experiences the family's problem
4. Carefully observing the family members' behavior with each other
5. Offering a major intervention that names a theme and a strength of the family
6. After some further discussion, proposing to the family that they need to learn a skill that is not fully developed
7. Teaching them how to do an experiment intended to enhance their functioning in the underdeveloped area
8. "Selling" the experiment to the family and making sure they understand its purpose
9. Watching the family work the experiment and occasionally coaching them if they get stuck
10. Asking them what they learned from the experiment and how they could practice their new skill at home

Sonia always follows through, completing every session by offering all the family members an opportunity to express how they feel.

Ideally, we need an hour and a half to perform this beautiful acrobatic ballet, after which the family leaves experiencing a sense of new learning and affirmation of their own goodness as human beings.

I learned from Sonia how not to waste words, how to conceive interventions with clarity and full intentionality, and how to show genuine appreciation for every family's effort to improve its lot in life. In all these years, I have never heard her say a critical word about a couple or family after they have left. Never! Such steadfast integrity is hard to come by in this world.

PART ONE

Theory

1

Our Common Ground

When Rabbi Noah, Rabbi Mordecai's son, assumed the succession after his father's death, his disciples noticed that there were a number of ways in which he conducted himself differently from his father, and asked him about this. "I just do as my father did," he replied. "He did not imitate, and I do not imitate."

—Rabbi Nachman of Bratzlaw

This book is about fully seeing and apprehending couples and families: a step-by-step building of skills. The first skill is to be fully present with one's full vision and compassionate relatedness: *being there.* Only when we have taken the time to be moved by others and their experience of being related (or disconnected) can we have the privilege of telling them, in the most compelling way, what we experience in their presence. After people become fascinated with themselves by feeling both *heard* and *seen* through the eyes and ears of another, they will usually consider

Note: The author wishes to thank the following people for helping with this chapter: Riley Lipman, Donna Rumenik, Roberta Tonti, Ed Harris, Penny Backman, Joe Melnick, and Paul Shane.

changing their behavior. The family has honored us by allowing us to sit with them as a witness to their struggles. This "sitting with" and articulating what we experience is an aesthetic and spiritual ritual. Besides enabling us to experience the beauty of the unfolding of healthy human interactions, therapeutic interventions also have aesthetic and spiritual dimensions that nurture this unfolding. A clear and powerful observation emitted from one's loving heart is magnetic, compelling, difficult to brush aside, and beautiful to behold.

This book teaches therapists how to create, develop, and complete this ritual. We learn how to sit with people, "to squint" so that we can behold them in their many forms: as an organism, a living being, a metaphor, a lovely or awkward dance. We learn to make the "dance" inside of us so that through our creativity we can evoke changes in "human choreography" to empower a couple or family to move with sure footing on the solidity of anchored strength. A "sick" couple or family are poor actors, and watching them is deplorable theater: they cannot rise above their habitual patterns into the excitement of dramatic authenticity; they cannot let go into the joy of their own comedy; nor can they reach down into the depths of their own souls for real tragedy. We teach them how to live authentically—the truthful spontaneity of immediate improvisation—from their hearts and guts, from their longings and laughter. And, in turn, we experience their revealed beauty.

We teach people how to live beautifully.

The creative arts of theater, dance, literature, poetry, painting, sculpture, architecture—all of these are more than just metaphors for the witnessing, participation, and articulation of living human interaction. The creative aspect of bearing witness to life and doing this work is a stance; a perspective; a visceral, motoric, and intuitive response.

Since the study of the soul was first proposed by Aristotle and others, the old armchair debate has existed about the definition of the psychotherapist's true role—*what we really do*. Is what we do a science, a discipline, or an art? This professional identity crisis became an especially thorny one not long after psychology fled the realm of philosophy in the late nineteenth century and modeled itself after physics in order to assume its rightful, independent place among the sciences. One's point of view in this debate seems to create a self-fulfilling prophecy: if you believe it is a science, you tend to approach it as a technician (one who is preoccupied with technique or numbers and measurements offered up to the twin gods of "reliability" and "validity"); if you think it is a discipline, you necessarily become a disciple (one who endlessly practices at becoming a "master"); if you experience your work as an art, you are an artist (one who is a creator-witness). There probably is no one pure type, for if there were, it would mean being only partially human, since all three viewpoints are different sides of the same investigation of human reality. Indeed, in the present work you will see all three stances combined, but I gravitate toward that of the artist. This is because an essential premise of this book, flowing like an underground river through our teaching of how to work with couples and families in the Gestalt approach, is to communicate that an aesthetic validity exists in *all* psychotherapies and in the moment of human interpersonal contact.

Becoming aware of being human is a creative adventure; assisting the growth of this awareness is an adventurous creation.

Most of my attitude comes from my long professional and scholarly experience, but some comes from the distressing observation that psychotherapy, in its historical struggle for recognition as a "physics of the psyche," has lost touch with its own name: the study and healing of the soul. Much of this has happened because its graduate curricula have slowly drifted away from classical education, the humanities and the arts in particular, toward empirical technology.

But regardless of educational deficiencies and the variety of theoretical persuasions, I contend that there is an aesthetic side to all human interaction and every therapeutic style. Every school of thought is founded on a group of principles and techniques. The choice of principles and techniques by their preferred selection and application alone implies the direction of the course of therapy and what "good" or "healthy" human functioning looks like. To make progress in a particular direction during the therapy hour means that judgments must be made—

what should be said, done, seen, heard, measured, recorded, and so on. That is, underlying each school of therapy is an unarticulated ideal toward which the work strives to carry its clients. This ideal, in turn, implies a set of values—what "good" is, what "healthy" is, what "growth" means, what a "family" is, and what a "relationship" is.

Thus, there is an "aesthetics of psychotherapy" as well as an "aesthetics of human interaction," since aesthetics is dedicated to the study of the expression of values. Our search for the good form of human interaction and the practice of psychotherapy that uncovers that good form is subjective, intuitive, and metaphorical.

This book is as much about aesthetic values—the creative appreciation of the "good form" of human relationship and therapy—as it is about the presentation of the Gestalt approach to couples and families; indeed, my entire therapeutic approach is founded on this aesthetic premise. I did not happen on my own value of aesthetic appreciation by accident, nor do I emphasize it without reason. My view, along with my theoretical and technical principles, began developing many years ago when I first entered serious education and training as a graduate student. I am the heir and innovator of and in a variety of traditions and philosophies. And so before you begin mulling over and assimilating this book, I wish to introduce you to our common ground.

Common Ground

Following World War II, Fritz Perls, a German psychoanalyst living in South Africa, became interested in concretizing abstract psychoanalytic concepts.[1] Fully involved in studying the individual, he realized that the learning process is much like assimilating food. In discussing mental phenomena as processes of psychic and physical assimilation, Perls spoke of a *mental metabolism*[2] and described various mechanisms of defense in the language of physical digestion. For example, introjection—a revision of a Freudian term—was a failure to adequately chew mental food. Infants introject readily because they do not have teeth; that is, they cannot challenge a speaker or ask questions before taking things in. Infants *can* spit and they do, but that is a gross act, not a subtle sifting of what is presented. Developmentally, introjection is fitting for a six-month-old but less fitting for a sixteen-year-old. In adults, therefore, introjection is a failure to ask questions, to express doubt, to chew and taste. It is a way of swallowing whole, a swallowing without chewing. (Note that in the context of imbalanced interpersonal and political power, it is probably much safer to swallow a rigidly authoritarian environment, where questioning is a form of insubordination.)

Perls spoke about other resistances[3]—brand-new ones—that had not been discussed in psychoanalytic literature. Retroflection was a mechanism by which people held in what they were afraid to express to others—as in holding in anger or withholding an expression of love.[4] Retroflection was not just a low-voltage brain transaction without awareness but an energy that constricted muscles and that was held in stasis. It caused actual physical pain and various secondary symptoms like headaches.

Even though this was clearly an interactional phenomenon—"I hold in what I want to do to you"—Perls's actual work was not focused on the interactional threat that caused the holding in, but on learning to undo the retroflection through movement and other expression. He helped his patients and students express anger toward an empty chair (the fantasized Other, such as a parent) or another person in a practicum, but he himself did not become fascinated by the living recipient's response to the anger as such. The recipient was a kind of dummy-volunteer, a blank screen, who was generally used in the service of helping others put forth whatever they retroflectively held in their bodies, causing the pain or anxiety.

Fritz and Laura Perls loved theater, dance, and other expressive experimentation in general, and so they both evolved into "improvisational behaviorists." Here is an example of improvisational work with retroflected anger.

If I am told that I am hurting someone and I have no awareness of it (other than perhaps a vague pain in my throat), it may be helpful to ask myself how and where I hold my anger in my body-self.[5] If, then, I become aware of a tightness in my throat, and if, with some support and encouragement, I manage to make a sound—an angry sound toward my spouse—two things tend to happen at once:

1. My own experience of the sound coming out of my body teaches me on the spot how angry I feel ("I sounded like some kind of wild animal!").
2. My spouse looks hurt and perhaps even frightened and I get an inkling of how, unaware, I impact him or her.

My insight about my anger is not something I have to take on faith from a therapist; it is something I bewilderingly discover in my voice, lungs, and belly and in the grimace of my spouse. This is a moment of what Gestalt therapists call *contact*—my contact with my own angry self and possibly the beginning of a contact cycle with my spouse.[6] A socially enacted event holds incredible possibilities for my rapid transformation and the transformation of those involved with me.

Perls once told a story of a concert violinist–patient who complained of dizziness and lack of concentration while performing.[7] After asking the man to bring his violin to the therapy session and play for him, Perls soon noticed that just gazing at the man felt aesthetically unpleasant. Attending more carefully, he saw that the man had little grace because he stood awkwardly, with feet held tentatively and much too close to each other. He also looked as though he was about to pass out because of not breathing properly. Later, when the patient was shown how to plant himself fully with all his weight on the floor, with legs separated and knees loose, and was told how to breathe fully and deeply, he instantly experienced relief from his dizziness and anxiety.[8] This enabled him to more fully contact his music and audience. Learning awareness and insight leading to contact were organismic events taking place at the boundary between the person (organism) and the environment. The transaction in that boundary was where the stuff of resistance to learning (or contact) occurred and was also the nexus of connectedness and transformation of the self. Poor functioning was a person's (or a system's)[9] "stuckness" (as in retroflection) in an unfinished situation. It involved a frozen awareness, in both body and time, that needed to be overcome by finishing a situation successfully—the *Zeigarnik effect.*[10]

I met Fritz Perls at what was to become the Gestalt Institute of Cleveland in the 1950s, when I was a graduate student—and continued to have contact with him until he died in Chicago in 1970. In those early days of the human potential movement, the Cleveland therapy scene was extremely conservative, with psychoanalysis holding a virtual monopoly. It was almost impossible for a Gestalt-oriented graduate student to obtain an internship in the analytically dominated hospitals and clinics. Many of us went "underground" about our Gestalt affiliation, especially in regard to the university and our professors. Fritz and Laura Perls were perceived at best as renegade analysts and at worst as quacks who encouraged the undisciplined "acting out" rather than the therapeutic "acting through." Fritz responded to this disparagement by pointing out that acting out took place without awareness, while acting through was behavior supported by full awareness.[11]

Another important teacher in my extracurricular studies in the early 1960s was Carl Whitaker. Whitaker was also an antiestablishment psychiatrist specializing in couples and families, and although I often wondered about the origin of his interventions, I certainly felt a kind of kinship with him. If Perls was my strange genius-father, Whitaker was a loving and supportive uncle.

I remember one event during that period, when one of the therapists brought a "difficult" couple for Whitaker to work with during a public demonstration. Here he was sitting in front of the nervous couple, having been told earlier that the wife was a schizophrenic. Whitaker sat back, gazed at them for a while, then asked innocently, "How did the two of you decide who would be the sick one?"

"Well," said the husband with a perfectly straight face, "Mary was to be sick because I had to go to work to make a living."

Both the question and answer were revolutionary events. They spelled out the notion that psychological illness was an unaware agreement supported, "held," and perpetuated in the couple or family system. This was a stunning event for me, because I was still steeped in intrapsychic theories, diagnosis through urine analysis, and ideas about "schizophrenogenic mothers." The effect of the Palo Alto research had just started filtering down in my direction, and I read with fascination about "paradoxical behavior" and the "double bind" in schizophrenic families.[12] I was told the story of a loving mother who visited her daughter faithfully in the psychiatric hospital. The twenty-year-old schizophrenic woman was seen walking and smiling with her mother. Mom even had her arm around her daughter's shoulder. One day after the mother left, the staff discovered numerous black-and-blue marks on the patient's upper arm. When asked about this, the patient responded calmly that her mother expressed disapproval about her behavior during these walks by quietly inserting her hand into the sleeve of the daughter's dress and pinching her severely. The benign expressions remained unchanged on the women's faces when this happened, as if all was well with both . . .

Broderick and Schrader describe Carl Whitaker as one of the leading founders of the family therapy movement (John Bell is considered its father figure). Here is how they characterize him: "From the beginning, Carl Whitaker has been noted as the most irreverent and whimsical of the founding fathers. In recent years, he has developed his approach into a finely honed therapy of the absurd—a therapy in which he often seems to drive a family sane by appearing more mad than they. It was in keeping with this character, then, to be one of those who early risked violating the conventions of traditional psychotherapy."[13] To me, Whitaker seemed to scare families into sensible behavior by playing from the depth of his psyche—often intuitively mimicking the system's primitive thinking.

Both Perls and Whitaker were dramatic characters (Whitaker still is!) who appealed to my desire to break out of the rigid psychoanalytic mold and to experience clinical work that enacted individual intrapsychic forces as well as interpersonal ones. People rediscovered themselves in acting through differentiated inner forces (top dog versus underdog) as well as those played out in their relationships with significant others. I slowly learned how bounded intrapsychic phenomena could be manifested in dialogues with an empty chair as well as how boundaries behaved interpersonally—how, for example, persons can "force-feed" each other in a well-choreographed yet unconscious dance of projecting and introjecting.

The notion of paradox was beginning to fascinate me: Why did the mother and daughter smile while one was hurting the other? Was the daughter the Christ figure volunteering to save the family? Was the mother holding on desperately to a young woman who was no longer the child whose presence kept the parents married? How did Whitaker get the couple to tell their unconscious "agreement"? How did he stimulate families to act more sanely when he imitated their unconscious "crazy" process?

Both Perls and Whitaker taught me and others to be more courageous in exploring our therapeutic hunches through a lively interactional process. The notion of *experiment* was born. The practice of therapeutic experiment—the "safe emergency"—is supported by the notion that Gestalt therapy is an integrated form of phenomenology and behaviorism. We share with the phenomenologist a respect for the individual's (or system's) perspective. Therapy is grounded solely in the client's experience and actual behavior. We use this behavioral and experiential material—grading and modulating it—in a carefully timed manner. This gives Gestalt therapy the unique quality of modifying the client's aware behavior in the therapy situation. An experiment in Gestalt therapy is a kind of systematic behavior modification growing out of the client's experience, need, and cooperation.[14]

The experiment is the cornerstone of experiential learning. It transforms talking about into doing and stale reminiscing and theorizing into being fully here with all one's imagination, energy, and excitement.[15] The experiment allowed therapists to modify both intrapsychic conflicts of the client and the interpersonal conflicts within couples and groups. We could play with exploring and shaping awareness at different levels with different systems. Careful work involved making clear where boundaries were drawn—so the client system understood what our intentions were and where the focus lay. Carefulness also meant that, unlike Perls, we in Cleveland did not cut through resistances but taught clients to discover something in a graded, timed, and well-supported manner. Respect for the client system's unfolding awareness was important to us; it soon became a key professional value grounding and guiding our work.

I also met Virginia Satir, a social worker with a powerful presence. She too specialized in couple and family systems. She was the only teacher I met who could magnetize an audience of several hundred therapists into an animated "family" event or "family reunion" where almost everyone could feel like a distant cousin, if not a sister or brother. Satir was one of the five major intellectual players in Gregory Bateson's Palo Alto group; the others were Jay Haley, John Weakland, and Don Jackson. These were a rich mixture of bright people with varied intellectual backgrounds, who initially studied families of the schizophrenic patients. They started with broad areas of communication and later discovered the nature of paradoxes and double binds. These ideas were grounded in systems theory, and, years later, the movement developed an epistemological orientation. Epistemology is the study of the nature and grounds of knowledge and the limitations of various theories of knowledge; the Bateson group's interest in this topic grew out of concerns with "What is actually happening in this family?" and "What can we say is 'true' about their way of being-in-the-world?"[16]

Our epistemology is embedded in existentialism (What is our existence?) and phenomenology (What is the language of a given existence?). This theory of knowledge brings us to how the system speaks to us with its varied and contradictory themes. It is grounded in the process of developing awareness and contact. Knowledge is not static; it is a process at the boundary of a given system or subsystem in a given unit of space and time. The meaning of a couple's or a family's behavior does not belong to any one member, nor does it originate in any one member. It develops spontaneously (systems theory) in the total circumscribed field of that system in the moment-to-moment process. The meaning (or some tiny portion of it) is articulated in an intervention of a therapist and, if it seems plausible or useful, is substantiated by the growing awareness of the members of the given system. Meanings are "confirmed" by the growth of contact and later by loss of interest in that very experience. The meaning is assimilated by the system, and the system is later ready, for the exploration of the next meaning, and so on.[17] Meanings are not only cognitive; they are living, ongoing, changing events perhaps more like choreographed dances—living works of art moving through time and space.

Satir, as one of the founders of family therapy, created an emphasis on process for systems.[18] She later wrote: "I have worked on a systems approach long before I understood about it and before I even heard the name for it."[19] She said she discovered what systems are about by reading Jackson's work on communication in schizophrenic families.[20]

The post–World War II period was a time of enormous creativity in the clinical field. It was a time of inventiveness, theoretical questioning, cross-fertilization, and the overlapping of interests between different mental health professions. Philosophically, I was influenced by a variety of existential thinkers and by phenomenology as it relates to pathology. I was drawn to Lewin's field theory,[21] Von Bertalanffy's systems theory,[22] and even Zen Buddhism.[23]

It was a paradoxical time for the psychoanalytic movement. Analysis, as noted earlier, was the dominant approach, especially in New York, but it began to spring exciting new branches that, in time, radically undermined its petrified stance: logotherapy, onto-analysis, and character analysis and its cousin, Gestalt therapy. Humanistic analysts—in particular, Victor Frankl, Wilhelm Reich, Frieda Fromm-Reichmann, Erich Fromm, Fritz Perls, and Eilhard Van Domarus—received increasing attention.

The emphasis seemed to shift from intrapsychic analysis of the individual patient to the notion of *encounter:* the encounter process between patient and therapist as well as the nature and meaning of encounter or contact within couple, family, and group systems.[24] Yet most analysts still believed Freud's dictum about the need to separate the analysis of individual family members. Said Freud: "When the husband's resistance is added to that of the wife, efforts are fruitless and therapy is prematurely broken off."[25] The notion of resistances being created by systems of persons was generally unknown or at least not yet widely written about. Although early efforts were made to describe such phenomena in families, few professionals became interested in psychotherapy with whole families prior to the 1960s.

We, the so-called Gestalt therapists, were the offspring of some of these revisionist analysts. The Second World War taught us to doubt any absolutist statements about being human—human beings were not born as essences to be developed in a lifetime. Instead, existence preceded essence: we took our lives into our own hands and took responsibility for ourselves.[26] Therefore, the process of therapy was existential in the sense that it took place in the here and now in an atmosphere of responsibility for one's own process. It was also phenomenological in the sense that it centered on the individual's experience as it unfolded before us.

Among the important post–World War II analysts was, of course, Wilhelm Reich. He analyzed character structure as it occurs in the person's body. Fritz Perls was his patient for a short period in Europe. Heavily influenced by Reich, Perls began to integrate the existential here-and-now notion with the character-body resistances model. And so what reached us as fledgling therapists in Cleveland was the notion of character as an expression of body, posture, breathing, retroflections, and the body's natural choreography under different conditions of interaction. We watched the clients' bodies as they revealed themselves in the therapy session.

On one level, our family tree looked something like the diagram in Figure 1.1.

This diagram partly describes our evolution into the 1960s and our thinking and methodology in relation to *individuation,* to working with a single person. If we are to include our concern with small *systems* like couples, families, and groups, we may pay tribute to the aforementioned mentors and theoreticians like Whitaker and Satir as well as inspired teachers and

Figure 1.1. Gestalt Therapy.

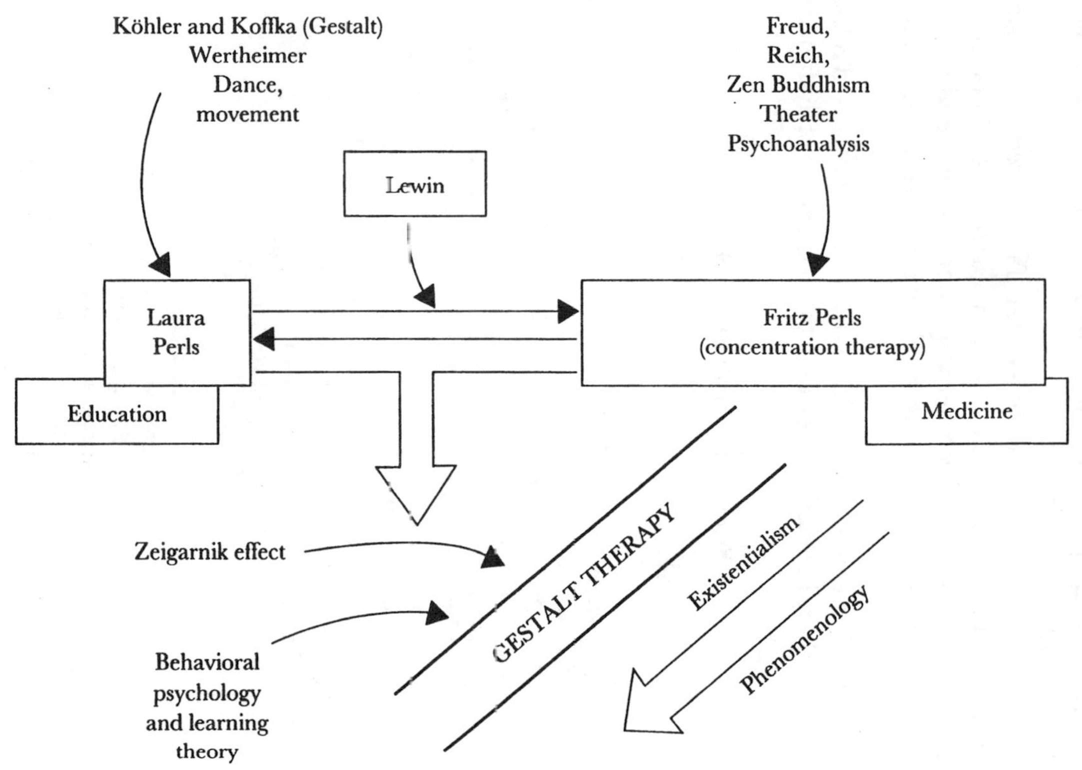

writers such as Gregory Bateson, Paul Watzlawick, Harry Stack Sullivan, and Margaret Mead. Creative therapists like Murray Bowen, Milton Erickson, Jay Haley, Cloe Madanes, Salvador Minuchin, Nathan Ackerman, and many others should also be added to the list.

When we combine the Gestalt family tree with systems thinking, the picture is as shown in Figure 1.2. If one studies Figure 1.2 closely, it becomes apparent that the resulting therapeutic assumptions are comprehensive in scope and power:

1. Developmentally, the child learns "who" he or she is in relation to others in health as well as in the acquisition of dysfunction.

Figure 1.2. Gestalt Family Therapy.

Systems theory; field theory; emphasis on awareness; learning as digestion; character and character armor; working at boundary of system; acting through

Zeigarnik

Systems theory thinking; epistemology; induction/suggestion; cutting and bypassing resistances; emphasis on outcome; paradox; power of therapist; enactment

Complete unfinished situation

Beauty of good function

Aesthetics; emphasis on process; *praising* competence and resistance; paradoxical theory of change; bring *what is* to foreground; respect for ongoing awareness; experiment

Metaphor

2. Developmentally, character styles and resistances to contact or contact styles[27] are learned in relationships and maintained by those relationships.
3. Unlearning certain resistances or contact styles is best accomplished in a social context, either with a significant other or in transference with a therapist.
4. Linear causality of psychological events is in question. So is reductionistic thinking about causes of individual and family pathology.
5. Historical studies of a family or other groups are at best arbitrary because they tend to follow a narrative or linear pattern. It is therefore deeply satisfying to identify *patterns* of interaction in a couple or family as they are observed in front of us in the here and now, especially when they are easily validated by family members.
6. The most potent methodological combination of systems theory and Gestalt study of the human body and awareness is an *experiment* conducted with the couple or total family. Reflecting an evaluation of the system's strength as well as its undeveloped side, the experiment is a specially tailored practice session in which the members of the system practice strengthening the undeveloped side of the total system.

I once observed Minuchin doing what he termed *enactment* with a family of a five-year-old who dominated the system. Minuchin asked the father to place his son on his own shoulders and carry him as the little boy gave out the orders. The family quickly learned that the parents must take charge of the resulting chaos. While Minuchin calls this *enactment,* it is clearly a Gestalt-like experiment.

Let us now speak briefly of *paradox.*[28] Essentially, in most schools of family therapy, paradox is the strategic assignment of the symptom to the family in an intervention. In the Minuchin example, the family would be told to spend a day together while the five-year-old is in charge of the activities. The paradox here is not an invitation for the family to change in a given way but to learn from what already is in an explicitly exaggerated form. In Gestalt therapy, our *paradoxical theory of change*[29] is similar: it asks the family members to observe themselves and report what they experience. Consequently, the more they know what they are, the more they become transformed. Although I may at times lean toward a more dramatic method of exaggerating the symptom, I prefer the more subtle process of emphasizing what is and how this "isness" changes the system's awareness and functioning. Later, alternative behaviors are more balanced and aesthetically beautiful.[30]

Strategic users of paradox, such as Haley and Madanes, are not especially interested in changing awareness. They want to see behavioral change in families. Foley gives the clearest summary of this outlook:

> Therapy is a power struggle in which the therapist must be in control if change is produced. Another factor in Haley's approach which is different is the role of awareness. It is not necessary for the family to become aware of their behavior for effective change to take place. This, too, is a departure from the traditional viewpoint of therapists.
>
> Insight, awareness, or knowledge of how the system operates are all unnecessary. What produces change is the therapist's intervention into the family system. The why of change is not important because only the fact of change matters. This is consistent with Haley's view of therapy as a power struggle.[31]

The same is true for the use of induction by Erickson and his followers. Here, new awareness may follow behavioral change. The emphasis is on a short-term process in which resistances are bypassed and behavioral change follows rapidly.

This is where we as Gestalt therapists stand in stark contrast to the strategic workers and perhaps other family therapists. As this book will demonstrate, *we work with awareness all the time,* and as we help patient-systems *articulate* their awareness, they slowly experience themselves changing. In a sense, it can be said that we still have a foot in the psychoanalytic camp; we value emerging awareness as it ascends from the darkness of unawareness.

In this connection, we are reminded of the question of the therapist's *power* in our system. As opposed to Haley, here the client empowers the therapist as authority and the therapist respectfully empowers the client's system as the prime mover of change. Therapists "create change" only because they earn the ability through their presence and skill. We value the resulting experiences of contact in which the family participates fully and then owns its own success.

Moreover, we do not bypass or cut through resistances to contact, as in behaviorism or hypnotherapy. Rather, we point out in the family's language how resistances are forms of creative survival. We congratulate and praise the system for saying no, for example. It is only when the "no" is seen, recognized, and appreciated that the "yes" becomes accessible to the entire family.

We identify strongly with the work of Murray Bowen's family systems approach, which examines structured, interlocking relationships within families.[32] Like Bowen, we attend to the balance of power, to the cooperative creation of individual pathology, and to the intricate connections of triangles within couples and families. Like Bowen, we recognize that a given family can change but that drastic changes in families may take several generations. We like to work with at least several generations at a time: mothers and sons, granddads and grandchildren, aunts and their elders, and so on.

We emphasize knowledge of a couple's and family's development and the centrality of differentiation from a family. Definition of self starts with a family and continues in a struggle for balance between autonomy and differentiation.

Much of what we do will not seem strange to family therapists. What will stand out is that people talk to each other, not to us, and that our interventions are based on data seen in the session in front of us. The following list highlights the key features of the Gestalt approach to family therapy (also see the Appendix).

Gestalt Family Therapy

Forerunners	Freud, Reich, Rank, Husserl, Koffka, Goldstein, Köhler, Lewin, Buber
Philosophy	Existentialism and phenomenology
Model	Systemic; organism-environment contact boundary; process oriented
Major influences	Perls; Whitaker; Minuchin; Bowen; Satir; systems theory
View of function	Graceful flow of gestalten formation along the Interactive Cycle of Experience; flexible boundaries; judicious distribution of family resources of power, care, concern, and connection
View of dysfunction	Chronic interruptions ("stuckness") along the Interactive Cycle of Experience; extreme permeability/impermeability of boundaries; imbalanced distribution of power, care, concern, and connection; frozen subsystems—no interchangeable flow
View of awareness	Primary; foundation for change; awareness theory based on awareness continuum and Interactive Cycle of Experience
View of change	Dependent on underlying change in awareness

Overview of the Book

The preceding comments have established the framework of this book. Now it is time to turn to its purpose. My intention has been to distill many years of learning and experience into a simple, practical guide, much like a compass. Often, the dynamics of working with couple and family systems can threaten to overwhelm therapists; this book is meant to be a tool that, if used properly, will help readers find their way home. And, like the design of a compass, this book, while it is intended as informative and useful, may appear deceptively simple at first glance. The style of writing is intentionally nontechnical, as conversational in tone as I could make it, given that we are dealing with complicated phenomena and principles. While this may seem foreign at first glance, I hope and believe that the reader will grow to appreciate it.

Overall, this book springs from the ground of my "search for good form," as discussed in Chapter Two. The Gestalt process of figure formation as well as the functioning of a couple or family system can be appreciated aesthetically, much like a painting or sculpture or other work of art. There is an "isness" to this living art that, when viewed under the critical eye of the therapist, provides a focus for therapeutic strategy and intervention.

Chapter Three provides an overview of couples and family systems as holistic phenomena. The most important point made is that a system is an entity unto itself and is larger than its individual members. The contributions of field theory, Gestalt psychology, and systems thinking are further explored in this chapter. I touch on the boundary concept here as well, setting the stage for its further explication in Chapter Seven.

The Interactive Cycle of Experience developed by Nevis is one of the primary phenomenological lenses for looking at system behavior. It is covered in Chapter Four. We also look at the concept of awareness and how it is interrupted within systems. In addition, this chapter outlines the role of the therapist as a participant-observer.

Awareness and its relation to change is further developed in Chapter Five. Here we look at different models of awareness and its connection to energy, action, contact, and resistance. The paradoxical theory of change and how it is used to support "what is" is described, as well as the danger of interpreting rather than intervening. The chapter closes with a review of actions that guide therapists in the typical couple or family session.

In Chapter Six, we examine resistances, both as contact styles and as unaware modulations of awareness. I discuss various types of resistances and provide examples of how they turn up as habitual characteristics of different couple and family systems.

Boundaries and their management form the primary focus of Chapter Seven. In this chapter, I show how boundaries create meaning and how therapists can learn to discern and attend to them, affect them, and support them. The chapter closes with a discussion of therapists' boundaries—more specifically, of the creation and management of these boundaries during therapy meetings and their relation to the system at hand.

These seven chapters form the part of the book titled "Theory." Even though all the chapters include both theoretical and practical material, the remaining chapters are intended to be more application oriented and to blend by discussion and case example the theory and technique given previously. I begin with couples in Chapter Eight and present the real "nuts and bolts" of intervening in two-person systems. Using awareness as a focal point, I show how to set up a therapy situation, how to choose an intervention, how to evaluate the system's strengths and weaknesses, how to work with content issues, how to work with skewed polarities, how to work with resistances, and the importance of complementarity and the middle ground.

Building on the principles and practices of couples work, I move on to working with families in Chapter Nine. The discussion is based on a series of basic assumptions and orienting principles that guide therapeutic interventions. These include the celebration of good functioning, the definition of family, family subsystems, and parent-child dynamics. The chapter closes with another case study. (The basic material in Chapters Eight and Nine was originally written by Nevis and subsequently elaborated further by the author.)

The next two chapters—Chapters Ten and Eleven—are devoted to two special issues that often arise within couple and family systems: lying and truthfulness on the one hand and grief and loss on the other. These ideas, like much of the rest of the book, were developed in continuous dialogue between me and Nevis.

In the final chapter, I return to the concept of good form and the aesthetics of the Gestalt approach by examining the core values of Gestalt therapy in detail. I sketch the development of values in the maturing of Gestalt therapy and summarize its cardinal values and guiding principles. Given that values enable choiceful, aware actions, we consider the "ethical regret" with which we must often make our choices.

Conclusion

This book comes from many years of work, from many evenings sitting and musing about life's problems with beloved colleagues, and from collegial friendships built on mutual respect and devotion that have contributed to a richer and better life. I hope that you will also be enriched by these efforts. I am pleased to give you—the therapist who follows in our footsteps, as I followed in those of my teachers—this book to help you on your way, to lighten your burden, and to brighten your path.

Notes to Chapter One

1. F. S. Perls (1947), *Ego, hunger, and aggression* (London: Allen & Unwin).
2. F. S. Perls (1947), *Ego, hunger, and aggression* (London: Allen & Unwin, p. 107). Interestingly, the idea of a "mental metabolism" originated in a paper written by Fritz Perls on oral resistances that was an expansion of Laura Perls's research on dental aggression. See E. M. Stern (1992), "A trialogue between Laura Perls, Richard Kitzler, and E. Mark Stern," in E. W. L. Smith (Ed.), *Gestalt voices* (Norwood, NJ: Ablex, p. 22).
3. F. S. Perls, R. Hefferline, & P. Goodman (1951), *Gestalt therapy: Excitement and growth in the human personality* (New York: Julian Press).
4. Whereas in the first instance I do to myself what I want to do to you, in the second case, I give myself what I want you to give to me (like stroking my hair, holding my hand, and so on).
5. J. Kepner (1987), *Body process: A Gestalt approach to working with the body in psychotherapy* (New York: Gardener Press). See also M. Schiffman (1971), *Gestalt self therapy and further techniques for personal growth* (Berkeley, CA: Wingbow Press).
6. J. Zinker & S. Nevis (1981), *The gestalt theory of couple and family interactions,* Gestalt Institute of Cleveland working paper, Cleveland, OH. Also see Chapter Four of the present work.

7. Personal communication.
8. Just a note to remind you that this story was related in the 1960s and that nothing was known then about the usefulness of beta-blockers in relation to this cardiovascular phenomenon.
9. J. Zinker & J. Leon (1976), "The gestalt perspective: A marriage enrichment program," in O. Herbert (Ed.), *Marriage and family enrichment* (Nashville, TN: Abingdon Press, pp. 144–157). See also J. Zinker (1980), *Complementarity and the middle ground: Two forces for couples' binding,* Gestalt Institute of Cleveland working paper, Cleveland, OH.
10. B. Zeigarnik (1927), "Über das Behalten von erledigten und unerledigten Handlungen (On the persistence of finished and unfinished tasks), *Psychologische Forschung, 9,* 1–85. See M. R. Ovsiankina (1976), "The resumption of interrupted activities," in J. Rivera (Ed.), *Field theory as human science* (New York: Gardner Press). Both Zeigarnik and Ovsiankina have experimentally proven that the persistence of memory for unfinished tasks is about two to three times greater than for memory of finished tasks.
11. C. C. Clements (1992), "Acting out vs. acting through: An interview with Frederick Perls, M.D., Ph.D.," in E. W. L. Smith (Ed.), *Gestalt voices* (Norwood, NJ: Ablex, pp. 10–17).
12. G. Bateson, J. Jackson & J. Weakland (1968), "Toward a theory of schizophrenia," in D. Jackson (Ed.), *Communication, family, and marriage* (Palo Alto, CA: Science and Behavior Books).
13. C. B. Broderick & S. Schrader (1991), "The history of professional marriage and family therapy," in A. S. Gurman & D. P. Kniskern (Eds.), *Handbook of family therapy* (Vol. 2) (New York: Brunner/Mazel, p. 26).
14. J. Zinker (1977), *Creative process in Gestalt therapy* (New York: Brunner/Mazel, p. 126). See also E. Kepner & L. Brien (1970), "Gestalt therapy and behavioristic phenomenology," in J. Fagan & I. Shepherd (Eds.), *Gestalt therapy now* (New York: Science and Behavior Books).
15. J. Zinker (1992), "Gestalt therapy is permission to be creative: A sermon in praise of the use of experiment in Gestalt therapy," in E. W. L. Smith (Ed.), *Gestalt voices* (Norwood, NJ: Ablex, pp. 51–53).
16. H. A. Guttman (1991), "Systems theory, cybernetics, and epistemology," in A. S. Gurman & D. P. Kniskern (Eds.), *Handbook of family therapy* (Vol. 2) (New York: Brunner/Mazel, p. 56).
17. See the interactive cycle as described in Chapter Four of the present work.

18. See V. Satir, J. Stachoviac, & H. Taschman (1977), *Helping families to change* (New York: Aronson), and V. Satir (1964), *Conjoint family therapy* (Palo Alto, CA: Science and Behavior Books).
19. C. B. Broderick & S. S. Schrader (1991), "The history of professional marriage and family therapy," in A. S. Gurman & D. P. Kniskern (Eds.), *Handbook of family therapy* (Vol. 2) (New York: Brunner/Mazel, p. 29).
20. V. Satir, J. Stachoviac, & H. Taschman (1977), *Helping families to change* (New York: Aronson).
21. K. Lewin (1951), *Field theory in social science* (New York: HarperCollins).
22. L. Von Bertalanffy (1950), "The theory of open systems in physics and biology," *Science, 3,* 23–29.
23. For an eloquent description of Zen, see E. Herrigel (1971), *Zen in the art of archery* (New York: Vintage Books).
24. B. Feder & R. Ronall (1980), *Beyond the hot seat: Gestalt approaches to group therapy* (New York: Brunner/Mazel). See also E. Polster (1969), "Encounter in community," in A. Burton (Ed.), *Encounter* (San Francisco: Jossey-Bass).
25. S. Freud (1915), *General introduction to psychoanalysis* (New York: Liveright).
26. For an in-depth discussion of the notions of responsibility, freedom, and creating oneself, see J. P. Sartre (1956), *Being and nothingness: An essay on phenomenological ontology* (H. E. Barnes, Trans.) (New York: Philosophical Library).
27. G. Wheeler (1991), *Gestalt reconsidered: A new approach to resistance and contact* (New York: Gardener Press).
28. L. Selzer (1984), "The role of paradox in gestalt theory and technique," *Gestalt Journal, 7*(2), 31–42.
29. A. R. Beisser (1970), "The paradoxical theory of change," in J. Fagan & E. L. Shepherd (Eds.), *Gestalt therapy now* (New York: HarperCollins). See Chapter Five of the present work for a more detailed discussion of the paradoxical theory of change.
30. See Chapters Two and Twelve of this book for further discussion of what I call the "aesthetics of good form."
31. V. D. Foley (1979), *An introduction to family therapy* (Philadelphia: Grune & Stratton, p. 85).
32. M. Bowen & M. E. Kerr (1988), *Family evaluation and approach based on Bowen theory* (New York: Norton).

2

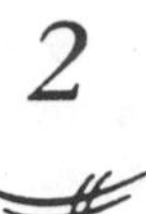

In Search of Good Form

I don't know if it's art, but I know what I like.
—Unknown

From the earliest days of my personal Gestalt therapy experience, I have noticed this truth: no matter what symptom I presented to my therapists, I left the consultation room feeling "friendlier" with the very source of the bothersome, painful experience I had brought to therapy. I left the therapy session with the recognition that my anxiety, obsession, or difficult image was a creative effort. Through time and experience, I learned that my "complaint" was not bad but was merely the best creation I could muster at the time to solve a life problem; that my symptoms had goodness, aesthetic validity, and special meaning; and that my "problem" was a search for a new balance, a good form. I therefore left the therapy session with the sense that my self was affirmed as good.

Gestalt therapy is a system and method for understanding and possibly changing ourselves as creative beings. One of its founders, Laura Perls, has explained that "the basic concepts of Gestalt therapy are philosophical and aesthetic rather than technical. Gestalt therapy is an existential-phenomenological approach and as such it is experiential and experimental. . . . Why do we call our approach *Gestalt* therapy? 'Gestalt' is a holistic concept (*ein Ganzheitsbegriff*). A gestalt is a structured entity that is more than, or different from, its parts. It is the foreground figure that stands out from its ground, it 'exists.'"[1]

The formation and destruction of gestalten[2] is an aesthetic process, not simply a utilitarian one. As with the individual, so with multiperson systems. When a couple or family struggles successfully through a dilemma, the experience feels whole, complete, right, good, and beautiful. Completed gestalten—fully ripened experiences of which we become aware, experience, assimilate, and eventually let go—are graceful, flowing, aesthetically pleasing, and affirming of our own worth as human beings. They have a "good form." Incomplete gestalten,[3] unsolved problems that repeatedly nag a couple or family, feel sad, faceless, ugly, and frustrating. They are aesthetically unpleasant.

The concept of good form is based on the smooth flow of gestalten structuring and destructuring through the process of awareness, energy mobilization, action, contact at the interpersonal boundary, closure (new learning), and withdrawal (reestablishment of boundary separation). From this simple, organismic process I am proposing an aesthetics of human interaction in the therapeutic situation as well as a good form to the therapist's interventions.

Life is a constant problem-solving process, from taking in the breath that sustains us to mourning the loss of loved ones. To see such a process as only a symptom, a pathology, or merely a mechanical response is reductionistic. Gestalt therapy envisions "pathology" as interruptions in a natural process that lead to repeated, often brave, efforts to solve a problem. Pathology is conceptualized as an interruption of process—a "stuckness"—which in turn only partially succeeds in solving the problem. It follows that every "symptom," every "illness," every "conflict" is an effort to make life more tolerable, more livable, though we and our loved ones pay a high price for such pathological interruptions. When a couple or family becomes stuck in its problem solving, repeating its failures again and again, it is interrupting its rhythm of moving apart and coming together. The moment we look at the couple or family as a single figure caught in a unified attempt to get "unstuck," we have an opportunity to see the goodness of the system's behavior, and to observe it trying to solve a problem as a total organism. When it is successful its actions are in synchrony, balanced, and complementary. For example, a family system stuck in a particular pattern is not in "bad form," but merely manifesting the best form it is capable of at this point in its life cycle; placing blame on one member or another misses the point. There is a kind of beauty when a family finds a good way of exploring with one another and solving a dilemma without naming the sick one, the problem child, the selfish one, or the one who loses his or her head.

The aesthetic of the "good form" of human relations is very much like comparing the merits of one painting to another; here we are not talking about criticism of style, content, and function, but an empathic response of appreciation to what is. The type of goodness that we are searching for is a sense of satisfaction in witnessing a family moving from

- Pessimism to hope
- Helplessness to increased competence
- Confusion and chaos to clarity
- Going around in circles to developing a feeling of direction for the future
- Mutual blaming and projection to ownership of an experience and an appreciation of each other's dilemmas

Although good form is difficult to describe, it can be seen and experienced; it has qualities and characteristics that can be explored. To realize this aesthetic viewpoint, you must first hold your perception of the human interaction in an "openness of being" to allow the key aspects of the system's process to emerge in your awareness. This means "being present" for the event, not unlike an audience member viewing a living work of art—theater, dance, painting, sculpture, musical performance, and so on. An event may occur, but if there is no one there to witness it, does it have any meaning? Our presence and interventions help to create change through heightening awareness and articulating meaning by supporting contact through dialogue and immediate encounter.

Second, you must frame your interventions in response to what's being witnessed and evoked in you. This is based on the therapists' own process of gestalt formation arising out of their "apperceptive mass"—the experiential ground of their full life history.

To look at something aesthetically in the Gestalt approach means to make judgments about its form. By *form,* I am primarily talking about process, although to a much lesser degree, I include content, qualities, characteristics, quantities, and so on. Making judgments implies the presence of values—for example, something is beautiful because it is perceived and valued as such. Values, in turn, imply that something is preferable or more important than something else.[4]

As stated in the previous chapter, I am making the obvious and fundamental assertion that all psychotherapies, regardless of philosophical approach, are based on a set of values. The definition of good form—in terms of human interpersonal behavior and therapeutic strategy and intervention—varies from therapy to therapy. We see clues indicating what is valued in the language used to define what is "healthy" or "functional": high functioning, equal distribution of power, efficient problem solving, self-regulation, self-actualization, maturity, self-validation, climate of trust, flexible boundaries, contact, authenticity, adaptation, stability, competence, being heard, greater connection, goal achievement, equality, role flexibility, intimacy, empowerment, nurturing growth, conflict tolerance, differentiation, attachment and separation, balance, homeostasis, and so on. Each term just named implies an underlying value that, through the judicious application of interventions, leads to an approximation of an intrapsychic, interpersonal, and systemic ideal: what I choose to call "good form."

Aesthetic Landmarks

I also recognize, after many years of work in the Gestalt approach, that therapists, to be successful change agents, must intervene with their own "good form." This is accomplished through four different, yet related, investigative modalities: the Interactive Cycle of Experience,[5] personal presence and boundary management, phenomenological apprehension and intuition, and the therapist's "apperceptive mass." While all of these will be discussed and demonstrated in greater detail in the chapters to follow, I present them here as part of an overview of my approach and to explain how they are used as steps along an essential and integrated path in the "search for good form."

Interactive Cycle of Experience

We look at problems of couples and families from a holistic, ecological perspective using the Interactive Cycle of Experience model (presented in detail in Chapter Four). The point(s) along the experience cycle that we choose to focus on depend on where we draw the boundaries for the given system level we are examining. When we create a boundary around a family, we can study how the family members relate to us at that boundary, how they relate to each other within it, and how we relate to them.[6]

The primary focus of Gestalt couple and family therapy is on the interactions between the couple and among the family members. We focus on the skills of these systems to organize themselves to complete a unit of work within an agreed-on time span.

Because the Gestalt couple and family therapist is interested in present interactions, the question of causality is immaterial. The causes of dysfunctional behavior in the present are the responses that represented the best possible solutions to difficult situations in the past; they were, therefore, functional at that time. When such behavior becomes habitual and unaware, when it is used in vain to solve present problems, it becomes interruptive and unresponsive to present needs. It prevents learning newer, more functional behavior.

In this way, the experience cycle is a theoretical model used as a kind of "external template" we superimpose on the interactional process of the couple or family system. The birth of energized gestalten flowing smoothly and gracefully from awareness through energy mobilization, action, contact, assimilation, and withdrawal is our aesthetic standard for good form and the basis for healthy, growthful human interaction. Our aesthetic values interactions that emerge spontaneously, achieve contact, and result in the satisfying resolution of a complete unit of work (that is, beginning, middle, and end) within a prescribed time frame.

Gestalt couple and family therapy focuses on heightening people's awareness of what they do well while showing them the ways they interrupt and block their process during the interactive cycle. Blockages or interruptions to this rhythmic movement—what we call *resistance*[7] to awareness and contact—are approached with both respect and appreciation of their paradoxical nature. On the one hand, resistances are lacunae or blind spots in awareness; they are conceptually held as the shadow side of good form. Yet, on the other hand, they are manifestations of the best functioning the system can muster at the time in order to achieve resolution to its interactive problem. Resistances in this regard are "static" attempts at contact and so are deemed healthy in principle, but in reality, they are not functional in promoting movement within the system. Working with resistances in the system's process is another way of heightening awareness, supporting choicefulness in behaviors, and experientially contrasting (through experiment) the different sides of the system's interactive existence.

In viewing the interpersonal process of the system, we attend to our own internal experience as we move through our own private cycle. We monitor both the system's movement through its awareness-contact path and our own experience of our separate yet corresponding position. From this internal ground of experience we are given phenomenological clues not only about our own internal, private reality but about what may be happening "out there." Gestalt couple and family therapists focus on their interpersonal responses to the shifting aspects of the therapy situation. We attend to our visceral, motor, metaphorical, and aesthetic experience of the system, as well as to what we see and hear. We scan for what is compelling and what is flat, what is rigid and what is fluid, what is energetic and what is lethargic.

For example, if you are observing family members interact and their energy appears to be escalating while your own energy level is still just warming up, this may indicate that the family as a system is moving too quickly through its cycle; it may indicate an inability to tolerate the slow, aware-full buildup of energy, or an effort to "hurry" contact, or just plain impatience or frustration in the individuals' process of relating to one another. In this way, the therapist's own experience cycle makes for an instrument to develop potential interventions. Related to this notion of being awake to one's own sensorium and using one's "self-as-instrument" is the concept of *presence*.

Personal and Boundary Management

The freedom of sitting with a couple or family while being outside its boundaries gives us creative opportunities to understand what is happening, to recognize and name major themes, and to invent experiments that enrich the system's awareness of itself.[8] As a result, the newly born curiosity of the system about itself along with the new awareness of its process contribute to change by allowing the members to move on with whatever is at hand without suffering major interruptions. The current phenomena, experienced against the ground of the interactive cycle, evoke a flow of figural material in therapists. We become "self-as-mirror" to feed back to the system what is evoked in ourselves and, like a mirror, when it is turned in a different direction, the image changes—it does not "stick."

Achieving this mirrorlike presence means having a clearly defined boundary in relation to the system at hand; otherwise, therapists are merely bystanders who make comments. But *true* presence, *real* presence, means more than just a strongly differentiated boundary. Presence means "to be present" as one's self with nothing added or missing. Authentic presence should not be confused with charisma, style, or force. Being present means to be fully grounded in order to allow the client system to emerge, brighten, engage, and be assimilated. While presence is easy to point at in the moment, it is difficult to describe in words; it is both a psychological state and a spiritual openness; it is the openness of the eyes and ears, but an openness of the heart as well. We become "self-as-witness."

Phenomenological Apprehension and Intuition

"Ex-sist" is from the Latin meaning "to stand out." In looking at a couple or family system, we look at what stands out for us in our own awareness of its immediate process. Eschewing content whenever possible, we seek direct perceptual apprehension of "what is." As various behavioral aspects of the system become evident to us, we make observation-interventions based solely on these phenomenological data. While not a pure "phenomenological reduction" in the Husserlian sense of the term, it is, nonetheless, an intervention methodology based on descriptive analysis of holistic phenomena.

> In its *pre-philosophical stage* this "phenomenological reduction" is a *descriptive analysis* of the phenomena under consideration. This descriptive analysis, however, should be sharply contrasted with the reductive analysis of the natural sciences which attempts to dissect its data into elementary parts and to reduce these parts to their merely quantitative aspects. The descriptive analysis of phenomenological reduction, on the other hand, is precisely performed *within* the act of intuiting the whole of the phenomenon and its manifold relationships. This descriptive analysis aims at revealing the phenomenon in its original "self-givenness," or in the irreducible uniqueness of the totality of its structural characteristics. Although at first blush this may sound surprisingly simple, the truth is that it is surprisingly difficult.[9]

Phenomenological apprehension ("to grasp") is founded on perception, specifically human vision. Sight is a central component of aesthetics (*aesthetics* coming from the Greek word *aisthanesthai,* "to perceive"). Indeed, seeing—literally or figuratively—has been considered the final measure of any theory of knowledge.

> For Husserl, the "final measure" of all theory is that which is "originally" given in simple seeing. The term "original" applies to that which can be experienced in direct observation; the "originally given" is something that is "naively" meant and possibly given as existent. That which can be "grasped" by simply looking is prior to all theory, including the "theory of knowledge." The phenomenologist is not disturbed by doubts as to the reality of the objects of experience, or by epistemological theories which try to prove that we are restricted to the immanent contents of consciousness . . . . The phenomenologist is interested in *that which is meant as such,* and that can be "grasped absolutely." That which is seen cannot be explained away, and this is the final standard in all truly philosophical thought.[10]

The phenomenological approach is based on "synthesis," not "analysis." We use phenomenological data to apprehend the behavior of the system as a whole and, in the process, through our presence, we allow this experience of the system to evoke figures, images, and metaphors in ourselves. This is what it means to intuit the system as a whole and is very much a "right-brain" creation based on "left-brain" data gathering. But where do these metaphors and other images come from? These emerge from what we call our *apperceptive mass.*

Apperceptive Mass

The apperceptive mass is one's personal ground of life history—the totality of experiences that have made us who we are. It is our essence, our facticity,[11] and our structured personal ground. The apperceptive mass, as ground, consists of memories, imagination, dreams, unconscious inspiration, spontaneous bodily sensations, and the like. From this ground, in response to what is evoked by being present with the client-system, spring spontaneous insights such as images, feelings, and metaphors that the therapist can develop into interventions to further heighten awareness. Such material from the apperceptive mass arises as an immediate creation, and its development by the therapist into metaphors that provide transcendent meanings or into creative experiments to foster contactful awareness is the artistry of the Gestalt approach. All of these concepts just presented—the experience cycle, presence, phenomenological observation, and apperceptive intuition—help make the therapists' own good form in their search for the good form of the client-system.

The idea of good form will be implicitly demonstrated in the following chapters, although not directly discussed again until the last chapter. I do this intentionally so as to allow the reader to become absorbed in the principles, techniques, and case examples. Then, in the conclusion, I return to the concept of good form and explore it in greater detail. In the meantime, to orient the reader and briefly illustrate what I mean by the search for good form, I turn to a session with the "Houghton family."

The Houghton Family: The Search for Good Form

Nadine and Jerry Houghton are in their forties. Nadine's face looks drawn and tight, her eyes always squinting. Jerry looks uncomfortable and seats himself away from his wife and son, Reggie. Reggie is a lanky fourteen-year-old boy. He carries a new football, which he throws up and catches every once in a while. He is fidgeting and looking out the window absently.

In previous sessions, the Houghtons have presented the following problems as their reasons for seeking therapy: Jerry's jealousy of Nadine's "overattentiveness" to Reggie, Nadine's flatness of feeling toward her husband and the couple's increasing distance from each other, Nadine's and Jerry's worry about their shaky marriage, and Reggie's love of sports and neglect of his studies.

In this session, Nadine and Jerry are talking and, without visible cause, she turns to their son. Jerry responds by accusing Nadine of being "selfish." In response, Nadine accuses her husband of "losing his head." Rather than focusing on underlying dynamics, the therapist attends to the raw data, to the phenomena developing in the present moment of the session. The goal is to support all three persons with compassion for their repetitive stuckness and stereotypical blaming behavior, which is now being played out before him.

Therapist: *I'm curious about the two of you: how easily you seem to know each other—whether it's "being selfish" or "losing your head." But I suspect that, in the heat of excitement, your curiosity and sense of inquiry fail. You simply tell it how you think it is, and both of you wind up feeling badly about the other. And you, Reggie, possibly aren't curious either.*

Here the therapist diagnoses how the family's interaction is an aesthetic failure by merely reporting some matters of curiosity along with the phenomenological impressions of "what is."

Jerry: *Yes, but she always turns to Reggie. She always takes the selfish step of attending more to him than to me.*

Nadine: *And he always loses his head, and doesn't care how I really feel . . . and doesn't ask.*

Reggie: *Sometimes I wish you guys would leave me out of this.*

You will notice that they are attempting to become unstuck by voicing their frustrations with each other. By naming the other's behavior, they assume that the behavior will change—that is, that the other will somehow miraculously become "selfless" or will keep a "cooler head." But it is a poor form overall, because it asks two or three people to accept self-deprecating characterizations of themselves. This mobilizes *resistance* to push away the characterization, rather than encouraging an interest in what is going on for the others. The therapist looks for a route that relieves pressure, avoids blame, and offers a simple way to be creative.

Therapist: *You really don't know what is in the other person's mind. Would you be willing to ask each other about what happened in that moment when everything went awry? Do you want to start, Jerry?*

Jerry: *Okay. Nadine, what were you thinking when you turned to Reggie? Why did you turn away from me?*

Nadine: *He was fidgeting and I was simply feeling distracted! I wondered if he really wanted to be here.*

Jerry: *Really?*

Nadine: *Yes, really. I thought, "I don't know why we drag Reggie in here. If you and I had our act together, he wouldn't be having trouble in school . . .*

Jerry: *I'm sorry. Maybe I really did jump the gun telling you you're selfish . . .*

Reggie: *I wasn't doing anything!*

Therapist: *You were just fine, Reggie. Now, Nadine, would you ask Jerry what he was feeling at that moment when you turned to Reggie?*

The therapist seeks good form by asking *all* to be curious, to open the field, to seek balance by gathering the raw data of the event. Asking Nadine—and later Jerry—teaches that inquisitiveness and inquiry pay off and legitimize the experience of all family members without becoming mired in name calling and interpretation.

Nadine: *(Her face softens for the first time, especially around her eyes) Jerry, what happened to you when I turned to Reggie? How did you feel inside?*

Jerry: *I thought, "There she goes again, wanting something for him and not for me—like my mom did for my brother." Dad would sit in his rocking chair reading the paper and she would be after Jack for something.*

Nadine: *I didn't mean to set that off. Your coming here is very important to me. It's our marriage we need to work on. I love you, Jerry.*

Reggie: *I'm restless because I have football practice in half an hour, and I wish you guys would keep me out of this. (He silently pauses for a moment and then says quietly) I didn't mean to distract you, Mom.*

Therapist: *By being curious about each other, you all got to find something new—and to express feelings that matter to each other. Keep going.*

Nadine: *Jerry, how would you feel if we asked Reggie not to come back next time?*

Jerry: *I think it's a good idea if you and I have a couple of sessions to work out some private stuff. Then I'd like Reggie back to talk about his relationship (turning to Reggie)—your relationship with me and your academic problems.*

Reggie: *That's okay with me, Dad.*

Jerry: *Is that okay with you, Doc?*

Therapist: *Yes, it is. Boy, you folks are getting curious all over the place! I'm so pleased. And these last few comments show some boldness and direction. You are all getting clearer about what needs to happen.*

Nadine: *Yes. Once we get the right idea, we sure go with it!*

Jerry: *We do well with a little help.*

Therapist: *I feel that you have a brand-new option to guessing what is in the other's heads. What are your options?*

Reggie: *(Turning to Jerry) To keep finding out what's going on, right?*

Jerry: *Right, son.*

The session ends with a clear resolution of how the Houghtons can move from habitual and unsatisfactory patterns of interaction to a sense of "good form" and balance. Everyone plays a part; no one was the scapegoat, nor was anyone the hero or "identified patient." As a result, everyone got what they wanted—the satisfying contact and closure—which is what we, as therapists, search for.

Conclusion

Good form in both the therapist's interventions and the family's interaction can be visualized as a reshaping of the "living sculpture" of the couple or family process. In the case of the Houghton family, we see a woman moving from her son toward her spouse without hurting the son. We see a father moving from a potentially abusive contact with his son to a concerned paternal closeness with him. We see a father who is able to maintain his sense of himself as a husband and of being a dad to his son. And we see a general decrease of anxiety in the whole system. The little experiment taught the Houghtons that they do not know each other as well as they thought, and that getting into the adventure of inquiry can bring them closer together.

The models for couple and family interactions are learned early in life and are generally acted on, indeed often acted out, without awareness. We therefore focus on living through these interruptive patterns in the present; however, we do not deny a concurrent interest in the past. All thinking people want to examine their lives, to review and know their past, to talk to others about it, to tell their story, and to know their place in the family and the family tree. Families yearn to know about their history, their ancestors, their roots.

To experience oneself as having a past and a future is good psychological health. The past and the future are best explored in the resolution/closure phase of a present experience. Mulling over what has been learned or experienced in the present can frequently offer insights into the possible "whys" of the past. Although the "whys" are myriad, and all behavior is multiply determined, the linear exploration of cause and effect continues to fascinate and sometimes even haunt all of us. But, even though we tend to cling to the idea of linear causality, the world has been fundamentally transformed by the impact of relativity, holism, and systems thinking on psychotherapy. How we and our world have changed is the subject of the next chapter.

Notes to Chapter Two

1. L. Perls (1992), "Concepts and misconceptions of gestalt therapy," in E. W. L. Smith (Ed.), *Gestalt voices* (Norwood, NJ: Ablex, p. 5, original emphasis).
2. A gestalt or image is formed to accommodate a given situation. It may be a concept that defines the situation and gives it meaning. When the situation changes, creative adaptation requires "destruction" of the old gestalt and redefinition of what is being created with the birth of a new gestalt that reorganizes the old.
3. The value system underlying Gestalt therapy will be discussed more fully in Chapter Twelve.
4. B. Zeigarnik (1927), "Über das Behalten von erledigten und unerledigten Handlungen (On the persistence of finished and unfinished tasks), *Psychologische Forschung, 9,* 1–85.
5. See Chapter Four.
6. See Chapter Seven.
7. See Chapter Six.
8. See the section in Chapter Seven titled "Therapists' Boundaries: Creating a Presence and Managing Boundaries" and the section in Chapter Eleven on "Witnessing."
9. B. J. Boelen (1971), *Existential thinking: A philosophical orientation* (New York: Herder and Herder, pp. 112–113, original emphasis).
10. M. Farber (1943), *The foundation of phenomenology: Edmund Husserl and the quest for a rigorous science of philosophy* (Albany: State University of New York Press, p. 203, original emphasis). Perls himself would have disagreed, because as he often said, if given a choice between his eyes and ears when doing therapy, he would rather give up his eyes—to him hearing was indispensable. I experience phenomenological apprehension with my full sensorium. But I feel that training in phenomenological vision is essential for training in psychotherapy. There is a simple training program along these lines in R. L. Harman (1990), *Gestalt therapy: Discussions with the masters* (Springfield, IL: Thomas). Here is an excerpt:

    J[oseph]: *Well, I was thinking that I would break a group of people into triads; you know how we do that. I would focus on the observer, not on the therapist. I would make the observation the most important skill. I would praise the observer. I would evaluate observation and the basic skill of attending to phenomenological data. And only then, once the therapists learn how to observe well, would I teach about intervening beyond the intervention of seeing "what is." I would elevate "what is" to the highest post, the highest level of goodness in training psychotherapists. I would make people do it for weeks, just for them to tell me what is, what they see, what they hear, and how they experience me, and not one word about my trying something or doing an experiment. So, I think we've come full circle. Ten years ago, I loved the experiment and I emphasized the experiment. Now I'm emphasizing the phenomenology of awareness. I think that I just assumed that everyone had the kind of phenomenological keenness that I had, so that I could build the experiment. Of course, it had to have some foundation, and people really don't see or hear. That's one thought I've had about training. Basically, the trainee would respond with a "what is" statement: "you're creasing your forehead, your mouth looks relaxed, your eyes are on me, and so on." I think that's why Fritz says Gestalt therapy is an awareness of the here and now. You can see how he would think that way.*

H[arman]: *What else would you have in the Joseph training program?*

J[oseph]: *I would have field trips. During the first segment in the Intensive . . . I would have field trips to the Natural History Museum, to the Cleveland Art Museum, to the Cleveland Institute of Art, to the Cleveland Orchestra, with specific thematic assignments. I would sit two students in front of a painting and say to them, "Write down five or six pages of what you see in that picture." I have made myself do that. I just did that about six months ago, and . . . I couldn't stop writing. It was like a seventeenth-century painting of a mother, father, and a child with a dog. It was incredible what I made myself see. So, one piece of the process was just to see it. The other piece of the process is to find a language for it* [pp. 52–53].

11. *Facticity* as used in this book is similar, but not identical, to the true existential term. An excellent definition is provided in J. Macquarrie (1972), *Existentialism* (Harmondsworth, England: Penguin Books, p. 190, original emphasis):

Existentialists use the word *facticity* to designate the limiting factor in existence. *Facticity* (the word has been coined to translate the German *Faktizität* and French *facticité*) does not mean the same as *factuality*. When we say something is factual we are pointing to an objective state of affairs observable in the world. Facticity, on the other hand, might be called the inner side of this factuality. It is not an observed state of affairs but the inward, existential awareness of one's own being as a fact that is to be accepted. No one has chosen to be. He simply finds himself in existence . . . . The factical is the given, and above all, the givenness of our existence. That *we are here* is, if you like, an inexplicable brute fact. . . . However, it is not just human existence in general that is a factical given. My existence, your existence, his existence, her existence are in each case characterized by facticity. We may recall from the introductory discussion of the concept of existence that a basic characteristic of it is "mineness" . . . I discover not just that I exist, but that I exist as this particular "I." I cannot exchange my existence for the existence of another. I am I. This sentence is no doubt a tautology, yet it also expresses a mystery—the inexplicable fact that I just happen to be this particular person and no other. I have this particular body; I am of this particular race and colour; I have this particular heredity, this particular intelligence quotient, this particular emotional make-up, and so on. Furthermore, I have been born into this particular historical situation in this particular society, and all kinds of forces are operating in the situation and in the society to shape my life and to limit what I can become.

Heidegger uses *thrownness* (*Geworfenheit*) as an equivalent term. I use *facticity* as a descriptive synonym for apperceptive mass because of its emphasis on the essential characteristics, life structures, and experiences that one finds one's self having without choice.

3

Systems: Couples and Families as Holistic Phenomena

The unleashed power of the atom has changed everything save our modes of thinking, and thus we drift toward unparalleled catastrophes.

—Albert Einstein

The world was orderly before the days of Einstein. Things were simple. Since Einstein, we have discovered warps in space, black holes, speeds that make time stand still, and a new geometry to calculate randomly arranged crystals and the structure of clouds. The linear world is going to pot; the straight line is becoming indeterminate. Numbers do not necessarily imply equal spaces between one another. The space between two and three may be different from the space between twenty-two and twenty-three. There are books about Zen in mathematics and Zen in nuclear physics; titles like *Zen and the Art of Motorcycle Maintenance*[1] have become commonplace. God is no longer up in the clouds (if she ever was), Freud could juxtapose seemingly different ideas in a book like *Moses and Monotheism,*[2] and the earth is not the center of anything.

Take, for example, the problem of relationships. If Mary is one and Paul is one, we have two persons. If Mary thinks only of herself (one), and Paul thinks only of himself (one), and there is no "magnetic force" between them, they are indeed two—a simple addition (Figure 3.1). But in a relationship, according to systems theory, there is the entity of Mary, and there is the entity of Paul, and there is the third entity of the relationship. The moment we look at a relationship on a more complex level, we say things like "the whole is greater than the sum of its parts."

So, what is the point of all this? Relationships are not arbitrary. To make sense of complex relationships, we have to designate boundaries around things, phenomena, or events. When you look into the dark sky on a clear night, it is filled

Figure 3.1. "Meaningless" Relationships.

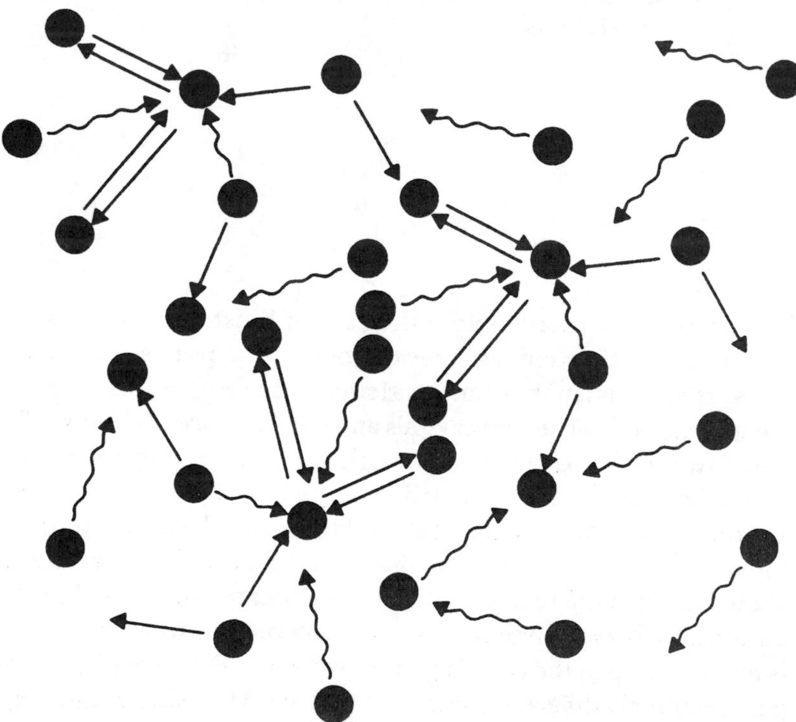

with stars. It is an unbounded panorama. But it does not stay unbounded because before long you organize your vision, your awe, with concepts (Figure 3.2). "There's the North Star," you say, or "There's the Big Dipper." This process of organizing the sky involves drawing imaginary boundaries to make sense of experience. We draw a boundary around a certain dense, bright pattern of stars and call it the Milky Way. This boundary, together with its inner content, is a system. The system's boundary denotes its relationship to its surroundings. We achieve a boundary by giving something a name: panhandle, Big Dipper, cell, or family. Attributing meaning to something is to give it a boundary (or perhaps a set of boundaries) to differentiate it from other things or phenomena.

Systems theory no longer allows us to think that Alcoholic A or Schizophrenic X came from Parents Z and R or from a substance called vodka. Alcoholic A is the product of many interrelated factors:

Figure 3.2. A Boundary Makes Meaning.

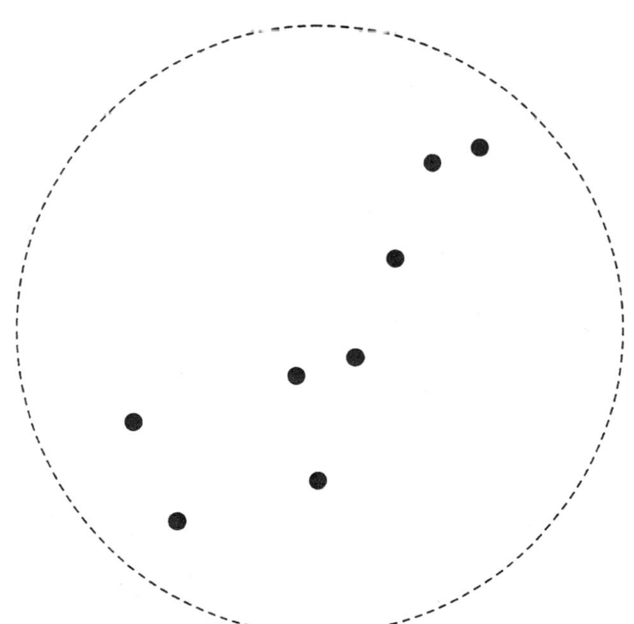

1.	Genetic predisposition	L
2.	Life circumstances	M, J, B
3.	Zeitgeist	B
4.	Parental alcoholism	K
5.	Other factor	Y
6.	Level of addiction	Z

These relationships are not necessarily ordinal, equal in value, sequential, or even additive. Figure 3.3 shows how their dynamic interaction may be arranged loosely. Human life circumstances and developing events do not stack up like numbers or figures or straight lines flowing from origin A to goal B. We now recognize patterns of events and, by studying whole patterns—gestalten—in their entirety, we slowly begin to make sense of the complex structures of small and large systems—families or corporations. Given this, there is little meaning in such pompous expressions as "a schizophrenogenic mother" or "a criminal family."

Figure 3.3. Alcoholic A.

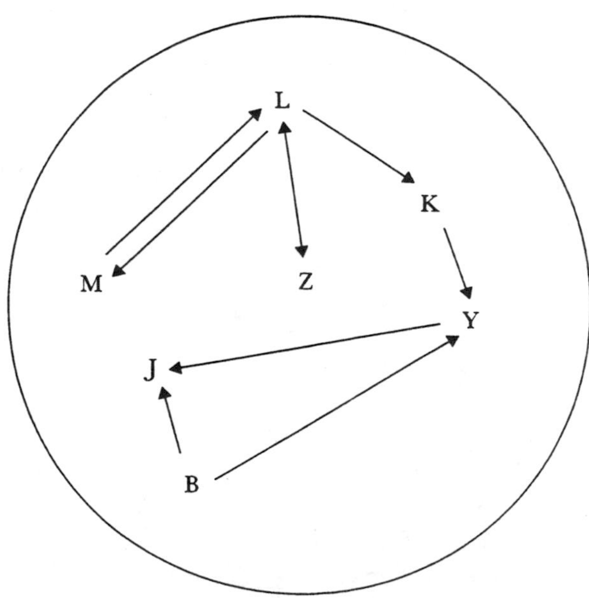

In dysfunctional marriages, it is naive to conclude that one partner or the other is the culprit, the troublemaker (though again, we may need to label and prohibit a particular behavior as abusive and unacceptable). To see this partner alone does not help the therapist understand the dysfunction, because another part of the problematic relationship is sitting at home or work unseen. So we study one partner, then the other, and then the "relational space" between them. Then we discover the influence of their respective parents, uncles, aunts, and children. To clinically investigate the system, *we define the family in terms of at least two generations* but, to manage it in our office, we say to ourselves, "At this time I will draw a boundary for this situation around parents and their children; this will be the *system* I will study and try to influence today."

Systems Theory, Field Theory, and Gestalt Psychology

Before moving on, the reader should be aware of the interconnection among systems theory, field theory, and Gestalt psychology. Notions of systems and fields came from the physical sciences. The field concept in physics was initiated by the work of Faraday, Maxwell, and Hertz. Their theories described electromagnetic fields in the nineteenth century and were followed by Einstein's revolutionary theory of relativity in the twentieth century. But field theory eventually left the realm of the physical sciences and was adapted by social scientists, specifically the Gestalt psychologists. Three German psychologists initiated the Gestalt movement.[3] These were Kurt Koffka,[4] Max Wertheimer,[5] and Wolfgang Köhler.[6] Their early work preceded World War I and was published in English in the 1930s and 1940s. They demonstrated that the way an object is perceived *is related to the total configuration in which it is embedded.* Perception is not determined by fixed characteristics of individual components, but rather by the relationships among these components.

Kurt Lewin was associated with Wertheimer and Köhler at the University of Berlin following World War I. Lewin, who created a psychological theory based on field concepts, is regarded by many as one of the most innovative and original figures in contemporary psychology.[7] It was Lewin who first applied the notion of psychological boundaries to intrapsychic processes, to the relationship between people and their psychological and physical environments, as well as to relationships among persons. Indeed, his first key paper was on how he, as a soldier, organized his perceptions of the battlefield.[8] And it was Lewin who described the various characteristics of boundaries, including their firmness-softness and fluidity-rigidity.

The intellectually fertile years between the world wars also produced the work of the German biologist Ludwig Von Bertalanffy. Between 1929 and 1941, he wrote a number of papers related to systems theory in physics and biology. In his most significant paper (for our purposes), he states that "a system is closed if no material enters or leaves it; it is open if there is import and export and, therefore, change of the components."[9] Von Bertalanffy's ideas about systems are congruent with Lewin's concepts of psychological fields. Here, too, we find the idea of boundary and its role of separating the organism from its environment. The nature of the boundary determines, for example, the difference between open and closed systems. In Lewin's language, closed systems have rigid, firm boundaries, while open systems have weaker, more fluid ones. Von Bertalanffy said that "living systems are open systems, maintaining themselves in exchange of materials with environment, and in continuous building up and breaking down of their components."[10] Social scientists and psychotherapists extended the notion of open and closed systems to the social situation, including the family. Von Bertalanffy would probably argue that all social systems are essentially open since they must interact with the environment to survive. However, therapists have loosely used the notion of closed systems to connote the relative impermeability of boundaries containing certain social processes and groupings.

Turning back now to the Gestalt psychologists, Koffka and Köhler discovered certain principles of perception. They found that when we look at certain patterns of dots, we complete them. While looking at .˙. we do not say that we see three dots. What we probably see is a completed gestalt—a bounded figure that we call a triangle. Human beings make patterns in their heads; we tend to look for perceptual closure. Indeed, this may be one of the primary shaping characteristics of homo sapiens, as significant as a larger cortex, opposable thumbs, biped motility, language, and year-round gestation.

The field of physics became a field of human experience. We organize the world within us and tend to synthesize experience in terms of wholes. When we manage to do this, we experience closure—satisfaction, completion, or insight. When an experience is difficult to organize and to complete, we feel disease or discomfort.

Laura and Fritz Perls met at the University of Berlin, where they were influenced by Lewin, Koffka, and Köhler. The Perlses bridged Gestalt psychology with Gestalt therapy.[11] Like Wertheimer, Lewin, and Goldstein before them, the Perlses were interested in extending the principles of perception to psychological health and disturbance. They theorized that health is signified by repeated experiences of closure, while "illness" is a state of chronic lack of closure. They adapted the notion of gestalten from perceptual patterns and organized wholes to gestalten as psychological-emotional-cognitive experiences within an oral-digestive model. If people are not able to organize a childhood experience fully into their lives—to chew it and assimilate it—they will be forever plagued by it. It will be a "disturbance" in their field—the so-called "unfinished business" of the Zeigarnik effect.[12] At the simplest level, we can say that the Perlses created a therapy to complete unfinished experience—to make them whole inside of us—so we can move on with life.

On the individual level, this means being able to bring the unfinished or unclear event into the present with our senses, awareness, energy, and expressiveness. The sense of completion is crowned by contact with what matters fully; and contact allows us to celebrate completion, let go, and move on to the next lively contact. As defined by Perls, Hefferline, and Goodman,

> Contact is awareness of the field or motor response in the field. It is for this reason that contacting, the functioning of the mere boundary of the organism,

> can nevertheless pretend to tell reality, something more than the urge or passivity of the organism. Let us understand contacting, awareness, and motor response, in the broadest sense, to include appetite and rejection, approaching and avoiding, sensing, feeling, manipulating, estimating, communicating, fighting, etc.—every kind of living relation that occurs at the boundary in the interaction of the organism and environment. All such contacting is the subject-matter of psychology.[13]

Perls talked about everything that involved the process of our development and its interruption. He was fascinated with what takes place at the boundary between people: contact takes place at the boundary; growth is at the boundary; figure formation and destruction occur at the boundary; health is in the color, brightness, dynamism, and grace of the interaction—the degree of spontaneous response—at the boundary. For Perls, relationships at the boundary include contact, organism-environment, novelty, excitement, self, consciousness, emergency situations, neurotic possibilities, resistance, and "human nature."

The ordinary state of affairs for the normal organism is to move fluidly from a state of need arousal to a state of need satisfaction, from tension to relaxation, from figural attention to homogenized disinterest. Well-functioning people are the ongoing process itself and do not experience themselves as static objects. Under circumstances of disturbance, of conditioned inhibition, of pathology, people interrupt their flow, segment their behavior, freeze their fluidity. Their psychic life is in a state of incongruence where a considerable discrepancy exists between behavior and awareness.

In the cycle of experience, we start with vague sensations, become aware of needs, become aroused, seek out what we need, and finally move to obtain what we want. If unimpeded, this is an example of individual or intrapsychic closure. The same phenomenon occurs in couples and families; mutual needs are discovered, actions taken, and contact is made to the mutual satisfaction of family members. When these interpersonal cycles are not completed but constantly interrupted, couples and families suffer.[14] Thus, what started as a discovery of physical fields in nature was incorporated as perceptual fields in humans, was expanded into a field model of individual need satisfaction, and finally was extended to phenomena related to couples and families.

My philosophy of intervening in small systems, then, is based both on principles of how to complete situations successfully and on principles of how systems operate. I now describe the latter principles in more detail.

Couple or Family as System

A couple or family is a system of individuals committed to staying together over an extended period of time, thus maintaining continuity. Such continuity may satisfy the urge to extend one's individual life span and one's individual awareness into future generations. This extension into future generations helps transmit values of the existing culture.

In addition to merely staying together, the members of a couple or family are committed to joint tasks. They create a home together and raise children and interact with larger systems; they comprise a subsystem within the larger systems of neighborhood, city, country, and world. The couple or family is a social, cultural, and economic unit of the community.

In modern times, the units take on many faces. There are adults living together, sometimes with combinations of children from one or more marriages. There are combined families of adults coming from divorced marriages to create a single household; there are homosexual couples living together; there are communal arrangements of various kinds. For the most part, families consist of one or more adults living in various arrangements with one or more children. These configurations have boundaries around them, making them distinct and separate from other families and groups in the neighborhood.

Within the boundaries of the family, subsystems exist. These include individuals, adults, children, and combinations of adults and children. Each subsystem has its own boundary. Under ideal circumstances, individuals treat one another with respect, allowing each other privacy and, at the same time, showing concern for and interest in each other (Figure 3.4).

Boundaries are constantly changing: sometimes a system is open to socializing and its boundary is semipermeable; at other times, it finds comfort in separateness and, in those moments, is firmly bounded. Individuals in well-functioning families know each other well enough to sense when to come together and when to stay apart. When questions arise about such matters, people feel comfortable enough to ask, "Are you available to talk about my problems at the office this afternoon?" Adults easily gather together in subsystems. They are the brains, the managers of the family. We expect them to make reasonable decisions about the family's daily life. Children get together to play, learn, and grow. Managerial interactions between adults and children are determined developmentally; a five-year-old will look to the parents for more daily guidance than a fifteen-year-old.

Well-functioning families are characterized by fluid, flexible subsystem boundaries among individuals and groupings of adults and children. People congregate for play or work. Dad takes a walk with his teenage daughter to talk about her boyfriend's transfer to another school. The kids go to the movies on Saturday evening while the parents go to a party. There is a common purpose, solidarity, cohesiveness, and responsiveness, as well as a respect for each person's separateness and specialness. A graceful rhythm prevails—from union and intimacy to individual autonomy. During stable times, people are able to leave each other alone. On the other hand, they give each other attention during periods of difficulty, stress, illness, or just plain interest. A similar graceful flow exists around the initiation, development, and execution of common tasks. Family members approach each other, negotiate what needs doing, do it, complete their tasks, enjoy the contact, and exit without clinging to each other or becoming stuck endlessly discussing what was done or not done. A healthy family is generally a good working team.

All families range from mutual protection on the one hand, to a lack of attention and sense of alienation on the other. No family is always in perfect balance. Families function with

Figure 3.4. A Well-Functioning Family.

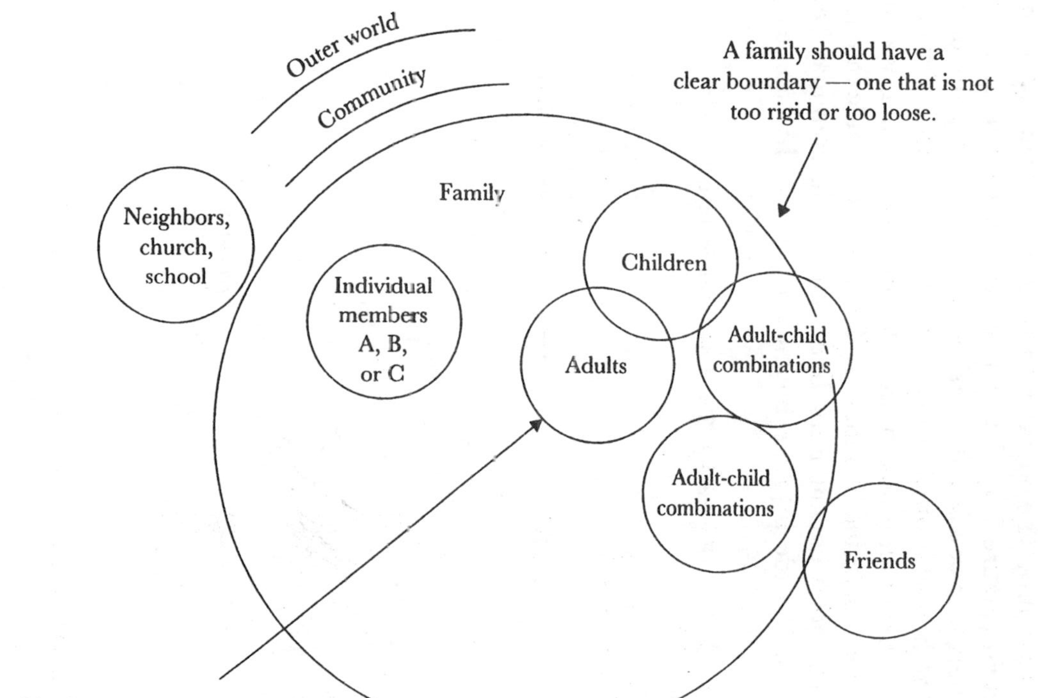

more or less clinging or looseness, and the sensitive therapist will attend to what works for a given family rather than to some absolute, monolithic principle such as "enmeshment" or "disorganization."

Families with impermeable boundaries overprotect themselves as a unit. The boundary around such groupings is thick and rigid (Figure 3.5). There is no easy exchange or activity with neighbors or friends outside of the system. They do not get together with others to attend lectures, movies, travel, or work on neighborhood projects. Within such families, we often find poor individual boundaries. The parents intrude into their adult or adolescent children's lives, and the children may be allowed to intrude into the business of adults. In one case, a

Figure 3.5. The Confluent System.

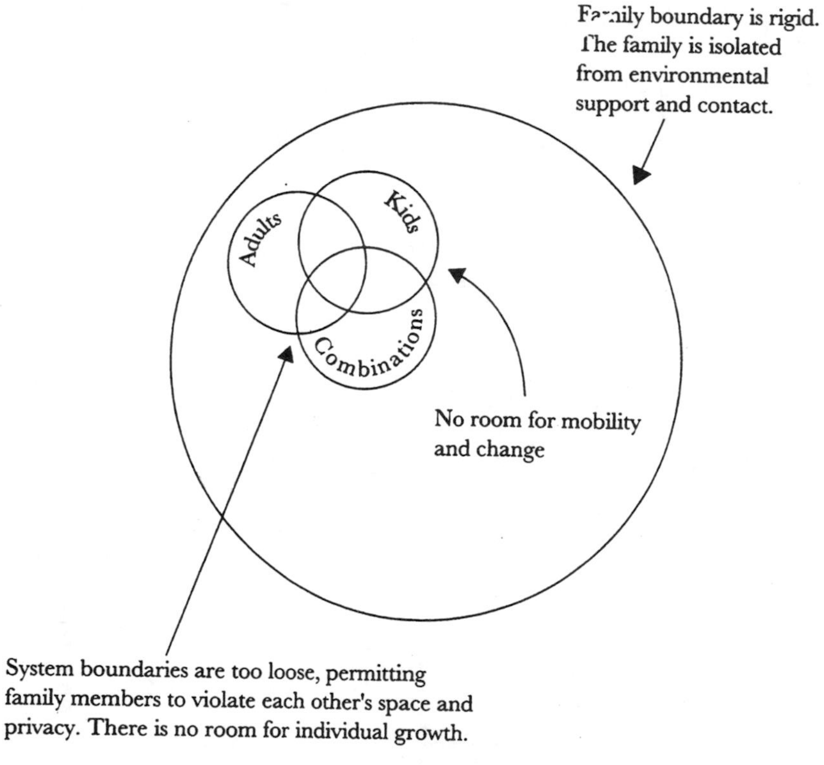

woman called her daughter-in-law daily to quiz her about her son's eating and excretory habits. Adults may have no privacy or secrets from one another. In another family, the adults removed doors from all bedrooms and bathrooms in the house. In less extreme cases, people can walk into each other's rooms without knocking. The same goes for their psychological lives: they may enter each other's inner lives without asking permission. While this kind of family has unusually rigid external boundaries, boundaries around subsystems are often too loose, too flexible, not allowing the individual or subgrouping a sense of autonomy and independence; everyone worries all the time about everyone else.

These can be termed *retroflected families*. To retroflect means "to turn sharply back against"; thus, retroflection is a resistance that contains energy and prevents its expression. Family members may suffer psychosomatic symptoms related to contained energy and inadequate expression of feelings. We see individuals suffering from a sense of being psychically choked; asthma, neckaches, constipation, chest pain, cramps, allergies, skin disorders, headaches, and anorexia nervosa may be some manifestation of these closed systems. Mothers and fathers are overly anxious about their children starting school, and school phobias in the children of these families are not uncommon. Children may have difficulty leaving home to marry or attend college. Parents and children are too vigilant about each other's lives. Too much concentration is within the family—too little is directed to the extended world.

At the other extreme of the continuum are the disorganized families whose external boundaries are too loose (see Figure 3.6). Here, people come and go without paying much attention to each other. Their homes may resemble a community recreational center, with neighbor adults and children coming and going without much ado or formality. Mealtime may find several spontaneous guest arrivals—if mealtime is managed as a regular communal activity at all. No one takes the time to inquire about the other's life, work, school performance, or significant relationships. Adults are alienated from each other and from the children. Children may be neglected psychologically and physically.

Figure 3.6. Loose Family System.

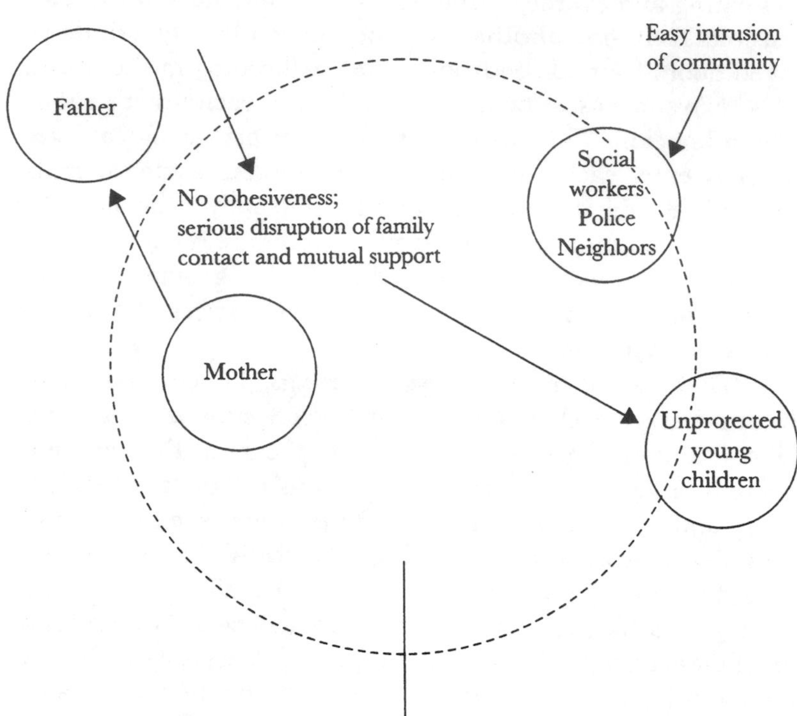

When a lack of intimacy and union exists, when family members cannot turn to one another for what they need, individuals may even resort to alcohol or other drugs to escape the chaos and try to grasp a sense of inner oneness, organization, or peace. Children are hungry for attention from peers, teachers, and neighbors. In some cases, they seek attention by stealing or otherwise taking what belongs to others. They may receive attention through disciplinary action from school or law enforcement officials. Their feelings are deeply buried, and their individual boundaries are not easily accessible. They are well defended against potential disrespect and pain.

Between these two extremes are the majority of families who function with more or less adequate external and internal boundaries, such that family members can feel a sense of belonging and love, as well as a respect for individual privacy and freedom to come home as well as to move out into the world. Children are not overprotected or underprotected: protection of children is conceived in relation to their stages of development.

The notion of systems is attractive to couple and family therapists because we have learned that no one member (molecule, particle, part, star) is solely responsible for the struggle of the family. The trajectory of the family's development is multiply determined. The whole, as we are fond of saying, is different from the sum of its parts. The concept of systems, therefore, allows us to honor the complex aesthetic quality of the couple or family.

By using the notion of boundaries, we obtain a diagnostic picture of the couple or family's functioning in the world. We can investigate the degree to which the couple or family unit extends itself into the world and allows the world to enter. Boundaries also exist around individual members of each unit, and we can analyze their relationships with each other in this way as well.

All systems, whether they are circumscribed clusters of bacteria or solar systems, have boundaries and a wholeness. Their processes include information exchange and change. One form of change is entropy—a tendency toward disorder. Negative entropy, on the other hand, is a tendency toward order. Systems "struggle" for stability or homeostasis, a balance of order with disorder. Systems can be more or less open or closed depending on where they are at that moment of their ongoing struggle.

In her book *Super-Mind: The Ultimate Energy,* Barbara Brown speaks of this subject in terms of awareness of patterns:

> There is still another area of "unconscious" awareness that is neither recognized nor utilized. We have no convenient descriptions of this kind of awareness, but it seems, as in Gestalt concepts, *to be an awareness of patterns of events, things or situations as wholes rather than awareness of specific elements within the wholes.* In some way, the perception of patterns leads to

> an unconscious direction of activity and behavior that is appropriate to a total situation or event. The phenomenon suggests that the mind appreciates, extracts, judges, makes decisions, then acts with considerable relevance and specificity to elements within the pattern.[15]

Within each system delineation or pattern, there is life and movement; separate entities exchange energy with each other (have a relationship). No one subsystem "causes" anything. Events within and among systems are multidetermined. No two things have a direct causal relationship. Processes are not simply linear but are complex and exist simultaneously at many different levels. The system world is like a galactically hierarchical arrangement of events. Past, present, and future are simultaneous events. Actions take place throughout nonsequentially, perhaps at the same moment, and no one event is wholly dependent or independent of another.

And so, in the human family, no one character causes the problem or is responsible for any given situation. All members act in concert to arrange or disarrange their lives in a way that contributes to their happiness and well-being or dissatisfaction and misery.

Moving from Individual to Couple and Family Therapy

Gestalt and other therapists accustomed to working with individuals will have to make a cognitive and perceptual leap from looking at the boundary of one person to experiencing the couple's or family's boundaries.[16] The organism becomes much larger and, in order not to drown in it, sensitive therapists move their chair back to see the family as a whole configuration. Because we are dealing with complex, multidetermined phenomena, seeing whole configurations rather than discrete parts, reductionistic language fails us and so we must think in terms of metaphor, analogy, and other images. The therapist's sense of metaphor and creative imagery will help make it possible to find the patterns of the larger organism.[17] The therapist must switch from analysis to synthesis, choosing to create wholes rather than taking things apart into smaller units.

The couple and family therapist attends to larger themes of which the family or couple is unaware. Thus, a family will argue about where to vacation, while the therapist attends to the positioning of their bodies, and while another family member wants to know which is the better babysitter for little Johnny, the therapist attends to the firmness or tentativeness of their voices or opinions. While a couple tries to express anger, the therapist will note that they continue holding hands. While the family focuses on Mary's eating habits, the therapist will look at how Mary, John, and the parents talk to each other or do not talk to each other, look at each other or do not look, ask questions, touch or stay apart, answer or remain silent, express appreciation or do not, criticize each other or refrain from criticism. The reader will note that in this approach to small systems, we are focusing on the *process* of the system rather than on the *content* of what the members process.[18]

Conclusion

The systems-oriented therapist will synthesize, not analyze; see complementary forces, rather than conflicts; avoid polemical directions while using metaphor and creative imagery to find integrative images and wholes; look for aesthetic forms in spaces between and around people, rather than focusing on individual circumstances or content issues. Because systems do not behave in a linear fashion, no matter what observed phenomena are pursued by the therapist, staying with the process will yield outcomes that enlighten the couple or family. This assumption is related to the principle of equifinality, which asserts "the equivalence of one form of behavior with another in reaching a certain goal."[19] Pursuing causes and effects is useless; it is like trying to find the pot of gold at the end of a rainbow or chasing your own shadow. Therapists will do well staying in the present and asking, "What are they doing? How are they impeding themselves from moving toward satisfaction? What processes are being repeated regardless of their usefulness? What's missing?" Answers to these questions form the ground-substance of interventions.

Finally, as a guide to orienting the reader to the Gestalt approach of working with couples and families as living systems, I have developed a list of thirteen principles, which have come out of my assimilation of systems theory and its application to couple and family therapy.

1. There is no linear progression in human relationships. There are no ordinary causes and effects—just complex interactions.
2. All events, including human relationships, are in constant process.
3. Relationships tend to triangulate.
4. No "identified patient" exists without a pattern of "unidentified patients."
5. History, whether of family or culture, is not a story but many events exploding all at once—a pattern.
6. Content is seductive and process needs careful observation and feedback.
7. The individual being, even in isolation, exists in relation to others.
8. Any event anywhere in a system, small or large, affects all other events; no event can be seen in isolation.
9. Couples and families are complementary: change the mood of one and the moods of others change.[20]
10. Reductionism is dangerous because it tends to harbor or stimulate polarization and the desire to destroy the Other.
11. We must face the problem of the apparent paradox between autonomy and relationship. Only truly autonomous persons can have "hot" relationships. (Confluent relationships destroy the spirit.)
12. The world is both one (pattern) and also pluralistic. Events in the world must be examined as interaction between whole-ness and politics. The world is made up of diversified voices crying, "We are all One."
13. Couples and families are "dissipative structures," since they tend to run out of energy at certain developmental stages. The ideal restructuring of these stages involves moving

upward into higher levels of functioning (imagine a spiral structure like the DNA helix).

Our job as therapists is to help the couple or family become aware of how and where the system becomes stuck and how to use their collective awareness and energy to overcome these stuck places in their interactions. Our job is basically completed when the couple or family can begin, develop, and complete interactions successfully, again and again.

Having made this fundamental point, let us continue in the same direction in the next chapter, which deals with the Interactive Cycle of Experience.

Notes to Chapter Three

1. R. M. Pirsig (1974), *Zen and the art of motorcycle maintenance* (New York: Bantam Books).
2. S. Freud (1964), *Moses and monotheism: An outline of psycho-analysis and other works* (London: Hogarth Press and Institute of Psycho-Analysis).
3. C. Hall, G. Lindsey (1957), *Theories of personality* (2nd ed.) (New York: Wiley, p. 207).
4. K. Koffka (1935), *Principles of Gestalt psychology* (New York: Harcourt Brace).
5. M. Wertheimer (1944), "Gestalt theory," *Social Research, 11,* 78–99.
6. W. Köhler (1947), *Gestalt psychology* (New York: Liveright).
7. K. Lewin (1936), *Principles of topological psychology* (New York: McGraw-Hill); K. Lewin (1951), *Field theory in social science* (New York: HarperCollins).
8. K. Lewin (1917), "Krieglandschaft" (War landscape), *Zeitschrift Angewandter Psychologie, 12,* 440–447.
9. L. Von Bertalanffy (1950), "The theory of open systems in physics and biology," *Science, 3,* 23.
10. L. Von Bertalanffy (1950), "The theory of open systems in physics and biology," *Science, 3,* 23.
11. F. S. Perls (1947), *Ego, hunger, and aggression* (New York: Vintage Books).
12. B. Zeigarnik (1927), "Über das Behalten von erledigten und unerledigten Handlungen" (On the persistence of finished and unfinished tasks), *Psychologische Forschung, 9,* 1–85.

13. F. S. Perls, R. F. Hefferline, & P. Goodman (1951), *Gestalt therapy: Excitement and growth in the human personality* (New York: Julian Press, p. 229).
14. The interactive cycle of experience is described more fully in Chapter Four of the present work. See also J. Zinker (1977), *Creative process in Gestalt therapy* (New York: Vintage Books).
15. B. Brown (1980), *Super-mind: The ultimate energy* (New York: HarperCollins, p. 274, emphasis added).
16. Chapter Seven of the present work discusses attending to and managing the boundaries of couples and families.
17. For further discussion of the use of metaphor and creative imagery, see J. Zinker (1977), *Creative process in Gestalt therapy* (New York: Vintage Books).
18. The therapist's work in attending to process is more fully described in Chapters Eight and Nine of the present book.
19. H. B. English & A. C. English (1958), *A comprehensive dictionary of psychological and psychoanalytical terms* (New York: McKay, p. 184).
20. See also M. Ferguson (1980), *The aquarian conspiracy* (New York: St. Martin's Press).

4

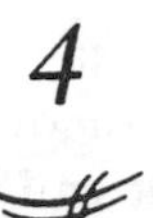

The Interactive Cycle

There is nothing so practical as a good theory.
—Kurt Lewin

Couple and family therapists are awed by the complexity of the interactions before them and by the wide range of possible interventions that could improve the existence of the people who turn to them for help. The complexity and range of choices may often appear so overwhelming that therapists risk being immobilized by confusion. Fortunately, these complexities can be made visible, organized, and comprehended with the use of a theory of human interactions that both identifies and explains which interactions are functional and which create difficulties.

Note: This chapter was originally written by Sonia Nevis; a revised version that I coauthored with her first appeared as a working paper produced by the Gestalt Institute of Cleveland, 1981.

Since the observable data of interactions are the same for all therapists, the therapist's theoretical stance determines what will be attended to and what will be ignored. A theory is good if it enables the therapist to see what is happening and if it supports deciding where to intervene. The strength of a theory is how useful it is for observation as well as intervention.

The Gestalt theory of psychological functioning has been refined and elaborated for the past thirty years and more by the faculty of the Gestalt Institute of Cleveland, among others. Our phenomenological description of intrapsychic process is referred to as the *Gestalt experience cycle*[1] (Figure 4.1).

On an intrapsychic level, we are grounded in awareness of what is relevant in the moment, what grabs our attention

Figure 4.1. Gestalt Experience Cycle.

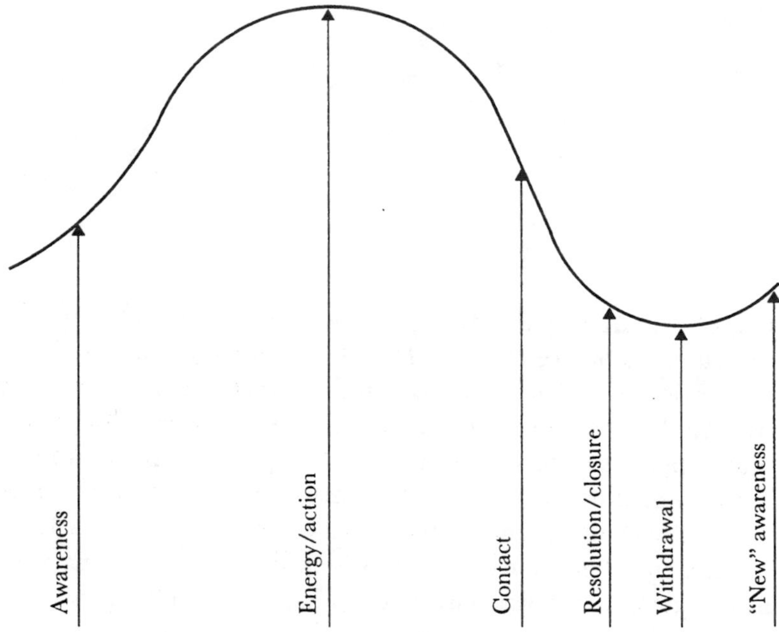

This is the "normal" cycle — with awareness being "fat" so that movement into action is well grounded . . . withdrawal is at the very bottom (where energy is relatively low and one can rest alone).

and stands out intellectually and/or motorically. This interest is invested with energy without which we would be unable to act. Ideally, our awareness is clear and rich. When awareness is sufficiently heightened by energy, we are able to move decisively toward what we want. Actions lead to contact with the environment and are followed by a sense of satisfaction, resolution, and closure. We are able to withdraw from the situation, relax, and let go. Withdrawal, when clean and complete, allows us to turn to a fresh experience without feeling the "drag" of something unfinished. A new awareness then comes to the foreground, and the cycle begins again.

Work with couples and families under this model is an extension of the intrapsychic experience cycle. Such an extension is used to describe intimate interactions in small systems. The principles are the same: full awareness leads to clear contact at the boundary between the self and the environment. However, the Gestalt interactive cycle focuses attention on the interactions between two or more people (Figure 4.2).

Phases of the Cycle

The phases of this cycle are continuous and sometimes overlapping, as one cycle follows from and intermingles with another. To show the flow within a single unit of experience, the cycle is artificially divided into the five phases described below. These phases are arranged in a sequential order that makes both logical and intuitive sense. At the same time, we know that each phase has elements of all other phases within it.[2]

Observation of the interactions between the two individuals making a couple, or among the members of a family, provides a therapist with a clear view of the system. In addition, observation makes evident the skills in the system that are a part of good functioning. Competence in the skills needed for moving through each phase of this process underlies satisfaction. A completed cycle, with each phase well articulated, results in a sense of well-being. An incomplete cycle results in dissatisfaction and "dis-ease." Observation of cyclical functioning brings out the resistances in the system that interrupt smooth resolution

Figure 4.2. Gestalt Interactive Cycle.

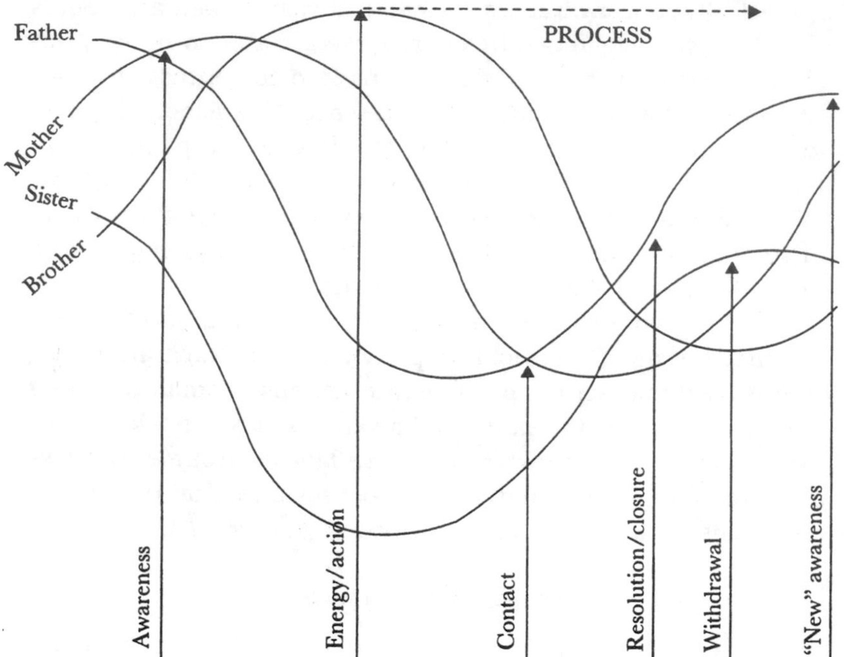

and that are, therefore, linked with dysfunction.[3] As the therapist identifies and helps to resolve breakdowns or resistances in the flow, a satisfying process is restored.

Awareness

"Awareness is characterized by *contact,* by *sensing,* by *excitement,* and by *Gestalt* formation. Its adequate functioning is the realm of normal psychology; any disturbance comes under the heading of psychopathology."[4]

Intrapsychic and interpersonal awareness exists before interaction. Individuals in a system are separate, with their own sensations, emotions, thoughts, memories, and hopes.[5] Each person's awareness is different: we live in our own self-defined worlds. The complexity of this awareness is well known. Some sensations, thoughts, or feelings are readily available and easy to articulate; others are dim, unclear, and require work to put into words or actions; some are unavailable to oneself, yet visible to others.

The turning from self to other(s) marks the beginning of the awareness phase in the interactive cycle. An individual alone may not need to articulate intrapsychic sensations: one may proceed from the "itch" to the "scratch" without the intermediate step of saying, "I itch."

Sometimes people do articulate for themselves—for example, in keeping a journal. However, in this case, attending to the response of another is optional; no one requires it. Turning to interaction requires work. It becomes necessary to say aloud what is obvious to one's self but what may not be to others: "I'm tired" or "I'm in the mood for pizza" or "It would be nice to play bridge tonight" or "Perhaps I'll try to finish reading my book before I go to sleep." Even more work is required in the struggle to say or do what is less clear: "I'm feeling low and don't know what it's about" or "I'm restless tonight—any interesting ideas?" or "If you hang around me now, we'll probably fight."

In addition to the work required to clearly express one's feelings, there is the work of listening, wanting to hear about the world of the other. Work is also required for noticing others, being willing to say, "You look tired. Why don't you relax tonight?" or "You're favoring your right leg—your knee must be hurting again." One must care enough about the experience of others to ask: "What happened at the meeting today?" or "Any thoughts about what we can do tonight?" or "How do you feel about what I'm saying?"

This interplay of saying and listening, seeing and being seen, touching and being touched, knowing and being known, moves us to clarify our similarities and differences. This increasing awareness of each other stimulates the energy necessary for the clear emergence of wants or desires: the emergence of a figure from the background.

The ability of a couple or family to engage in such exploratory activities is visible to a trained observer. If awareness skills are sparse, a limited awareness phase will either provide little energy for action or the ensuing contact will be superficial or stereotypical (the narrow band of interaction that is typical of the system); the ensuing phase will also be stereotypical or bland. In such families, we hear the same things repeatedly discussed and the same activities engaged in again and again (Figure 4.3).

A varied and enriched exchange of awareness is related to a rich and interesting family life. However, when strong conflict exists and when the system is dealing with difficult life tasks, the skills for staying long enough in this exploratory, testing-out, trial-and-error awareness phase will probably be a major factor in determining whether or not the system can come to a satisfactory closure and to a mutual sense of a task well done. And this will be one of the major criteria defining "good form."

Figure 4.3. Limited Awareness Phase.

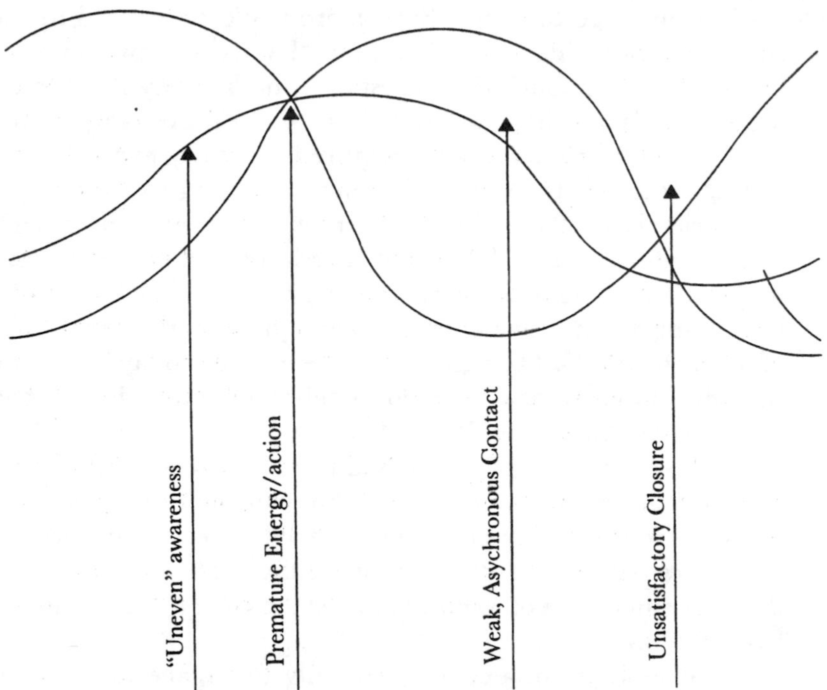

A limited awareness phase will either provide little energy for action or the ensuing contact will be stereotypical.

The first therapeutic task in the awareness phase is to encourage fuller articulations of wider bands of self-awareness, then to teach the skills of noticing, seeing, and hearing the other. In addition, the therapeutic task will be to focus attention on the strengths as well as interruptions or resistances in exchange of awareness between people.

Although resistances to awareness are varied and will be explored in more detail later, the common ones during this phase are introjection and projection. Resistances are often described as though they were intrapsychic processes; while they are often conceptualized as opposing internal forces (needs versus wants), they are made manifest in observable interpersonal phenomena with significant others. The therapist's observations of a couple or a family system provide a startling view of how certain responses are learned, as well as how they are repeated. Such eventual habituation may indeed lead to the increasing unawareness that characterizes resistance.

Introjection—the "swallowing whole" of a foreign body without assimilation—can be observed in a couple or family when there is (1) a force feeder—one who expects food or opinion or information to be swallowed as given—and (2) a swallower—one who absorbs all that is given, rather than selectively chewing and then spitting out what is not wanted. Introjection and other resistances to contact are always in interaction: the swallower cannot exist without the force feeder, and vice versa.

Projection—the unaware transference of unwanted qualities of one's own self onto others—can also be observed during the awareness phase. It requires one person who offers little personal information and deflects or discourages questions, another person who is willing to guess and fill in the gaps, and others who will not interfere. Conversations are characterized by: "You must be hungry" or "You won't like what I'm going to say" or "You'll love school."

Such interruptions in the flow of awareness to the common pool of information available to a couple or family provide the clues for therapeutic intervention in the system. The major aim of these interventions is to seize the attention of the system and direct attention to the couple's or family's style of moving through the cycle. The intervention must focus on the strengths of the system as well as the patterns of resistance, not on one person's action or inaction. Awareness of its own process enables the couple or family to become interested in how it functions, rather than in who is to blame for the difficulties. When such interventions are made sensitively and with compassion toward all members of the system, people want to learn more about the intricacies of their interactions.[6]

Energy/Action

In this phase of the cycle, an individual's excitation or energy continues to grow and to organize awareness so that a want or a desire emerges clearly; that is, a gestalt forms and becomes figural. Energy becomes invested in a dominant interest, and competing interests or wants recede into the background. A healthy person can form and focus on sharply delineated figures that emerge out of a rich and varied ground.

A similar process takes place in a couple or family system. From the pool of awareness, interest in or caring strongly about something emerges and becomes a shared figure for all members of the system. This process is interpersonal: individuals want different things, are interested in them to differing degrees, and exhibit their caring in different ways. The task in this energy/action phase of the cycle is to manage the complexity of these differences so that the resulting figure (want, care, concern, interest) is clear, lively, and invested with sufficient energy for moving through the process to contact and resolution.

A competent couple or family can work toward a melding of wants by developing a common figure that both encompasses and transcends its differences through a combination of pushing and patience. Difficulties in achieving such a melding occur when the system is either impatient or lacking energy.

Some active skills required for working in this phase are suggesting, creating, influencing, or enticing. Some receptive skills required are an openness to being influenced, a willingness to be enticed, an interest in suggestions, and a willingness to encourage and support the creativity in others. Give and take, as well as a combination of seriousness and lightness, are characteristic of this phase.

Daughter: *Mom, I want some of those cookies.*

Mother: *I think you should wait until after dinner.*

Daughter: *Then let me eat now.*

Mother: *Okay with me, if you don't mind eating alone.*

Daughter: *Well, maybe I'll wait.*

Wife: *Let's go out and get something to eat.*

Husband: *I don't have much money, but I don't want to cook either.*

Wife: *Let's see if there's anything easy to fix in the house.*

Husband: *Okay, just so it's simple, like a picnic inside.*

The therapist's task during this phase of the cycle is not only to encourage the active and receptive skills described above but to look for and support a respect for the other. This is the kind of respect that neither pushes too hard without checking on the effects of the pushing nor fails to push hard enough because the other might be "fragile." Good interactions during this phase are like playful fights. Everybody gets a workout but nobody gets hurt. Interruptions or resistances in this phase are marked by a drop in energy or interest when differences are aired. The system becomes either compliant or resistant rather than imaginative and lively.

A common resistance during this energy/action phase is confluence—the loss of boundaries between self and other. Confluence is apparent when power is misused or abused: suggesting or influencing becomes bullying or demanding; enticing becomes seducing. When power is clearly in one person or in one part of the system, the potentially common figure becomes a confluent figure. The energy in one part of the system wields too much power and the energy of the other part becomes depressed, hidden, underground—although observable as placidly confluent.

Another common interruption or resistance during the energy/action phase is retroflection: a turning inward of energy. Couple or family members do not reach out to each other—not in warmth, in anger, in curiosity, or in attempts to influence one another. Such resistance is maintained when no one protests or insists on reaching out; everyone colludes in the belief that boundaries must be overrespected, that intrusiveness is forbidden. In retroflective families, every subsystem obeys these rules: parents protect children by having their own secrets, and children shield parents by withholding their feelings, their questions, and their guesses (Figure 4.4).

Retroflecting families can also be damaged by their isolation from the world outside the family. These systems have tight boundaries; they keep their concerns, worries, and troubles to themselves and do not readily seek help. They place an excessive emphasis on privacy. A therapist has no difficulty in

Figure 4.4. Limited Energy Phase.

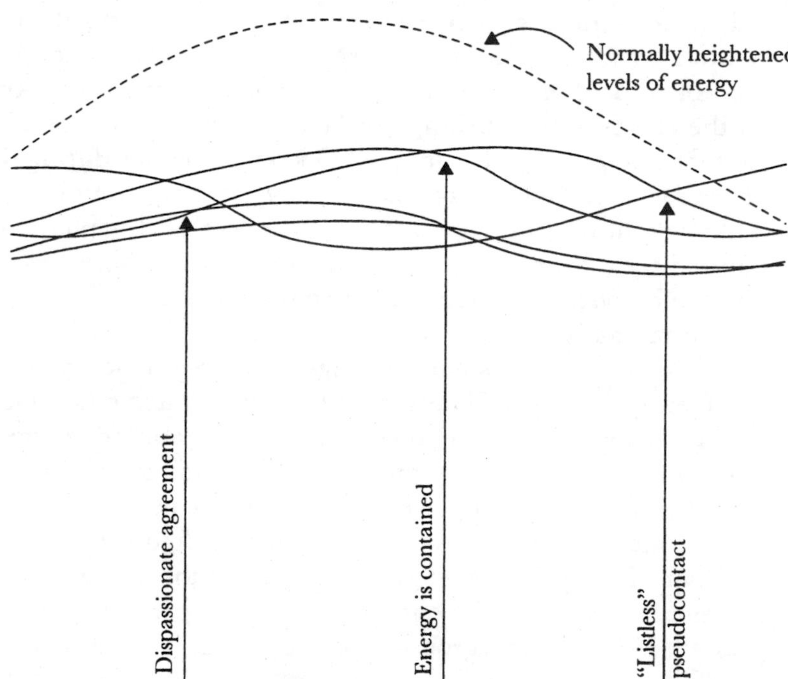

In a system marked by retroflection, energy is contained or withheld and people do not reach out to each other.

recognizing retroflecting families: one soon notices that these family members rarely turn to the therapist for help when they feel stuck, nor do they take kindly to suggestions offered when they do ask for help.

Contact

Contact is the awareness of difference (the "novel" or "unlike") at the boundary between organism and environment; it is marked by energy (excitement), heightened presence or attention, and "intentionality" that mediates what crosses the boundary and rejects what is unassimilable.[7]

The contact phase of the cycle is the fruit of the labors of the energy/action phase. Wants or concerns have been melded by interactions into a newly created whole—a whole that is different from its parts. The emergent figure is made up of the different wants; it does not belong to one-half of the couple or to one member of the family. Rather, it is owned by all, for it has been formed by a mutually influenced process. Contact, then, is the sensation of mutual ownership, the glow of satisfaction at work accomplished.

When contact is strong, energy is ample for carrying out the agreements, the understandings, the insights into the future. Plans to meet for lunch are realized, not postponed; enthusiasm grows for having a party, and the party takes place. Agreements are fulfilled. Saying no takes place less often; instead, people make positive suggestions. Promises are kept to play a game after the chores are done or to read stories before bedtime. The therapist's task at this point includes being alert to any signs of healthy mutuality and a moving toward each other—to note responses like "okay," "yes," "seems right," "let's do it," "count on me," or "let's forget it," "that's the way it is," "nothing we can do."

The therapist is also alert to any trace of resistance that may have started in the action/energy phase (confluence and/or retroflection) and resulted in an ambiguous figure that is fuzzily delineated or confused. The common goal is not supported by any or all parts of the system. When confluence is a major resistance in the energy/action phase, the contact that follows is incomplete, half-baked. The shared figure is characterized by identifying statements such as "That's sort of a good idea," "I guess we should do that," and "I'll try to remember." Weak interest and apathetic agreement will be reflected in the voices, bodies, and words of couple or family members (Figure 4.5).

Couples and families that are prone to being confluent are those that overvalue agreement, similarity, and avoidance of conflict. They reach the contact phase of the cycle quickly in order to avoid the airing of disagreements. They avoid the work necessary for finding new ways of viewing situations and solving problems. The contact they achieve is often stereotypical

Figure 4.5. Incomplete Contact Phase.

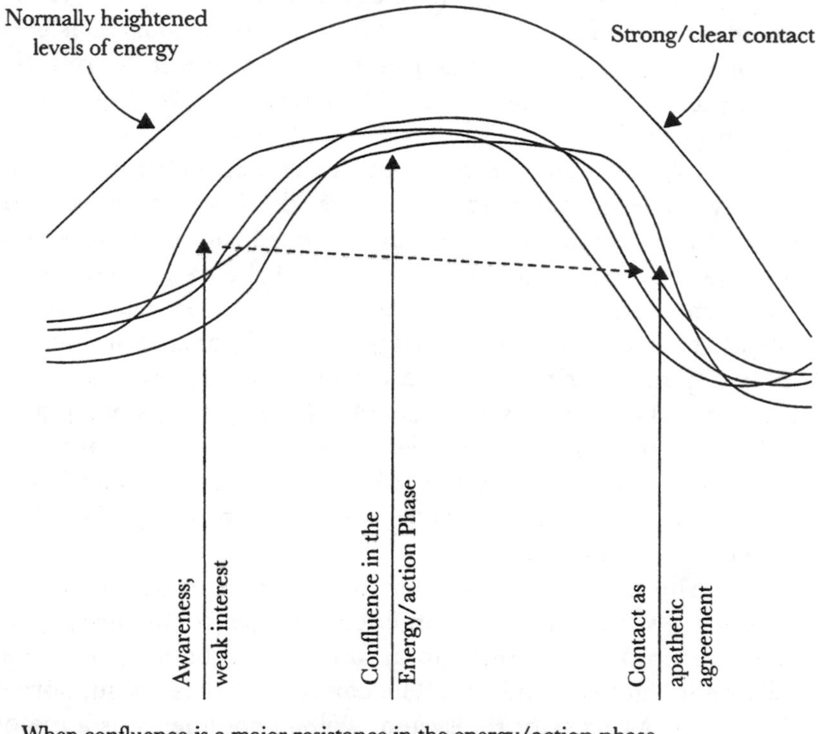

When confluence is a major resistance in the energy/action phase, the contact that follows will be incomplete.

of their previous contacts; liveliness and interest are minimal. Thus, the emerging figure, idea, or goal is not memorable and is not infused with caring; it is easily forgotten. Agreements are neglected, plans are aborted, and insights are blurred. Such couples or families develop a relationship with the therapist that resembles the one they have to each other. They readily agree to all the suggestions, insights, and prescriptions of the therapist, and then act on none of them.

When retroflection is a major resistance in the energy/action phase, contact is not achieved and premature withdrawal occurs. This can be true for the family as a whole: family members often stop treatment and try to solve problems without outside help. Or it can be true of parts of the system: an individual or subsystem withdraws energy to wait for another time or to try to work out things alone. A child who has been bullied appears to agree if the resistance is confluence but subsequently withdraws into sullenness, anger, or confusion, becoming unavailable for contact. A spouse who is overwhelmed by demands or recriminations may also withdraw, either to a room alone or internally, remaining unavailable for contact.

When the interactive cycle is interrupted, the tensions of incomplete situations accumulate. The therapist must then turn the couple or family members back to the beginning of the signs of resistance, must interest them in how they interfere with their process, and must work to undo the resistance so that contact and resolution can occur.

Resolution/Closure

In this phase of the cycle, the couple or family reviews what has happened and finds ways to express the experience, checking for a common understanding of agreements, appreciating themselves and each other, and regretting together what could not be. The system summarizes, reflects, and savors the experience, then nails it down. Characteristic words or gestures include the following: "Hey! That's good." "Too bad we couldn't go visit grandma." "Now remember, we're going to save as much money as possible this month." "You didn't shout as much this time." and "You really listened."

This "chewing over" during the resolution/closure phase of the cycle allows the energy to diminish gradually, ending when all interest, curiosity, and feelings are dissipated. Then closure becomes possible. The stronger the feelings and the interest and the greater the risk in the new commitment, the longer the time and attention needed in the resolution/closure phase. A simple figure, easily achieved—"Let's go to the movies" or "Okay, let's see the new western"—will probably only require, "That was a good idea," in order to close. A large figure—say, going back to school—will need repeated review, follow-up, planning, readjustment, and reassurance all around. Either way, closure permits letting go, followed by healthy withdrawal; both are necessary before turning toward new sensations, new awareness.

The therapist's skill during this phase involves noting the presence or absence of the necessary activities for resolution. When a system is skilled in resolution, the individuals feel a sense of completeness. When the situation feels incomplete, the therapist may intervene by saying, "Tell each other how you felt about what just happened" or "Tell each other what you learned from this." If the activities of resolution go on too long, one can say, "I suggest just one more sentence from each of you" or "Finish by looking around and seeing how everybody appears now."

The resistances in this phase take the form of either letting go too soon or hanging on too long. A system that characteristically lets go and closes too quickly does not learn from each resolved cycle. The resolution does not include enough time to chew, swallow, and assimilate what is useful and to spit out or reject what is extraneous. Such hurried people are often inadequately nourished by their experience.

On the other hand, a couple or family that hangs on too long endlessly discusses, dissects, and drains the experience dry. Such a couple or family repeats things over and over and talks on and on when interest is diminished and even long gone. Rather than swallowing and allowing assimilation to take place, the experience is endlessly chewed until the flavor fades away.

The therapist recognizes couples' or families' resistances to resolution and closure when they do not finish a unit of work within the agreed treatment time. Such couples or families either consistently run overtime or abruptly start something new when the closing time approaches. With these systems, the therapist encounters difficulty in closing the therapy session.

Withdrawal

Withdrawal marks the end of the cycle. During this pause before a new cycle begins, people separate, turn inward, and let go of the other(s). We need to be able to make contact and withdraw, to touch and be touched, and then to let go. This is our dance of life.

Withdrawal can draw the boundaries closely around a person, subsystem, or the couple or family as a whole, thus accentuating its distance from the outside world. The system's ability to do this, to contact the boundaries and then to start the process of expanding them again, is a healthy process.

The task for the therapist is to watch for the signs of letting go that mark independence and self-sufficiency—those signs in body, in concern, and in attention that begin to separate individuals and groups from each other, thus marking the end of an experience. These signs also may be verbal indications that individuals or subsystems are turning toward a consideration of what they want to do next. Example statements would be: "Well, I'm satisfied." "What shall we do next?" "I'm feeling good, nothing's coming up for me at the moment." It's a period marked by long, comfortable silences and verbal expressions of satisfaction or neutral statements; the participants are gently present for one another in a relaxed atmosphere, much like a lovingly comfortable postcoital embrace.

This initial turning toward the next event is often subtle. The absence of such signs of new interest suggests interference or resistance; it indicates an inability or reluctance to withdraw and let go. The system's inability to move on may become fixed in habitual withdrawal that lasts so long that the amount of contact between people is dramatically reduced.

When resistant to letting go, couples and families can be characterized as clinging to each other, to other family members, or to the therapist. They have difficulty being alone. Togetherness is overvalued and privacy devalued. These couples and families nurture dependence and frown on independent behavior as secretive or asocial.

When withdrawal is prolonged in couple or family members, they spend a great deal of time alone or with those most similar to themselves. Individuals, subsystems, or the couple or family are always removed from contact with people different from themselves. They have difficulty casually turning toward others. Self-sufficiency, needing no help, and "It's nobody's business but our own" are the norms (Figure 4.6).

Figure 4.6. Prolonged Withdrawal Phase.

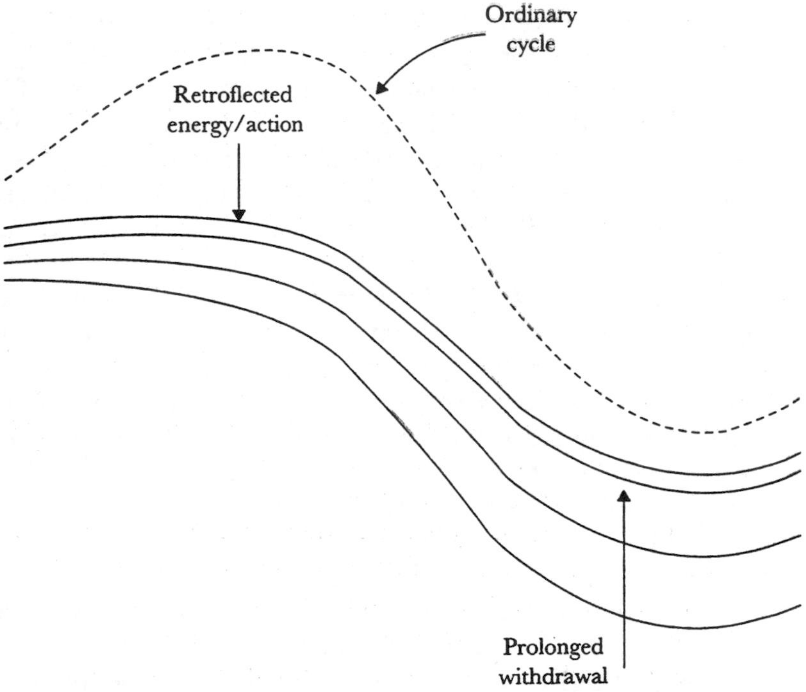

When withdrawal is prolonged in a couple or family, they will spend a great deal of time alone.

John and Diana: Moving Through the Cycle

The following session illustrates one couple's movement through the interactive cycle. This is the couple's third session. They have been married for seven years and have two children. John is an engineer and Diana is a rehabilitation psychologist. They came to see us because they sensed that although nothing had dramatically deteriorated between them, there was a "rift," a "dullness" between them, as Diana put it. John says, "We have good sex but we don't make love." Both are beginning to spend less private, one-on-one time together and seem to be more interested in other people than in each other.

Therapist: *I would like for you to turn to each other and talk about something that matters to both of you. I'll sit with you and listen and if you get stuck or need any help, please turn to me and I'll be glad to help out. Okay?*

John: *I talk to her all the time and all I get back is that it's all my fault, that something is wrong with what I did or said. I want to please, and I don't please.*

Therapist: *I'm glad you are able to say that. Just say it directly to Diana and if I see that what you say happens, I promise to comment on it.*

John: *Like I was saying, you always blame me.*

Diana: *(Starts crying softly) I am a romantic woman and when we were in New York last summer, I asked you to take me to a special place, just the two of us. And what happened? We wound up going with other people. Why? Why are you so mean to me?*

John: *I took you all out and paid for it, didn't I? I wish you would appreciate my generosity.*

Diana: *I am not making a point about generosity, John.*

Here, a long silence ensues. Both John and Diana look dumbfounded, dismayed. Diana turns to the therapist, just looking, not saying anything.

Therapist: *You both got started wrong and now you're stuck. Does that happen at home, too?*

Diana: *Yes. After a while we both seem to get tired and then there are long silences.*

Therapist: *In the beginning, you have good energy. You both go in trying to solve the problem. You both do your best to move in with all your feeling.*

Here, the therapist tells them about their competence, what they do well.

John: *Sure, I have feelings about not being appreciated.*

Therapist: *You have strong feelings but you don't* hear *each other very well. Each of you says something important that the other doesn't acknowledge. Can you both feel that?*

Because of previous repeated failures to make themselves heard by each other, the couple runs out of energy early in the awareness phase of the cycle. They are not able to stay long enough with the talk, to give it more energy so as to come across fully to one another.

Diana: *He doesn't hear about my birthday request.*

John: *You see, Doc, here we go again.*

Here, the couple is in the awareness or *clarifying* stage. They are trying to identify the problem—to articulate it and, later, to find a common ground with the therapist in coming to an *awareness* of each other's point of view.

Therapist: *I would like to help you both to hear each other better. What I want you to try is to start all over again—but this time, before you respond to the other, I want you to tell what you hear each other say. Do you know what I mean?*

Diana: *Yes.*

John: *I think so. I want to be appreciated. I want to be praised for my goodness. I'm always feeling criticized by you, Diana.*

Diana: *(To therapist) Now you want me to tell him what I hear him tell me before I answer?*

Therapist: *That's right.*

Diana: *He says he wants to be appreciated. (She pauses now as if the words are stuck in her throat. She clears her throat.)*

Therapist: *Would you say that to John, please?*

John: *(Appears excited and somewhat angry) What's the matter? Can't say it to my face?*

Here, it's hard to tell their mounting excitement from their words. But they look more aroused and drawn to the work required of them.

Therapist: *(To John) Please stay out of Diana's thing. She is doing her best. Your turn will come.*

Diana: *You're a hard man to praise and appreciate. But it's true . . . I hear you tell me that you want to be praised for your goodness.*

John: *Yeah, that's right. I want you to see how hard I try to please you at other times. Maybe it's not exactly your way, maybe it's not very romantic, but it's from my love that I try to please you.*

Having been heard has touched John and he is able to talk from his feelings, even his passion.

Therapist: *Now it's your turn, John, to tell Diana what you heard her tell you. Tell her, not me. I'll hear it.*

They practice hearing each other for a while. Although the couple are now able to achieve a little more contact through awareness, their energy is not heightened because they are not looking at or *seeing* each other. Each is programming the other with words but without passion.

Therapist: *You are both doing well* hearing *each other but you are not* looking *. . . Remember when you first met? . . . How you couldn't keep your eyes off each other? What happened? Here is what I want you to try: look at each other silently for a while and take turns saying what you see. No editorial comments . . . only what you actually* see.

John: *The first thing I see is your blue eyes. I can't always tell what you feel when you look at me like that, except that I* love *that look.*

Diana: *I like your romantic-looking* eyes. *They're dreamy . . . Remember how we used to look into each other's eyes while dancing?*

John: *Yeah—dancing at the Pump Room at the Ambassador in Chicago? Yeah, and me looking down at your cleavage!*

Therapist: *Could you tell each other some feelings you have as you keep looking?*

Diana: *Nostalgic feelings—when I look at you and your face looks softer, I feel warm and cozy with you.*

(Their faces soften as if entering a deeper layer of feeling with one another.)

John: *I'm such a fool—I had a chance to have you all to myself and I blew it! I've worked myself into tears (his eyes are filled) like a fool. I don't know why I'm so dumb sometimes. You want me to do special things on your birthdays, like this trip to New York. You wanted to be alone with me and I didn't pay attention to that in New York. (Diana's eyes redden and she extends a tentative hand to John.)*

The therapist, having stretched the time so that each could think and feel the other's problem, allows the couple to move toward resolution. Both experience their energies moving them toward more understanding of the other.

Diana: *I can't tell you how much it means to me when you show me your feelings and your vulnerability. (Diana's head is tilted and John is looking at the floor, sheepishly.)*

Here, the *contact* phase begins.

John: *I'll tell you what we can do. I'll be finished with my project at Metro by the end of next week. How would it be if you leave that coming weekend open . . . and I'll plan a surprise weekend for us. I'll get the babysitter and all!*

Diana: *Oh honey, you can be so sweet. We can get Robin to come over.*

John: *I'll call her, okay?*

Diana: *Great!*

Because John and Diana developed a full understanding of each other's experience, they were able to spontaneously create a situation that gave them both pleasure. You could feel and see the mutual ownership and glow of their caring. They connected. They made contact.

(Both of them spontaneously turn to the therapist, smiling.)
Therapist: *So what happens when you both listen to each other and acknowledge what the other person wants?*

Diana: *I don't know if it's always so, but it looks like if I repeat what John wants, then somehow I get off of myself and want to respond to him.*

John: *Yeah, me too!*

In briefly reviewing their experience together, the couple knows what helped them make contact and behave as if they can repeat this successful experience later on. The *resolution* phase of their process comes with this sense of mutual congratulation.

Therapist: *Good! You got unstuck very quickly when you heard each other and it became clear to each of you what was at stake for the other. Then you could be generous.*

To summarize, all couples and families have their own style of moving through the phases of the cycle. Some move fast, some linger, some stay longer in one phase or another. Families in pain have characteristic ways and places of interrupting their flow. A healthy process has organization, order, and clear form, while an unhealthy process is disorganized, disordered, and unclear in form.

The repetition of successful experiences in complete cycles develops a sense of well-being in couples or families, a sense of growth and accomplishment. Such repeated success helps to build the stabilizing middle ground of easily achieved, common figures.[8] Gestalt small systems theory proposes that this stable and ever-expanding middle ground supports the system's enduring strength over time.

Ideally, a couple or family learns to focus attention on its interactive process, to form clear and common figures, and to complete situations. The following specific outcomes are related to the skills necessary for negotiating the various phases of the interactive cycle with a minimum of resistance.

1. The boundaries of individuals, subsystems, and the complete system will be clear and flexible, so that graceful contact is possible.
2. Members of the couple or family will allow each other to differ. They will learn to appreciate differences and to encourage a full expression of what is seen, felt, and thought.
3. Couple or family members will learn to encourage each other, to show appreciation for each other, and to support each other in a variety of nurturing ways.
4. The couple or family members will appreciate their own struggle and will have compassion for the struggle of others. They will learn mutual respect and loyalty.
5. They will learn to stay in the present, to finish an interaction before starting something new, and to identify interruptions in their process.
6. They will learn to have patience, to develop staying power when life gets rough, and to let go when necessary.
7. They will be authentically curious about each other's feelings and views and will be bold, experimental, and sometimes playful when creative solutions are necessary.

Role of the Therapist in Couple and Family Therapy

Against this background of the interactive cycle, a Gestalt therapist observes the couple or family interact. A specific phase becomes figural for the therapist, either because the system is particularly skilled at moving through that phase and is unaware of this, or because there are resistances or interruptions of which the couple or family are unaware. The therapist's interventions aim to provide awareness to the couple or family of how they interact: their strengths, what they already do well, and their weaknesses, what they need to learn.

The first task of the couple or family therapist is to stimulate the interest and curiosity of the system in its own process, to teach couples or families to notice how they interact. The therapist then helps to resolve the resistances, thereby restoring good function to dysfunctional systems.

The Gestalt therapist attempts to teach the couple or family to attend to its interactive process and to struggle to improve its movement through the interactive cycle. The therapist is a participant-observer, with emphasis on the observer.

While observing the couple or family, the interactive cycle is used by the therapist to identify the system's process skills, as well as its breakdowns or resistances. The therapist also uses his or her own responses to the system as an important part of the phenomenological data available.

As participant, therapists organize the therapeutic situation so that couple or family members interact directly with each other, rather than focusing their attention on the clinicians. This structure frees therapists to observe and evaluate the clients' ways of relating to each other. Therapists then organize their observations and responses to choose a figural point for an intervention that will make memorable some aspect of the process that the couple or family can use to know more about its own situation. Thus, therapists create fresh awareness that opens people's eyes and gives them more choices.

Therapists suggest relevant experiments to create new situations for enabling a couple or a family to learn new behaviors, to experience new feelings, to acquire new insights.[9] Thus, clients learn to use their new awareness, here and now, with the therapists present as coaches and witnesses. They learn to enlarge their competence. Therapists may introduce experiments at any phase of the cycle where new learning is needed. They may point out where boundaries become too "mushy" (confluent and merging) or too rigid (tight and impermeable) and may suggest experiments to alter the interactions between any two people or between parts of a system.

Therapists may report on their personal experience of the unfolding scene, using imagery, metaphor, and fantasy to provide the couple with a new awareness, a new way to look at itself. Therapists also watch for and work with polarities, taking great care to teach the couple or family, often with experiments, the creative possibilities inherent in all aspects of a given dilemma.

Finally, Gestalt therapists are a grounded, caring presence who affirm, appreciate, and praise all struggle, all strengths—all that is moving and personally touching. Therapists are compassionate people who become a model for the couple's or family's own behavior.

Conclusion

At the risk of sounding obvious, it can be safely asserted that effective therapy is based on effective interventions. The effectiveness of one's interventions, of course, depends solely on the validity of the *intended purpose,* the intentionality of the therapist. Intentionality is grounded in the therapist's aware presence and the phenomenological data filtered through the lens of the Interactive Cycle of Experience. But what is the intended purpose of each intervention? The answer, based on the "logic" of our theory and technique, is to direct and support the positive change in the system, and this can only be accomplished by a preceding change in awareness, individually and collectively (since these terms are mutually inclusive in any system). Therefore, our theory of change is based solely on awareness, which will be explored in greater detail in the following chapter.

Notes to Chapter Four

1. The cycle of experience as developed by the Cleveland school is essentially an expansion of the "instinct cycle" first proposed in F. S. Perls (1969), *Ego, hunger, and aggression* (New York: Random House). This eventually became the forecontact–contacting–final contact–postcontact sequence of "creative adjustment" developed by F. S. Perls, R. F. Hefferline, and P. Goodman (1951) in *Gestalt therapy: Excitement and growth in the human personality* (New York: Julian Press). A fuller description of its application appears in J. Zinker (1978), *Creative process in Gestalt therapy* (New York: Vintage Books). The cycle is the existential process underlying systems thinking, described in Chapter Three of the present work.
2. For example, awareness itself is driven by its own energy, although the energy required to think is much lower than the energy used in the action phase, which often involves the movement of muscles.
3. I have pointed out elsewhere that "a resistance is what the therapist experiences. The client is merely the person he thinks himself to be; his experience is that of taking care of himself" (J. Zinker (1978), *Creative process in Gestalt therapy* (New York: Vintage Books, p. 24)). See Chapter Six of the present book for a discussion of resistances.
4. F. S. Perls, R. F. Hefferline, and P. Goodman (1951), *Gestalt therapy: Excitement and growth in the human personality* (New York: Julian Press, p. viii, original emphasis).
5. Goodman makes an interesting distinction among the phenomena of awareness, consciousness, fantasy, dream, hope, and faith:

> Awareness is simple presentness, both perceptual and motor. Experience, in Aristotle's sense of the grounds of inductive truth, is present memory and habits. Consciousness is limitation of presentness to be subvocal and the safe perceptions, and the confining of motor response to the deliberate and the delaying, excluding the stronger passions which are motoric. Fantasy and dream are largely pure consciousness. Hope is largely fantasy and merely conscious, but the unlimited present component in hope is faith, in the fixed attitudes of ambition, determination, confidence, risking. In its most precise form, rather than in its fixed attitudes, faith is always "groundless," although *a posteriori* its grounds are generally apparent [P. Goodman (1966), *Five Years* (New York: Brussel and Brussel, pp. 19–20, original emphasis)].

6. Chapters Eight and Nine of the present work provide a detailed discussion of interventions in couple and family systems.
7. Contact, in Gestalt theory—as Wheeler (1991) shows in *Gestalt reconsidered: A new approach to contact and resistance* (New York: Gardner Press)—was originally conceptualized in a confusing and somewhat contradictory fashion. Contact is variously defined in F. S. Perls, R. F. Hefferline, and P. Goodman (1951), *Gestalt therapy: Excitement and growth in the human personality* (New York: Julian Press), as (1) awareness and movement toward creative resolution and assimilation/rejection at the contact boundary between the organism and the environment field, (2) an aware response, and (3) the process of figure formation of the organism/environment field.
8. A fuller description of the concepts of middle ground and its counterpart, complementarity, will be made in Chapter Eight. The reader is also referred to J. Zinker, "Complementarity and the middle ground in couples," *Gestalt Journal, 6*(2), 13–27.
9. For more about the creative use of experiments, see J. Zinker (1978), *Creative process in Gestalt therapy* (New York: Vintage Books).

5

Awareness and Change

You could not step twice in the same river; for other and yet other waters are ever flowing on.
—Heraclitus

The flow of life's events impinges on the couple or family, bringing change. Children are born, grow up, and leave; offspring marry and parents remarry; illness or death occurs; grandchildren are born; jobs are lost and new work is found. New information constantly flows through a family: schools, newspapers, television, books, new friends, new places visited. A healthy couple or family is always changing.

When a couple's or family's skills are inadequate for assimilating change, when its process is fixed rather than flexible,

Note: I wrote this chapter under the auspices of the International Gestalt Center in Tortola, British Virgin Islands, in January 1985. I gratefully acknowledge the consultation and financial support of Edwin Nevis.

then couple or family members, individually and as a system, become troubled. They become anxious (energy is detached from awareness), or they act out (behavior unconnected with their needs), or they may exhibit physical symptoms (blocked energy). These couples or families frequently seek help or are referred for help.

In couple and family therapy, healthy change can occur as the people involved become interested in their interactive process, as they become engaged in the struggle to become aware, and as they work to resolve their resistances or interferences to healthy change.

Determinism and Idealism

The history of psychoanalysis and psychotherapy is generally grounded in the notion of growth and change through awareness. What was unaware comes to light and change is then possible. Awareness provides opportunities for choice. Unawareness is acting naively, blindly, and without conscious choice. The opportunity to choose with awareness is what philosophers refer to as *free will.*[1]

I know that the notion that awareness and choice can change our lives, our destinies, is a wildly optimistic point of view, yet I maintain that the ideal life comes from choices made possible through deepening of awareness. I assume that when people are informed and aware of the wants of self and others, they will make the best possible choices for themselves as well as for each other as members of couples and families.

Deepening awareness, widening of consciousness, and the concomitant responsibility for choice that these entail are the philosophical underpinnings not only of Gestalt therapy but of all psychodynamic therapies.

Is all change predictable in that effects follow causes? If so, all we need is to find the many determinants of a given phenomenon and then to influence that phenomenon. Is this possible in a system where antecedent conditions exist for subsystems and where subsystems change each other in every possible interactional combination? The world would have to be constructed in a very simplified, linear fashion in order to make reliable predictions within human systems.[2]

Figure 5.1 shows what actual systems, especially open systems, look like. Causes and effects can only be arbitrarily assigned because of the enormous complexity of a given experiential field. Systems do not have simple cause-effect characteristics and cannot be reduced to a deterministic model of behavioral change.[3] A deterministic model of change that ignores awareness and resistances to awareness might look like the model depicted in Figure 5.2. Some therapies—for example, behaviorism—offer change without the responsibility required for making choices. The client or client system changes without actively participating in the change-making process. When therapists skirt awareness by "ramming through" resistance, they do not gain consent for an experiment and simply tell the client to do something that will result in more adaptive behavior. Bypassing awareness takes place in therapies where the patient's unconscious is addressed directly and is commanded to do some-

Figure 5.1. Typical Open System.

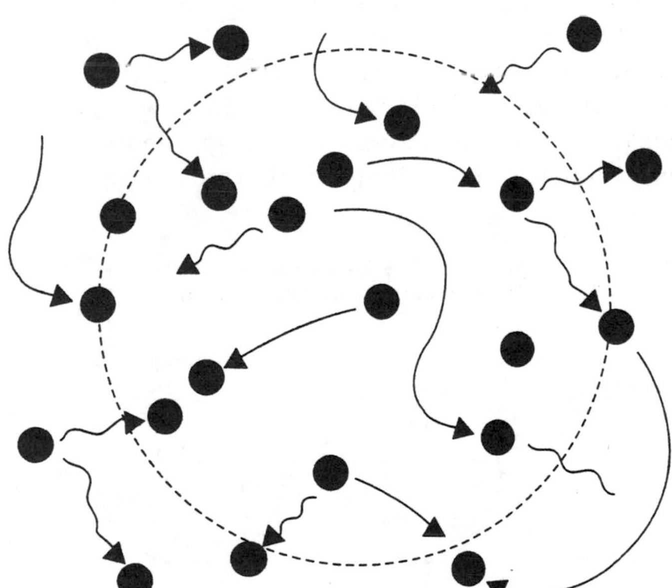

Figure 5.2. "Ramming Through" Awareness.

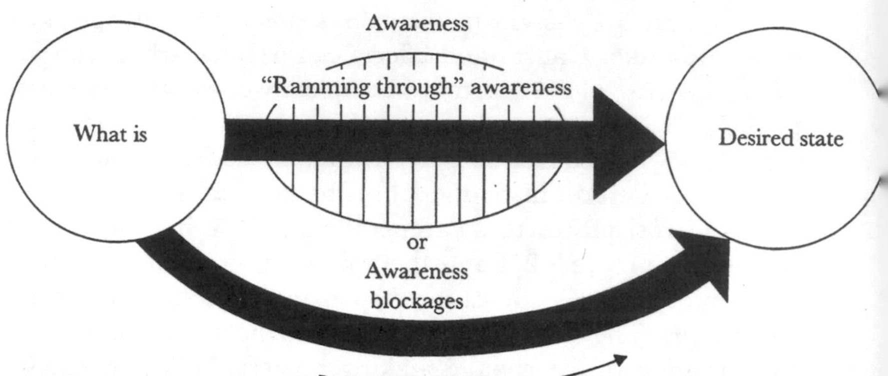

thing when encountering certain stimuli. This happens in post-hypnotic suggestions: "When you see your mother next time, and she gives you advice, you will thank her for it, and then proceed to do what makes sense to you. When you wake up you will not be thinking or worrying about this. This will happen only when you talk to your mother."

Another method of not engaging a system's awareness is by dissolving the existing awareness as if one dipped it into a solvent and then reconstructed it in the desired state. This model may look like the model in Figure 5.3. Here we see a technique by which awareness is "loosened" through the use of paradoxical explanations, storytelling, deliberate "crazy-making," or

Figure 5.3. The Dissolving of Awareness (Awareness as a Means to an End).

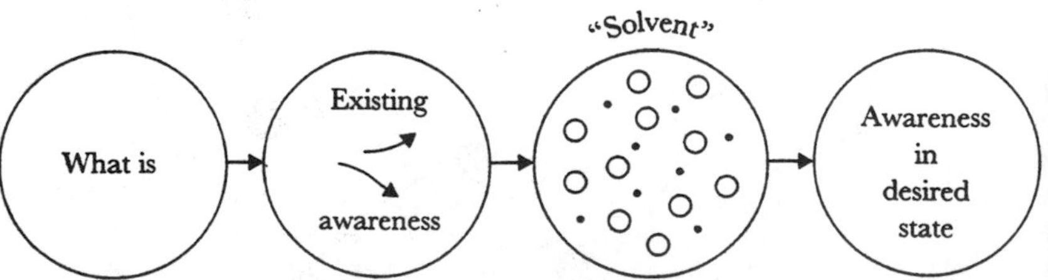

disorienting interventions that force the client system to examine itself anew, then see itself in a novel perspective or frame of reference—which, in turn, leads to the desired state of awareness.[4] Awareness is seen as a means to an end and not a therapeutic goal in itself. The focus is on outcome and not on awareness as such. Blocks to awareness or a struggle to make sense of something are ignored in favor of achieving a swiftly efficient movement toward the desired state.

People change without knowing why. They may feel gratified but unknowing. When the given procedure is repeated again and again, the undesirable behavior often disappears. I am not underestimating the importance of removing painful symptoms in a client who is miserable. Milton Erickson describes a case of a medical student and his bride, both of whom were enuretics.[5] He did a brilliant job using a very simple technique of suggestion and paradox,[6] and the couple stopped wetting their bed. We would consider this an interim measure to relieve stress, followed by individual or couple therapy to heighten the couple's awareness.[7]

The Phenomenology of the Here and Now

The reason deterministic models are successful at inducing functional change but fail at achieving meaningful change is that they are based in the history of causality rather than in the "what is" of the present moment. In a Harvard talk many years ago, the poet e. e. cummings said to his audience:

> You haven't the least or feeblest conception of being here and now, and alone, and yourself. Why (you ask) should anyone want to be here, when (by simply pressing a button) anyone can be in fifty places at once? How could anyone want to be now, when anyone can go whening all over creation at the twist of a knob? . . . As for being yourself—why on earth should you be yourself, when instead of being yourself you can be a hundred, or a thousand, or a hundred thousand other people? The

> very thought of being oneself in an epoch of interchangeable selves must appear supremely ridiculous . . . remember one thing only: that it's you—nobody else—who determines your destiny and decides your fate. Nobody else can be alive for you nor can you be alive for anyone else.[8]

The term *phenomenological* implies that the psychophysiological process that one experiences is uniquely one's own; adding the dimension of here and now gives these personal phenomena existential immediacy. These ongoing phenomena (and more) constitute a person's world. When people die, assuming that their awareness permanently ceases, their whole world will be forever finished and, phenomenologically, *the* world will come to an end.

By now, the expression "here and now" has become almost a cliché. It has been warped into a demand for extracting the other person's immediate awareness, as if the other always experiences the choice of sharing his or her self. It has become an extorted handing over of feelings using a few descriptive words. Carl Rogers pointed out long ago that the phenomenological world is the experienced world.[9] That is, I am what I experience myself to be in this moment, and if you ask what I feel right now and I say "nothing," you can safely assume that in this moment I live in a world colored by "nothing," that I feel "nothing" inside of me, that what I experience within I interpret as having the value of "nothing" in my communication with you. And so, instead of respectfully understanding the "nothing" of other people's experience, some therapists and group leaders tyrannically press them for more, as if they never responded to our question.

Experiencing the here and now begins with sensation. In the organism with a small cerebral cortex, the sensory moment-to-moment function is primal, since the cognitive process does not become conceptually elaborated. Not so in human beings. Sensory experience is automatically named, cognitively elaborated, and embellished: "I see a light. It is a yellow light. It streams directly downward and upward from a table lamp with a matted glass base shaped like a holiday whisky decanter. The lamp has an off-white paper shade. It is ugly. I don't like it. I want to get rid of it . . . and so on."

Generally speaking, we forget that our language has sensory roots and that our words stem from concrete referents. We often treat words as if they are prime experiences. The pedantic manipulation of abstractions removes and alienates us from the immediate impact of a personal reality.[10] To be in direct sensory contact is difficult in an increasingly automated world in which we are constantly distracted and rendered passive by an omnipresent process of secondhand cognitive noise.

Phenomenological reality always exists temporally in the present. Even in terms of the most profound and clear awareness, memory, and anticipation, there is no way of experientially living one's yesterdays or tomorrows. We are all temporally anchored to this ongoing moment. Images of yesterday are tinted by this nowness—they are like postcards pasted in an album, an audiovisual reference library in one's head: mere "about-nesses." The whens of our lives are devoid of a pulse, of a liveliness especially when we try to verbalize them. We can pump life into the whens by reenacting them *now* as if they are now taking place. The memory seems to come to life when it is revivified and brought into the present. We can enliven a fantasy or a dream or an anticipation in the same way. But these reenactments become present events and are not to be confused with the actual events that took place or are about to happen. The reenactment is inseparably fused within ourselves.

Phenomenological reality always exists spatially right here. The range of our "here" is determined by the phenomenal space occupied by the range of senses and instruments that extend those senses. In actual experience, we allow the thing being sensed to come dynamically into our own being. If we are clearly in touch with something in space, the distance between the person and the object choice is phenomenologically foreshortened; the object is experientially next to us. The dynamic point at which we and this sensation meet is called the *contact boundary*. An object perceived as having a negative valence may be spatially pushed away and visually contracted: "There is distance between us."

The phenomenological here and now, therefore, represents a highly personal sensory experience at this moment in time and place.

Actuality as it is experienced is a private affair. No one else can experience our inner lives for us. Sensitive people may express what they experience when they are with us and this expression may touch something within us, but if they were to make an interpretation of the "real" meaning of my behavior, the purity of our experience as it is concretely revealed at this moment would be lost. The significant point here is that we as individuals are the sole owners of our separate phenomenological lives. The experiential here and now, therefore, does not exist in a vacuum but is rather owned by a self, a person, a me.

The content of my experiencing is as valid a datum for me as another person's experiencing is for him or her. There are no "good" or "bad" experiential phenomena; things "just are."

Having sketched out my conception of phenomenological reality, I am ready to present my model of the phenomenon of interactive awareness as it takes place with energy and action within this reality.

Awareness, Energy, and Action

What is awareness? How is awareness generated? How does it grow? How does "full awareness" produce change? Is change lateral, linear, or is it somehow three dimensional? The Freudian model of awareness looks like a partially submerged iceberg (see Figure 5.4). This model stresses several important assumptions about awareness: that we live mostly in *un*-awareness, that awareness may be three dimensional, that it is in motion, and that we must deal with our resistance to knowing. It does not portray vividly that awareness may expand or contract, that it may become more complex and/or more distilled and layered.[11] Awareness certainly is not linear, as in Figure 5.5.

Awareness is in a constant dynamic state: it organizes stimuli, comes into sharp focus (figure formation), builds into energy and action (contact), disperses itself (withdrawal), and then scans for the next set of stimuli. This process must be multi-

Figure 5.4. Freudian Model of Awareness.

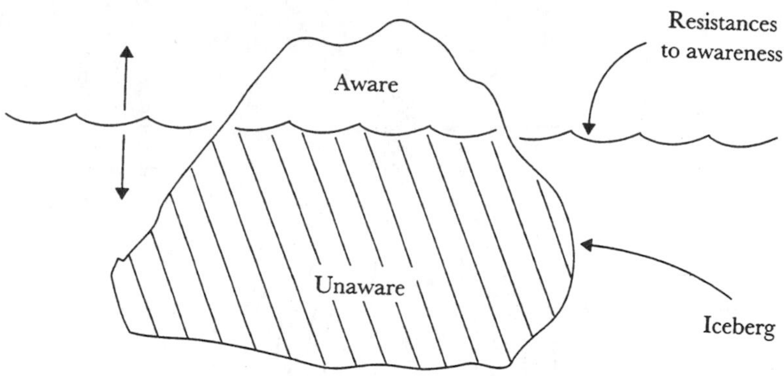

plied several times, since we are quite capable of organizing a number of our experiences simultaneously, letting go of some while holding onto others at the same time (Figure 5.6).

This model looks like two onions arranged horizontally and connected at their stalks and roots. The notion of an onion is fitting, since onions are layered from center to periphery, connoting growing richness accumulated over time. As the enriched analytical base narrows, thinking becomes distilled, focused, and synthesized—ready for action.

Awareness contracts and expands. Configurations appear as complex and varied organizing bands, then change into sharp-

Figure 5.5. Linear Model of Awareness.

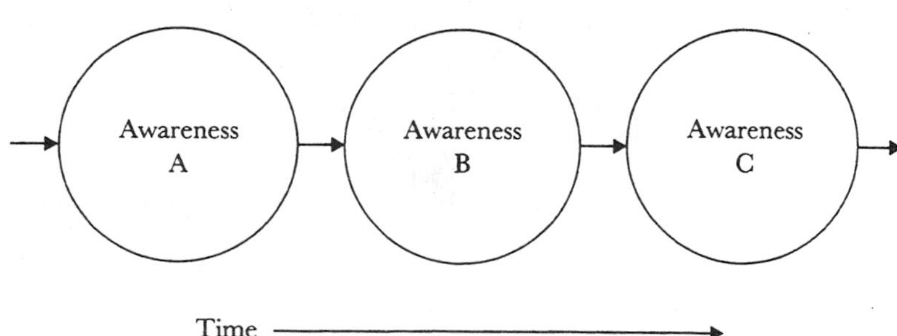

Figure 5.6. Dynamic State of Awareness.

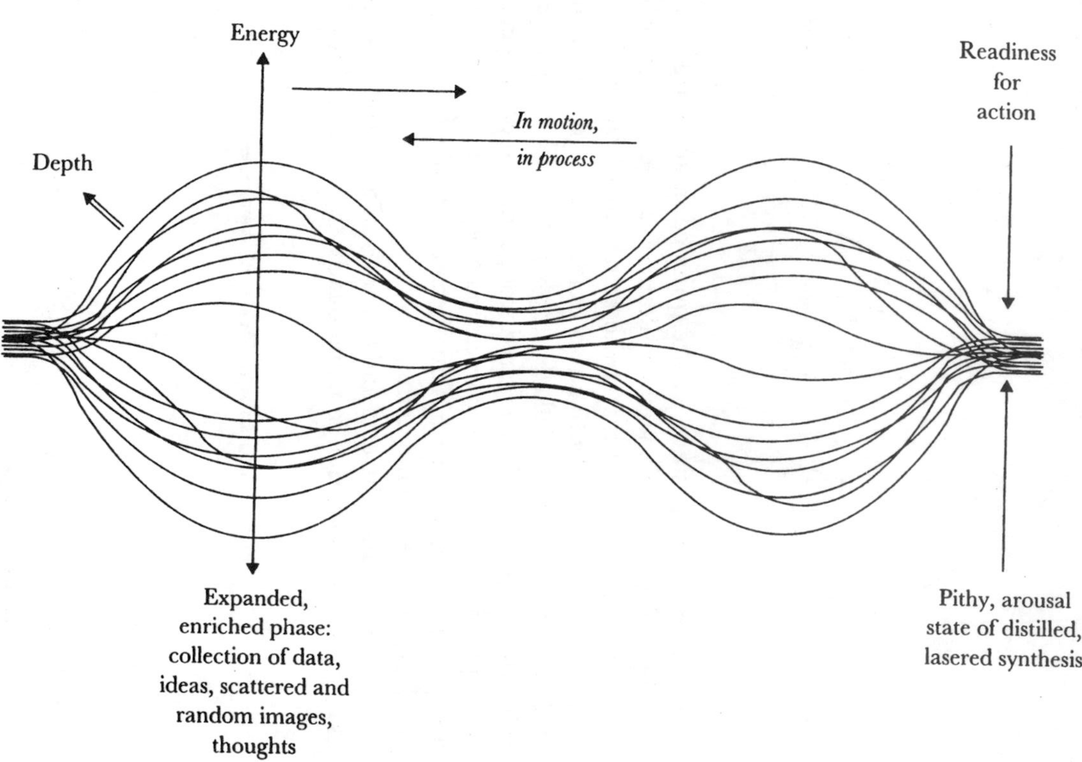

ened, distilled images from which potential action may spring. Expansion follows distillation in a rhythmic pattern of organizing experience, acting, and so on.

When awareness is thin, limited in depth and variation, unipolar and monolithic, actions tend to be tentative, awkward, and indecisive. There is a vacillation or ambivalence of behavior, as with a child who feels an urge, yet not being sure what to do, shifts from leg to leg to alleviate discomfort. Similarly, when a couple or family members do not make the effort to listen to each other's ideas and sentiments about something that matters, if not enough common awareness is generated, actions emanating in and from that system are weak. They cannot be fully supported by the whole family; they are poorly executed, with little pleasure or enthusiasm.

When a system's awareness is shallow and not all parts are engaged, the group's energy tends to be weak, with some members carrying more than their own share to make something happen. For example, while some individuals push and work hard, others drag along and complain, acting distracted or uncooperative. The total effect is that the couple or family does not experience much pleasure, has difficulty making decisions, and is a poor work unit. There is a kind of domino effect when awareness is not fully developed in the system. Shallow awareness does not generate adequate energy to carry out a given task. The energy is weak because awareness is not sufficiently enriched. The action is weak because it is not propelled by enough energy.

Awareness, if unobstructed, changes constantly. In psychotherapy, the witnessing of this process helps clients articulate fully and clearly their awareness in the moment (feedback). They receive the message: "Your awareness of yourself and the world is good and useful. This serves you well. It helps you survive and move on." Clients learn: "My thoughts and feelings are valid. My organism helps me understand my world and organizes my experience of it into meaningful units. I feel competent and good." Clients can continue examining their lives articulating what they already understand. The moment they know themselves, they begin to be curious about what comes next and, just as when they have finished a chapter in a good book, they are eager to turn the page and see what happens next (Figure 5.7).

Figure 5.7. Cycle of Experience with Awareness as Focus.

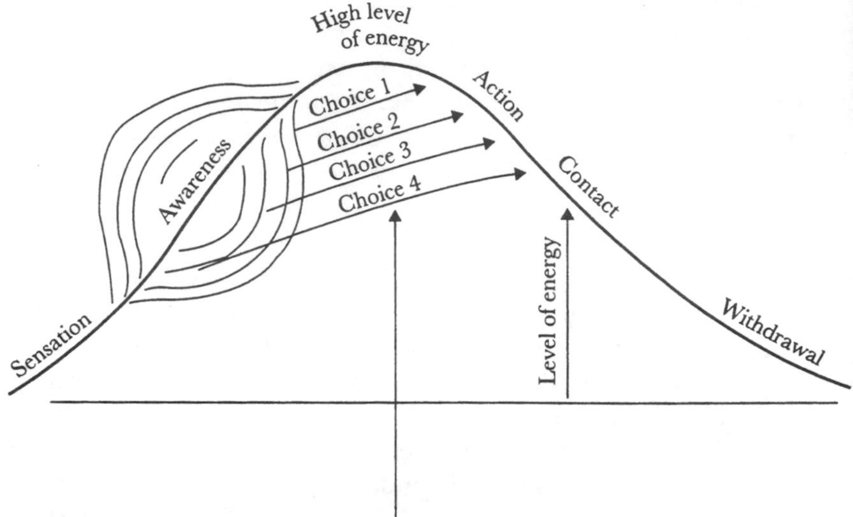

Expansive awareness makes for wider bands of choicefulness for a given action. The couple or family are free to do what feels right to them. Their actions are stronger, clearer, more decisive, more grounded, more lasting. There is ample energy to support the system's actions.

John and Nelly Mathienson: Getting Awareness in Synch

Young John and Nelly Mathienson always questioned conventional beliefs and values about sexuality. Coming from conservative Irish Catholic parents, John struggled with guilt feelings about masturbation and was angry with the nuns in his school who had conditioned him to think of his "spilled semen" as a sinful, dirty act. Nelly came from a New England family of atheistic scholars who did not care much about lovemaking one way or the other.

John's sense of doing the forbidden stoked his passion, while Nelly was more cortical about their periodic lovemaking. "So, I didn't have an orgasm tonight," she would say to her distraught young husband, "it's no big deal!" But John knew that repeated lovemaking without orgasm left Nelly feeling unenthusiastic, and that when she did reach a high peak of arousal, her orgasms opened her skin, her pores, her throat, and, it seemed, her very soul. At such times, she would simply glow.

When John and Nelly took time to discuss these matters of sexual arousal, they discovered that John would begin to have sensual fantasies hours or even days before actually approaching Nelly to make love. Nelly was fascinated by John's sharing and asked him to share his fantasies with her when they would first begin to occur to him. In contrast to her husband, she did not seem to fantasize anything sexual until he was already caressing her. John began to report his sensual thoughts to his wife, occasionally calling her at work to whisper some things he was envisioning about her. This kind of talk aroused Nelly to a smoldering excitement that lingered in her mind and body for hours before they came home at the end of the day.

After some weeks, Nelly reciprocated by calling John to tell him about how she could practically "smell the fragrance of your manly arms." The sexual energy built between them, and they experimented with ways of signaling each other when they wanted to make love. Often, they waited for weeks before approaching each other. At those times, they were blissful before even touching.

What they discovered was not only that their combined talks, images, and fantasies aroused them both, but that, together, they experienced a kind of colorful, sensual energy that inevitably left them both satisfied and drained after their lovemaking. Often, each appeared to match the other's anticipation of a novel aspect of touching the other. Gone were Nelly's heroic reassurances to John about "making too big a deal about coming," and John did not have to feel like a "naughty boy" to experience the power of his arousal for, and satisfaction with, Nelly.

In the beginning, the couple were in danger of falling into a kind of stereotypical relationship—the hesitant husband approaching a reluctant wife who accommodates him out of kindness and duty but without much pleasure. Increased awareness about their sexual fantasies led to a mutuality of anticipation and arousal. Together, they discovered the art of synchronously combining sexual interest with libidinal energy, and they found a variety of ways to please each other in and out of bed.

Paradox and Change

In his 1970 article on change, Beisser defined the paradoxical theory of change as follows: "*Change occurs when one becomes what he is,* not when he tries to become what he is not."[12] Edwin Nevis has defined the therapist's role in change this way: "Change does not take place through a coercive attempt by the individual or by another person to change him, but it does take place if one takes the time and effort to be what he is — to be fully invested in his current positions. By rejecting the role of change agent, we make meaningful and orderly change possible."[13] What does it mean when we say we look at "what is" in a couple or family? We give the couple or family an opportunity to examine what is experienced, what is done, what actions take place, what feelings and sentiments are available and expressed, as well as what may be held back.[14] We encourage the couple or family to see and to experience the goodness, the usefulness, the creativity of what they discover when they examine themselves. Couples and families are often unable to see the goodness and competence of their present positions. The discomfort of their predicament takes precedence.

When a couple or family members begin to experience their competence and creativity even in their troubles, they experience affirmation and dignity that were not previously available to their awareness. This, in turn, gives them the courage to look at what is missing in their system, what is on the other side of their strengths. They can then say, "We do this well, but we pay a lot for it. Perhaps we could try doing things another way that may not leave us feeling as lonely and as isolated as we have been." Going more fully into "what is" allows the journey to continue moving toward what is optimal and more fully adaptive in the life of the couple or family.

The paradox is that the more the couple or family experiences what it is and how it operates (rather than how it "should" be), the greater the chance that it can move on to a better life, a more fulfilled way of being together (Figure 5.8). On the other hand, the more a family is pushed to change its ways of thinking and doing, the more it will resist change. Accepting "what

Figure 5.8. Paradoxical Theory of Change.

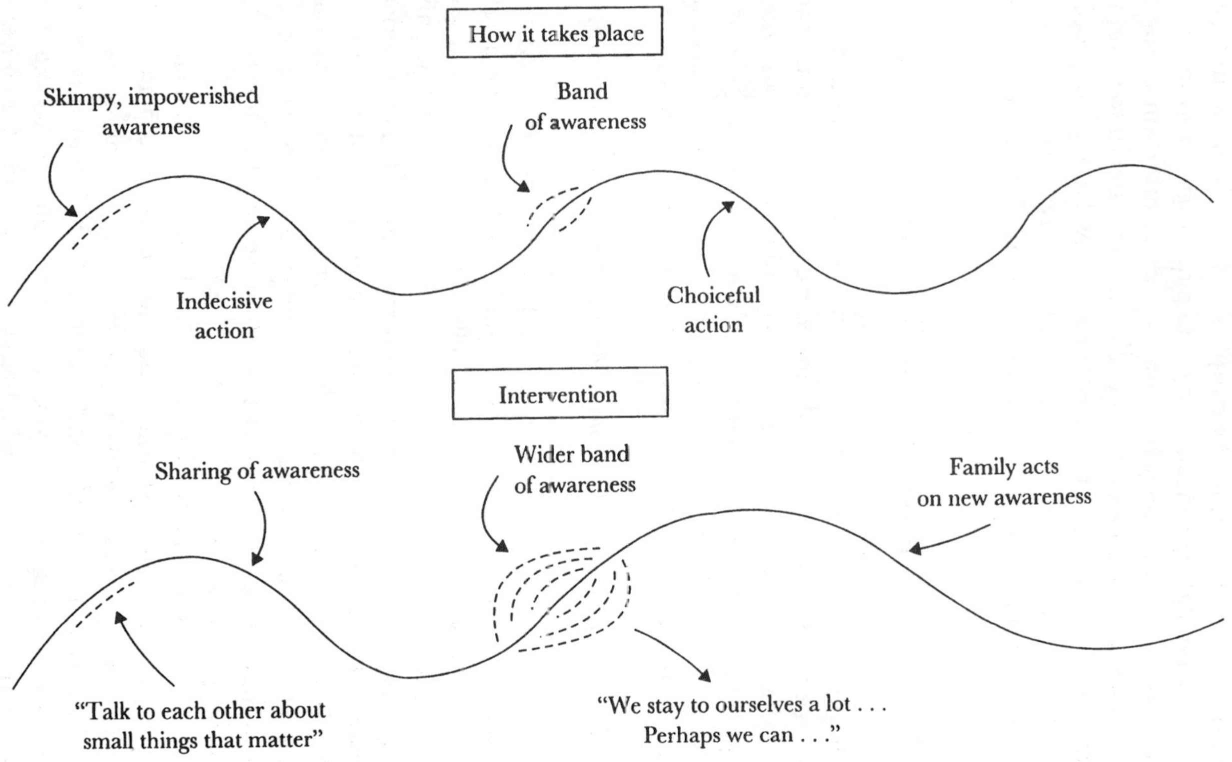

is" is the cornerstone of my therapeutic position. As therapists, we insert ourselves into the couple's or family's life at the level of curiosity and awareness. We try to pique their curiosity about how they are, how they function, what is important to them. The moment they can look at each other and begin to examine what they are—at that moment they are involved in the process of change. The level of their combined awareness changes. Greater, richer awareness gives them more choices and, therefore, a better chance for a good life.

Awareness and Resistance

Change is often unpleasant. Constructs of oneself or one's family are ego syntonic and well embedded: "I am a kind person" or "We are a close family" have been built over time and have been constructed for developmentally sound reasons. The self-image of a family or couple evolves during early encounters with each other, with grandparents, parents, and community.

The Madiar Family: Becoming Aware of Changing Boundaries

Having been isolated in the industrial and socially impoverished sector of their city, the Madiar family witnessed their neighbors being intruded on by bill collectors, social workers, and the local police. The grandparents, who came from Europe and still spoke their native tongue after many years of life in America, prided themselves on self-reliance, hard work, and keeping the family intact by refusing help from others. The parents, Gregor and Dotty, spoke Hungarian to preserve their privacy, and the two children learned not to tell family secrets to their friends in the parish school.

Gregor was an industrial worker; Dotty was a homemaker. There was a sense of shame about their poverty and about the father's periodic bouts with alcohol. He kept his drinking a secret, and his wife protected him by telling the kids—at least when they were young—that he was ill. The two adolescent children, Mike and Theresa, carried a heavy responsibility for chores at home and spent hours scrubbing floors, changing beds, vacuuming, helping with the shopping, and cleaning up after dinner. Homework was done late in the evening. They were "good kids."

Because of the pervasive secrecy, Mike learned not to say much at home when he got into trouble at school. Occasionally, his mother would find out that he had played hooky. She would report the incident to the father at suppertime, and Mike would get a beating later in the evening. "I'm doing this because I don't want you to turn out like those Mairowitsky boys," Gregor would say.

The family's containment gave them all a sense of being in a secure fortress. Other children were rarely allowed to visit Mike and Theresa, and although they never stopped complaining about their sense of isolation, they comforted themselves with the conviction that their parents were the "best parents on the block."

This was their definition of a good family—a construct supported by their best awareness of themselves for many years. Although in its original situation this "closeness" served the Madiar family well, later, when life became easier and they moved into a middle-class suburb, their way of taking care of each other did not change. They continued their vigilant turning away from the world with a concomitant clinging to each other. The neighborhood was safe and friendly, the father worked as a manager in a factory, and the mother had new leisure. Mike and Theresa were soon in high school. The old insistence on staying "close to the fort" continued, despite the fact that it had outworn its usefulness. The potential for a more interesting and varied life was ignored. The "closeness" persisted as a kind of lockjaw, acquiring its own functional autonomy, even though its adaptive purpose was outgrown. It was as if all the family members were trying to squeeze themselves into the same jacket, despite the fact that each had his or her own ample wardrobe.

When a therapist questions or interprets the meaning of a system's construction of itself, healthy resistance occurs: "Don't you see that your closeness is not a real being together at all, but . . . " This method of attacking the problem, of diagnosing and interpreting it, mobilizes the family's efforts to protect and defend its special way of seeing itself that has served it well, which was the best possible action, albeit with a heavy price, for so many years. The family's response is to protect its integrity. Intervention based on interpretation of pathology stimulates and mobilizes resistance. The family sees itself as being what they are and so feels threatened or invalidated and moves to defend against the perceived assault. A therapist's effort to push a new awareness into the system meets with stubborn silence or respectful nodding, but certainly not with enthusiastic appreciation.

Why not? What is lacking? After all, the family has come for help and the therapist offers what seem to be useful solutions. However, the family has not been given an opportunity to examine itself in such a way as to appreciate its own adaptive wisdom, its own creative efforts in coping with dilemmas in its history—difficulties which made "closeness" the most useful way of surviving as a cohesive, living, functioning unit.

The Gestalt couple or family therapist first gives the system an opportunity to look with respect and dignity at the nature and quality of its style of being together; room is made for exploring members' experience of closeness, for seeing themselves as competent people, for becoming aware of themselves as intrinsically good. Only when the collective awareness of the family unfolds or opens can they begin to feel comfortable enough to ask themselves the more difficult and provocative questions: "What have we done—or not done—to have gotten ourselves into this mess?" "Why is our closeness not helping us get along better?" "How are we getting in our own way?"

The impetus, energy, and curiosity for change must come from the family. This energy is stimulated when the therapist first asks members of the system to talk *to each other* about something that they are all concerned about. The experience of talking in the here and now allows for self-examination in the presence of a supportive witness. When the question "What matters a lot to all of you?" is raised and the therapist culls out of the many responses that *closeness matters a lot,* the Madiar family perks up its ears and begins to listen intently. The Gestalt therapist may initially make the following intervention:

Therapist: *I notice that when you talk to each other, everyone gets to say what they think of the other's ideas. You ask each other a lot of questions. You seem to get hurt when one of you disagrees. It's important to you to have consensus, to hang in there together. I can understand how this might make you feel stronger as a family when there is trouble. You are really good at pulling together.*

This is an example of working at the family's awareness level and supporting "what is"—supporting the family's awareness of itself. In response to this, everyone takes a breath of relief, everyone feels affirmed in the way they have coped, everyone feels well received, seen, respected, appreciated, and understood.

The therapist has the satisfaction of having supported the Madiars as they really are, touched a central theme of the family's previously unaware view of itself, and brought this view to awareness. There is genuine competence and goodness in every couple or family, regardless of how poorly organized or dysfunctional it appears.

Family members begin to experience a special regard and respect for the therapist, trusting the clinician's initial perception and support of the family's process. They also feel encouraged to continue to explore each other with interest and curiosity. The therapist has "hooked" them. What happened to the resistance? The Madiars have nothing to resist. They hear their own hidden voices revealed in the phenomenological observations of the therapist. They feel complimented and understood. The therapist merely describes what is, what is given, and puts it into simple language to be freshly grasped by the client system. The therapist moves with the system's process rather than pushing against it. Having given up the role of change agent, the therapist serves as a compassionate witness invested in observing and understanding the Madiar's way of being with each other. The therapist "glides" with the family, rather than flying into the wind.

Ordinarily, if the Madiars felt accosted by an outsider, especially given their developmental history and the way they have collectively organized themselves, they would hold back, treating the stranger with respectful acknowledgment or silence. In this case, resistance is kept to a minimum because the therapist is experienced as a supportive, affirmative figure who is able to understand the Madiars's earnest, well-meaning efforts to "raise a decent family." Nothing is said that aesthetically offends or threatens them.

It is only in a later session (or perhaps later in the same session) that the therapist can afford to encourage the Madiar family to look at the other side of the coin, the other side of their closeness: "What do all of you pay—what is the price for being so agreeable and so close all the time? Is there a price?" Heightening awareness means that we not only look at *what happens,* but also at *what does not happen;* not only at what *is,* but also at what *is not.*

The father does not seem to hear the therapist's question and asks that it be repeated. The therapist poses the question again and, after an uncomfortable silence, Theresa ventures a response.

Theresa: *I don't get to go out to Mary's house (glancing furtively at her parents).*

Mike: *Mom, why do I have to hang around the kitchen when I'm through helping you?*

And so, with the encouragement and support of the therapist, the Madiars begin to pose some difficult questions for themselves about the shortsightedness of their closeness. The therapist avoids becoming polarized by carefully supporting both the children and the parents.

Therapist: *It sounds like, by looking out for each other so much, none of you get to have much fun out there in the world with other folks. Is that true or am I way off base? (Giving them an opportunity to resist, the therapist adds) Perhaps I'm not seeing this right.*

Gregor: *Dotty and I go out to the movies once in a while and the kids come along if they wish.*

Dotty: *(Raising the ante slightly) I'm always worried that Theresa will get mixed up with the wrong kids in the neighborhood.*

When resistance is encountered, it is a signal that the family needs more time to assimilate new awareness and that they need more support before upsetting their constructs and leaping forward. Sensing the need for support and, at the same time, recognizing the delicate balance between the needs of the adolescent children and those of the parents, the therapist responds:

Therapist: *It's clear to me that you are good parents. You really care about the welfare of your children. But,* on the other side of the scale, *Theresa and Mike do have a legitimate dilemma. How are they going to meet the good kids out there? They are getting to that age when these social contacts are important.*

So far, both sides are acknowledged and the intervention is balanced. The therapist continues:

Therapist: *Talk to each other some more. Try to figure out how you can keep looking out for each other and, at the same time, let each other go outside the family a little more.*

Quite simply, our approach yields a deceptively simple, yet extremely powerful, three-step intervention formula that was implicitly demonstrated in the above session with the Madiars. This formula will be repeated again in the chapters that follow. I now recapitulate the "what, how, and why" of my therapeutic strategy.

1. The therapist begins by encouraging the family to talk to each other about something that matters to all of them. This gives the practitioner an opportunity to observe the family's level of awareness within its own boundaries. After obtaining enough phenomenological data, the therapist makes some observations. *This is the first intervention.* The observations are based on real data. Their purpose is to support the family's competence, goodness, and sense of creativity; what exists is brought to the family's awareness.

The therapist allows time for the system to respond, find exceptions, change meanings, and enrich its awareness of how they are as they are. The therapist "glides" on the system's generated energy, rather than pushing against that energy. As the family feels supported, it becomes hooked on the therapeutic process.

2. The therapist then focuses on the other side of the family's competence, namely, what they pay for their goodness. This is the negative side of the system's operation; it involves uncovering their incompetence. *This is the second intervention.* Often, this brings up a major area of difficulty, and the therapist should expect meeting potential resistance in the form of denial, shame, guilt, anger, or just plain unawareness. This is a subtle turning point where the system's awareness of itself is potentially stretched; the therapist encounters much questioning and discussion.

Resistance, as it arises, is always supported. The family is encouraged to chew fully on the generated data, rather than to swallow them whole. Experienced practitioners are aware that if the couple or family accepts their views too readily, learning and change do not take place. All parts of the system are supported equally. Interventions are balanced. This approach also minimizes polarization[15] within the system as well as among parts of the system and the therapist. Parents are supported in their sense of cautiousness, and the adolescent children are supported in their needs to move into the world. Only when everyone's needs are legitimized can the system let go and open up to the world.

3. The therapist can then move on to raising questions about what can be done (operationalizing what is learned) to change the implicit rules of enmeshment into explicit behaviors that support loosening of boundaries between the family and the environment. The Gestalt therapist uses experiment for this purpose. *This is the third intervention.*[16]

When the family's awareness is enriched under its own steam, there are more choices and more possible actions to pursue. The family generates its own energy and the ultimate decisions about the children's freedom can be supported by all. Mr. Madiar joins the soccer team at his company, while Mrs. Madiar enrolls in an adult education class.

Conclusion

In summary, what are the paradoxes of our theory of change?

1. If you support what is, and not what should be, change will take place.
2. If you support resistance to change, little resistance will be encountered and change will take place.

Enriched awareness will allow the system to function more fluidly, both within its boundaries and in its dealings with the community. The members then go on to develop in their own right and to move into the world without losing the sense of caring for the others. Since working with resistances and boundary management are integral pieces in the mosaic of our approach, we turn to these topics in the next two chapters.

Notes to Chapter Five

1 I am not so foolhardy as to embroil myself in a philosophical competition that has probably been raging ever since Aristotle first crossed swords with his master, Plato. In this section, I merely try to state my position regarding the importance of awareness. For those interested in further discussion, I recommend the following: A. Castell (1965), *The self in philosophy* (New York: Macmillan); L. A. Pervin (1978), *Current controversies and issues in personality* (New York: Wiley); P. Young-Eisendrath & J. A. Hall (Eds.) (1987), *The book of the self: Person, pretext, and process* (New York: New York University Press); A. Wandersman, P. J. Poppen, & D. F. Ricks (Eds.) (1976), *Humanism and behaviorism: Dialogue and growth* (Oxford, England: Pergamon Press).
2. See the discussion of systems theory in Chapter Three.
3. W. Buckley (1967), *Sociology and modern systems theory* (Englewood Cliffs, NJ: Prentice Hall); M. Shaw & P. R. Constanzo (1970), *Theories of social psychology* (New York: McGraw-Hill); E. Laszlo (1972), *Introduction to systems philosophy* (New York: HarperCollins); R. Becvar & D. S. Becvar (1982), *System theory and family therapy* (New York: University Presses of America).
4. This brings to mind the koan puzzles told by Zen masters to their students. No answer to these puzzles is either "right" or "wrong."

5. M. Erickson (1982), *My voice will go with you* (New York: Norton).
6. The "paradox" used here was the technique of strategic couple and family therapies.
7. For current thinking in this area, see C. J. Kershaw (1991), *The couple's hypnotic dance: Creating Ericksonian strategies in marital therapy* (New York: Brunner/Mazel).
8. e. e. cummings (1971), *Six nonlectures* (New York: Atheneum).
9. C. Rogers (1961), *On becoming a person* (Boston: Houghton-Mifflin).
10. This is not an attack on the use of concepts, since without them, this book could not have been written. Without concepts we could not record our history, develop mathematics, write literature, or create a theory of relativity. Without concepts we are not human beings, but with concepts alone without basic sensory exploration and evaluation, we are reduced to the position of computer automatons.
11. These works discuss the nonlinear complexity of awareness as seen through the lenses of psychoanalysis, biology, and physics: J. Winson (1985), *The biology of the unconscious* (New York: Anchor Press/Doubleday); M. F. Reiser (1985), *Toward a convergence of psychoanalysis and neuro-biology* (New York: Basic Books); F. A. Wolf (1985), *Mind, consciousness, and quantum physics* (New York: Macmillan).
12. A. R. Beisser (1970), "The paradoxical theory of change," in J. Fagan & E. L. Shepherd (Eds.), *Gestalt therapy now* (New York: HarperCollins, p. 77, emphasis added). I also recommend L. Selzer (1984), "The role of paradox in Gestalt theory and technique," *Gestalt Journal, 7*(2), 31–42, and K. J. Schneider (1990), *The paradoxical self: Toward an understanding of our contradictory nature* (New York: Insight Books).
13. E. Nevis (1987), *Organizational consulting: A Gestalt approach* (New York: Gardner Press, pp. 124–140).
14. By rooting ourselves in "what is," quite literally the "isness" of the system, our approach philosophically reaches back to Husserlian phenomenology ("to the things themselves") and Heidegger's ontological notion of *Dasein* ("being-there). In this way, Gestalt therapy, as Fritz Perls was so fond of saying, is "the philosophy of the obvious." The reader is also referred to L. Binswanger (1963), *Being-in-the-world: Selected papers of Ludwig Binswanger* (J. Needleman, Trans.) (New York: Basic Books); H. L. Dreyfuss (1991), *Being-in-the-world: A commentary on Heidegger's being and time, division I* (Cambridge, Mass.: MIT Press); M. Heidegger (1962), *Being and time* (J. Macquarrie & E. Robinson, Trans.) (New York: HarperCollins).

15. Polarities and polarization are key concepts in Gestalt therapy but have been a part of philosophy, psychology, and theology since ancient times. Polar qualities in the human psyche are very much akin to the Hegelian dialectic of thesis-antithesis (with psychological integration yielding synthesis). Polarities are defined by I. Polster and M. Polster (1973), *Gestalt therapy integrated: Contours of theory and practice* (New York: Vintage Books). They state: "There is nothing new about looking at polarities in man. What *is* new is the Gestalt perspective that each individual is himself a never-ending sequence of polarities. Whenever an individual recognizes one aspect of himself, the presence of its antithesis, or polar quality, is implicit. There it rests as background, giving dimension to present experience and yet powerful enough to emerge as figure in its own right if it gathers enough force. When this force is supported, integration can develop between whatever polarities emerge in opposition to each other, frozen into a posture of mutual alienation" (p. 61, original emphasis). I also recommend R. Fantz (1973), *Polarities: Differentiation and integration* (Cleveland, OH: Gestalt Institute of Cleveland).
16. For further explication of the use of experiment in Gestalt therapy, see J. Zinker (1978), *Creative process in Gestalt therapy,* Gestalt Institute of Cleveland working paper, Cleveland, OH.

6

Resistances to Contact

All happy families resemble one another, each unhappy family is unhappy in its own way.

—Leo Tolstoy

Everybody seems to know what a happy couple or family is. A happy couple or family has characteristics that we can point to and on which we can probably agree. What are these characteristics? Happy couples and families, by our definition, usually possess some combination of these features. They

- Hear each other
- Own their feelings and ideas
- Exchange ideas so that a good fit is achieved
- Ask each other questions, rather than making assumptions
- Disagree and accept differences without fear
- Accommodate each other
- Fight for what feels "right" and "good" for each other

- Start, develop, and finish a discussion or event and then let it go
- Share pains, curiosities, regrets, resentments, tenderness—a variety of needs and wants
- Learn to accept a "yes" gratefully and a "no" graciously without holding onto resentment
- Move from one experience to another without getting stuck
- Let go of wanting something that is hopelessly unavailable
- Laugh at themselves
- Influence each other
- Support each other's interests and projects
- Show pride and compassion for each other's accomplishments and setbacks
- Respect each other's privacy and, at the same time, intrude when another withdraws in pain
- "Mind each other's business" when it comes to important matters
- Tolerate strange and novel ideas from each other and dream together

To practice these behaviors is admittedly difficult. First, good functioning requires work—often hard work. Second, couples and families are generally poorly educated in the art of family life. Education of each generation is one of the functions of the preceding generation. Poor functioning is passed on from one generation to the next as a form of dis-ease; a family "character flaw." Since these patterns of poor functioning are largely unaware, we find that for every force in us that longs for "good" functioning within the couple or family, there is an unaware force of equal valence that pushes against it, that "resists" good contact among couple or family members. Third, some awareness is too painful to bear, some actions are too difficult to perform.

Unbearable Awarenesses and Too-Difficult Actions

We often do not hear each other: it is too painful to know something awful, or embarrassing, or shameful, or even beautiful about ourselves, or about those around us. It is hard to hear it and it is hard to say it.

We do not own our feelings and ideas of resentment, jealousy, anger, stupidity, shyness, pettiness, selfishness, over-embellishment of small things, overstatement of uninteresting ideas, close-mindedness, awkwardness, and the like. These are also too hard to hear.

And we do not exchange ideas to make a "good fit" with each other because we may not want to let go of our side of an opinion or because every time we tried to fit in in childhood, we were beaten up, shamed, compromised, abandoned, insulted, teased, belittled as being silly or stupid, and then left alone to suffer. It is too difficult to let such pain into us (or out of us).

We do not ask each other questions because we may be told that we are too intrusive, or we may be afraid of sounding stupid. We may hear answers that make us feel awful about ourselves, or we may discover hidden secrets about ourselves that make us sick inside. We may discover how poorly we have behaved with another, or our questions may be treated as invalid. Such awarenesses are too painful to carry in our minds and hearts.

We may not want to accept differences between us because it is simply unacceptable that a spouse or parent or brother or sister would "think that way" or be so insensitive, naive, idealistic, stupid, nasty, narrowminded, or uncaring. So why should we want to knowingly accommodate such a different point of view? It is a curse to be aware that way; it hurts too much.

Why should we fight for something when we repeatedly "lost" in the past, when we were too weak or too clumsy to stand up to our spouse or our parents or our siblings? Why should we push ourselves at others when we have been called "selfish" in the past? Why fight for something when we have always been outflanked by our spouse or family for "another way" of doing things? And why should we fight for something when, in the past, our voices have not been heard or understood or appreciated?

The list of our unaware objections to such ideals—ideals borne of youthful dreams and optimism—is endless. We have had plenty of experience of being rejected, profoundly hurt, and disappointed. And our unaware self carries these hurts.

It is easy to talk about growth as a wonderful, liberating, mind-expanding process. But it is not easy seeing what is really there, and it is not easy to bear one's responsibility for what one does or does not do. Living with the losses, the inevitable failures of ourselves and of others that matter to us, and seeing the condition of the world and living with it, is often unbearably painful. To be fully awake to all these things is a heavy burden. It is a blessing to know, yet with knowing comes the curse of suffering that knowledge.[1] It is no wonder that most of us are partially asleep. This sleepy wakefulness, this creative adaptation to the pain in the world, is expressed in our lexicon as *resistance to contact* and *resistance to awareness*. In this way, resistance is a type of contact in that it allows the avoidance of one type of contact in favor of maintaining contact with something other than the immediate experience; unawareness becomes for the organism the "lesser of two evils." In this discussion, however, I will be presenting resistance in its more traditional conceptualization as a dysfunctional form of avoidance to contact and awareness.[2]

We are never alone in our resistances. They develop in our childhood in cooperation with our families, and they extend from there into our present significant relationships. It takes at least two players to resist, and a whole family can participate in the blockage. Resistances serve an adaptive survival purpose. They are adopted and developed through conscious or unconscious cooperation in the family milieu and so are both systemically inherent and inherited. Finally, they are carried outside the system into the world at large into other relationship systems.

Phenomenology of Resistance

All movement engenders resistance. Since experience is in constant flow, it too takes place against an inner resistance. Our inner resistance is experienced as a reluctance to change our ways of doing things. It is only natural to take comfort in that which has constancy. We also take comfort in our experiential flow, but this constant internal change needs to move at a rate that is safe and smooth: a change that enhances the experienced self.

Resistance, unfortunately, is a term that connotes external observation of a person's reluctance. Although we may be observed to resist some behavior, an idea, an attitude, or some way of looking at things, our own experience is that we are acting to preserve, maintain, and enhance ourselves and psychological integrity. What appears to you, on your observing surface, as a casual reluctance to change, may be an inner crisis for me, a fight for my very life. This is the phenomenological definition of *resistance*—a definition that stresses the validity of the person's inner experience, the inner life.

A few basic comments may be helpful here. Our process of being and experiencing is constantly colored by the state of our needs and their frustration-satisfaction cycle. As highly complex and easily programmed organisms, we can learn to block our need satisfaction. This blocking can occur at every level of the ingestion and assimilation process, including sensory inputs, glands and other internal organs, muscles, and various other vital, supportive functions like respiration. Blocking also occurs on the cortical level in the form of ruminations, obsessions, and repetitiously stereotypical thoughts. This is what is meant by *fixation;* fixation blocks the continuous development of the organism. All psychopathology may be thought of as an extensive and often chronic interruption of the temporal-spatial process by which the organism gracefully moves to fulfill its full range of needs. The person is not robbed of integrity; experiencing merely changes to accommodate this halted state of affairs. Crippled behavior has its own special characteristics, and what appears "sick" to us is actually a state of accommodation to blockage in the other person.

Even though the human organism is complex, its hardware—its neurons and other cells—are discrete and finite. To the degree to which human hardware is manipulatable, conditionable, and capable of relatively permanent storage of information, to that degree it has the tendency to retain its own functional stability. The organism perpetuates its specific way of functioning. Therefore, one of the central polarities of our existence is of stability versus change; the need to know versus the fear of knowing. The human organism is a habit-bound, behaviorally repetitive being, constantly struggling to improve its lot and modify its future. Much of our energy is consumed in the tension between these two forces. Any technology that intends to modify behavior must deal with these polar resistance phenomena as being in the foreground of behavior. It stands to reason that no matter if we deal with the "cooperative" or "resistant" sides of the organism, we have a tendency to move toward its motivational center. All parts and forces in the organism are integrally connected, both structurally and functionally, such that each minute part leads toward a fuller sense of the whole.

Types of Resistance

In the discussion of the interactive cycle in Chapter Four, I described what happens to people at an optimal level when they experience, live through, and complete any event. I also touched on the topic of resistance, which I will now take up in greater detail, with special emphasis on its *interactive* aspect and function. Interactive resistances interrupt process prior to or during the various phases of the interactive cycle, so that a couple or a family is not able to start something, collaborate in developing the conversation or project, complete it with satisfaction, let go, and move on to something new. Let us look at all the ways that unaware blockage may take place in each phase of the cycle.

In the beginning of the awareness phase, sensation is organized into an identified experience between two people. People hear the sound of each other's voices, feel each other's skin, look at and see each other, and smell and possibly taste each other when they are close. Awareness is fired by these stimuli: needs are aroused and identified, sentiments come to the foreground as figure, and ideas are developed and acted on later.

The resistance that develops during the sensation phase of the cycle is called *desensitization.*[3] In this phenomenon, people look at each other with little concentration; they scan each other's language superficially or do not bother listening at all. They either avoid touching each other or, when doing so, they block "full entry" of sensations into their bodies, minds, or hearts. Subtlety of contact disappears even before there is an opportunity to feel understood.

When stuck at this early level of interaction, couples and families feel bored, uninvolved, and intellectually asleep or not present for each other. Couple and family members do not stimulate each other, and they maintain a dull, boring, uninteresting home. They accept boredom as a way of living together, not recognizing the boredom as such but as a kind of "grayness" perhaps filled with the color of television or some other distracting substitute for an activity or intellectual pursuit with one another. Their system does not value arousal of sensations and ideas. They lead dull lives and thereby feel safe and contained within their guarded, personal boundaries.

Desensitized couples and families keep from hurting each other, or being hurt, by not feeling. They often succeed, but at the price of not knowing how much they miss in life.

The main resistance to contact in the awareness phase itself is *projection*. Projection exists when one person, without asking questions, fills in the information for the other. The other neither gives information nor corrects the projected information. For example, the person who projects might say, "You must be hungry. I'll fix some food," or "You must be cold. I'll turn up the thermostat." There has to be somebody on the other side who does not give information and who allows the other person to fill in. The other does not say, "No, I'm not cold," nor is he or she willing to answer questions clearly.

The projecting couple or family are often clearly unsynchronized: the person who projects moves faster, and the person who absorbs the projection is slower on the uptake. The projector is impatient. If I ask you, "Are you hungry?" and you need a lot of time to think about it, I might become impatient and not wait for your answer. If you wait long enough without searching inside for what you really want, I will fill it in the way I want. Having a faster rhythm than yours makes it a painstaking process for me to wait and say, "Well, you look like you're thinking it over. All right, I'll wait until you decide." In a way, projection is saying, "Come on, *let's get on with it!*"

When you project, you make some assumptions and take your chances on being wrong on a certain number of them and then you get on with things. When the guess is correct, both people can move on and appreciate the outcome. If one person starts by asking, "Are you hungry?" and the other person is not sure, it is often nice for somebody to make the decision about preparing a meal or going out to dinner. But if guessing becomes chronic, the individuals get stuck in their own worlds and nothing new ever happens between them.

Projections tend to repeat themselves, because as the attributer fills in what he or she wants, the relationship among family members gets stereotyped, lacks variation, and acquires a deadening quality. A couple or family who supports a projective life-style tends to have a "go-get-em" leader and passive, listless followers. There is little discussion or lively debate. Those who do not speak up tend to accumulate resentments, which the whole family pays for with exaggerated outbursts of anger bearing little, if any, relationship to the size of the precipitating event.

"Agreements" among family members are, at best, weak and without vitality. The resulting behaviors are only half-appreciated and undervalued. Once the couple or family gets to the restaurant, one person is not really hungry, another does not like the cuisine, and a third wants to go to the movies. The anticipated feast turns out to be a bore at best, and a disaster at worst. A similar scenario and outcome can be extrapolated for any other family decision or activity; the problem here is a dysfunctional process rather than an issue of content.

When awareness in a couple or family begins to gather energy, *introjection* is the lazy system's way of resisting the awareness. The idea or solution is force-fed by one and swallowed whole by others. Introjection requires an investment of only a small amount of energy instead of the greater energy need for the fire of questioning or argument. Discussions and efforts at getting a "good fit" for all take energy and time. Introjection avoids the expansion of energy through arbitrary agreement. The family agrees not to chew things over, and there is no investment made to get everyone on board.

As in projection, introjection avoids lively discussions. The family values doing business as usual, using old rules of thumb rather than creating new, updated ways of doing things. Listlessness and lack of arousal are evident in such couples and families. A sense of false security is achieved by keeping group awareness narrow, stable, and unchanged. Conformity to the rules results in a kind of communal slumber. As in the main system, so in the internal subsystems. Individuals in this type of family need to conform to authority—for example, parroting information and opinions from the media or other influential sources—and so tend to do well in highly structured environments that do not require much creativity or independent judgment. They often do things by the book and value "standard operating procedure." When entering a new job, they are often very anxious about the rules—that is, until they learn them. They are usually more concerned about "what the boss will think" rather than with making the right decision, since the "right decision" in their minds is predicated on "what the boss will think." They swell the ranks of bureaucrats, soldiers, and compulsive consumers.

Retroflection is another method the family unknowingly uses to avoid awareness and contact. It takes place between the energy and action phase of the interactive cycle. Energy needs to be released from individuals and invested in a common cause for a couple or family to move vigorously into a project, activity, or any collective action. In the retroflected system, people turn inward and do to and for themselves what they would want to do to, or get from, the other members of the family. Couples or families hold in anger, aggression, and sexual expression and do not ask for support, comfort, and touch. Everyone feels somehow isolated and, at the same time, safe in their inner struggle.

This struggle is often imprisoned in the muscles, vocal cords, or other body parts of the potentially expressive mechanics of the human being. Individuals carry the petrified energy in the tension of their bodies, thus developing a myriad of physical symptoms. It feels dangerous to let another "have it," to notice that another is in pain, or to offer to help another get out of a predicament. People feel safer turning to work, alcohol, or a drug rather than to a parent, sibling, or friend.

Members of retroflected couples and families are isolated from each other. They do not share their anger or their pain, nor do they offer comfort or solace to one another. Their boundaries are overly rigid. Privacy is overrespected, and members are embedded in their own loneliness. Self-sufficiency is valued more than making connections.

The retroflected family, as a whole, has similar characteristics to that of its internal subsystems. Its boundaries are thickened and not easily crossed. It does not easily ask for help from neighbors, friends, or therapists. Nor does this kind of family move into the world of friends with pleasure, such as by having people over for dinner, giving parties, or enjoying others. Family members try to shelter themselves behind the ramparts of their own psychological castle.

It is easy to imagine how this sort of system keeps its energy pulled in and how expressive behavior is frustrated. Contact among family members is limited to essentials, and there is little meaningful exchange. The family is isolated from its surrounding community. It is secretive, both within its own system and within the world. Mom says, "Now don't tell your father." Sisters and brothers hold onto their own individual secrets. Adults do not share ideas, feelings, concerns, or insights with children. Children hesitate to ask questions of adults. The intellectual climate is arid. Although individual productions of journals, diaries, and such may be profuse, they are rarely shared. Illness, guilt, and a variety of self-destructive behaviors are typical, yet often, such families are "correct" and well-behaved when in the outside world. Almost always suffering in quiet misery, they pay a high price for the sense of safety and security.[4]

These individuals are the "strong, silent types" who value autonomy. They rarely participate when part of a group, yet they usually make good team players because they tend not to voice their concerns or resentments, preferring to tough it out. Their constant "poker face" makes it difficult to know what they are thinking. They conduct themselves in life as if it is "me against the world."

Deflection is another way a couple or family avoids enrichment in the contact phase of the interactive cycle. Here, people avoid connection by shifting the contact to some other topic that provokes less anxiety.[5] Here are two typical interactions with my own family of origin, which was rather deflective in nature:

Joseph: *(Greeting his parents after a long separation) That trip took forever! Hello! Hello! I've missed you.*

Father: *Hello, your hair is a mess. Why don't you get your hair cut?*

and . . .

Joseph: *(After his mother's operation) How are you feeling? I'm worried about you.*

Mother: *I have some pain over here. So, tell me, are you just going to stay for the weekend?*

Instead of making solid connections, messages ricochet off each other. By not noticing the deflection, the system collaborates to accept unfinished business. Deflected couples and families cannot build a solid theme to be explored to the group's satisfaction. One experience melts into another and disappears. There is little development or solid resolution of issues. Boundaries between persons are vague and ill-defined, and so interpersonal discomfort is avoided.

Deflection is dizzying and "crazy-making" in the sense that members of the family do not feel rooted or fully connected with each other. Voices travel "over" each other, start in the middle of sentences, change topics. At their most extreme levels, deflective people talk all at once, and no one feels a sense of belonging or of being understood.

Confluence is yet another way members of couples and families avoid discomfort with each other. Confluence is common in the awareness part of the cycle, as well as in the resolution and withdrawal phases. It is a basic way of disregarding differences. In the awareness stage of the cycle, people prematurely jump into agreement before examining issues with truly separate minds and voices. A similar phenomenon occurs during the resolution portion of the cycle when separation and differentiation are required for good health but cannot be accomplished; people have to "jump out of agreement" in order to move on.

Confluent families also tend to be retroflected. There is little encouragement to "chew" on each other's ideas and respond honestly to each other. There is a kind of intellectual laziness wherein people do not bother to think seriously about what is being discussed. They skip into agreements that are half-baked and, on closer inspection, do not always make sense. The work of loving *always* involves disagreement and the active fleshing out of the issues at hand. Confluence always prevents this work from occurring and so diminishes the experience and amount of love within the system; energy is neutralized.

Confluent and deflective families do not do the work that results in a loving closeness born out of pushing against each other, insisting on being heard, provoking anger or sympathy, arguing a given point of view, and siding with or resisting easy solutions to complex problems. Deflection and confluence result in stereotypical expressions of love that do not feel trustworthy, because they have not really been tested. People in these families cannot fully count on each other or feel real solidarity among themselves as a group.

In the withdrawal part of the cycle, the confluent couple or family members have difficulty letting go of each other. They cling to each other. They hang on, fearing that the separation that accompanies the end of an experience will result in losing each other's support. These are the service workers such as salespeople and advertising agency account executives, who are paid to be liked through their manipulative subservience. These are the "yes people" or "organization people." They are as noted for their diplomatic skills as they are phobic about conflict. Indeed, confluence usually arises in those who are so insecure or unaware of their own internal power that they are frightened of any external power.

As we look at these various creations called *resistances,* we repeatedly see that they are protections against the risk of psychic pain, hurt, discomfort, difficult confrontation, rejection. At the same time, we witness the price paid: listlessness, lack of intellectual spark and color, depleted energy, depression, loss of humor and playfulness, and a sense of rarely working things out to everyone's satisfaction. (See Table 6.1 for a summary of resistances and their effects.)

Table 6.1. Summary Definitions: Resistances, Collaboration by Others, System Supports.

A *Phase/model resistance*	*B* *Resistance occurring prior to or during the cycle phase*	*C* *Collaboration*	*D* *System supports*
Sensation/desensitization	Blocking of sensation through dulling of receptors, including selective hearing; tactile insensitivity; inability to distinguish subtle, or even obvious, qualities in others. Results: boredom and disinterest.	Maintenance of a stimulus-reduced environment; acceptance of the resulting boredom.	Absence of system cultural characteristics that stimulate; devaluation/fear of arousal.
Awareness/projection	Attribution of one's own arousals (thoughts, feelings, beliefs, and so on) to others. Results: internal phenomena are experienced as if belonging to others.	(a) Projector; (b) recipient who may (1) offer little personal information and discourage attempts to gain it; (2) accept projections without countering.	Limited communication and vocabulary; devaluation of talking things over; no sharing of awareness.
Energy/introjection	Accepting without discrimination ideas, information, values, beliefs, and so on; acting as one "should" without questioning results; identifying with the environment and annihilating the self.	(a) Introjector; (b) donor who force-feeds opinions, instructions, and so on. May resist efforts to destructure and assimilate—for example, by "talking things over."	Valuing of doing business as usual with little demand for contemporary system values to meet present situations. No energy to do it differently.

Action/retroflection	Turning inward of energy; doing to oneself what one would like to do to the environment; manifested in avoidance of aggression, avoidance of possible disappointment, maintenance of "self-sufficiency," and substance abuse. Results: self-destructive behavior, illness, and guilt.	Acceptance without discrimination of other's somaticizing of emotion/arousals (for example, inward-turned anger resulting in headache). Members offer nothing. Nobody asks for anything.	Overvaluing of self-sufficiency and interpersonal boundaries; system supports and reinforces physical symptoms as expression of feelings.
Contact/deflection	Turning aside of one's own or other's feelings and arousals by shifting attention from this contact; reducing the voltage or charge of an interaction.	Acceptance or aid in deflecting; satisfaction with "unfinished business." Willingness to go on with the new business without finishing old business.	Promotion of extraneous contact items; ill-defined boundary process that allows contact deprivation within the system; devaluing of conflict within the system culture; system vocabulary lacks conflict words like *fight, quarrel,* and so on.
Resolution/confluence	The blurring of boundaries between self and others and/or the environment; disallowing separation and differentiation of self.	Separateness is intolerable; hanging onto one another; agreement to stay joined	System has limited history of resolving issues; system mechanisms or rituals counter aggression or disagreement; "Don't rock the boat" values.
Withdrawal/confluence	Difficulty in letting go—hanging onto contact beyond the energy available in the contact experience.	Partner experiences anxiety at letting go, separation, and differentiation; like holding hands in a movie too long: "A dead hand."	System in which inactivity and quiet time are countered by ritual and process that cut them short, such as continued talking until all agree and achieve sameness.

Source: Lester P. Wyman, Ph.D. I am indebted to Dr. Wyman and the Gestalt Institute of Cleveland for allowing me to use this material.

Much of therapy with couples and families focuses on these unaware forces. A goal of therapy is to bring these resistances to awareness so that the couple or family can choose to transform itself into a more contactful unit. The therapist's job is to invite or entice a couple or family members to a curiosity about how they manage these phenomena, what is avoided in the way of difficulty, and the price paid for staying safe. Because we are optimists, we often hope that such awareness will produce change for the better, and we are often pleased to see such change.

The Franklins: One Family's Resistances

It helps to talk about resistances in the context of a given situation. Let us look at a specific situation to see how a therapist can treat resistances and avoid mobilizing resistances in the family. In the Franklin family, there seem to be no dramatic resistances. Contact is encouraged, and all members feel free to ask questions and be inquisitive of each other. But is it possible that members are allowed to intrude on each other's boundaries in the name of contact? When, for example, too many questions cause people to feel intruded on, should they feel free to refuse to tell something personal? That should certainly be possible in a healthy family.

The father in this family is a forty-three-year-old teacher, and the mother is a forty-two-year-old physician. There are three boys: Matt is seventeen and about to go away to college, Les is fifteen and still in high school, and Jerry is twelve.

Matt: *I don't want anybody to throw any low blows.*

Mom: *I don't want any low blows, but I don't always know what low blows are. When you raised that concern like you were worried that might happen, it made me curious and concerned about you feeling that way.*

Dad: *Most of the things that come up will be things that are important to us.*

Matt: *I'm not saying I don't want to talk about anything important. I'm just saying I think you should see that there's a certain line.*

Dad: *That's fine and I respect that, but I don't know what would be a low blow.*

Matt: *I think you both know a low blow—when you say something and feel "why did I say that?" An example of a low blow would be bringing up what happened during Christmas vacation in the islands with me and Chris, and you'd express your feelings to someone like you were disappointed.*

Dad: *Granted. You're right in assuming it would be smart not to bring something like that up. Good point. But I think the door should be open for talking about emotional things. Just because they're emotional doesn't mean they're low blows.*

Matt: *All right.*

Resistance between family members takes place at the *awareness* level. Because "low blows" are difficult to define or be owned by family members, there is a sense of mystery about the phenomenon—mystery invites *projections,* because meaning is not agreed on and uncertainty is the norm.

Introjections are possible when someone is called a name and does not question it or someone is accused of something and accepts it without challenging a parent or sibling.

Solving a problem with ease can take place in several ways: you can deny doling out "low blows" or you can explain them away. You can also admit that one invites "low blows" by denying the validity of what others are saying or otherwise upsetting them constantly.

Therapist: *I was about to say that I was impressed by how quickly you found something that interested you all. You worked and talked about it and came to a conclusion. That was active. Most of the families I see are not as active or as quick to do that. That was nice for me to see. Is it familiar to you that something comes up and you seem to solve it with some ease?*

In focusing on the family's strength and competence, the therapist supports the family: "Look how good you are! Look at the skills you have—how easy this is for you! I'm impressed." The implication is that not every family allows people to join in and take part in conversations so readily.

Another way of putting this is as follows: "I know you folks are good and basically competent, and if we hit a snag in the future we will deal with it knowing that *I am on your side*. And, while there is this lighter side, there may be a darker side in this family—things you may not like about yourselves—but I can carry this as well." The therapist has both the privilege and the burden of carrying the light and the dark sides of a family system; the burden of awareness brings with it the privilege of being the family's witness.

This intervention does everything to keep resistance from increasing. It promotes good feelings among the family members and avoids polarizing them. It says, "You came here to look at your dirt and you are probably anxious. If I jump in and join you in exploring the low blows that I see, surely you will feel badly. You might push back against me and say, 'Well, we don't have that many low blows—we are mostly a loving family.'" By joining the family members in their competence, the therapist actually lowers the resistance to contact among them and also between the family and the therapist. The practitioner forms a working alliance with the family.

The intervention also provides positive reinforcement in general. It says: "Keep going, you're doing well." Later, in asking them if they "solve things with ease," the therapist encourages the family to be curious about its interactional process.

The therapist supports the family's strength and, as noted at the end of the previous chapter, this is the first intervention and not merely a simple-minded compliment. It is a reminder to them about a basic form of their familial competence, which is that they are able to name a problem and discuss it readily. Often, families do not appreciate what they do well. Rather, they focus on their "problem," the content, their stuckness.

Dad: *Les and Jerry, have you thought about what it's going to be like next year with Matt gone?*

Les: *Matt's been away for trips, so I don't think it's going to be that much of a change.*

Jerry: *When Matt went away on trips, we knew he'd be back in due time. This is a different experience. I don't know what to expect.*

Dad: *I think the same way. Matt, what do you feel about leaving the nest?*

Matt: *I feel good about it—not in the sense that I want to get away. What I think about is coming back—it takes a little time to get back into the swing of things. I'm sure I'll be homesick for the first couple of weeks, but I know I can handle it.*

Mom: *I was real proud of how you planned the whole trip to school, figured out the flights by yourself, and made arrangements to have dinner with your friends.*

Matt: *Mom, you don't talk to your own brother that much. It doesn't sound like you and Dad are really close to your brothers and sisters. I'm curious about it.*

Dad: *I've wondered about that too, when I think about when you boys leave—how close are you going to be with one another or with us?*

Les: *How do you know when you're close or not?*

Dad: *I would hope that we can stay in communication.*

Jerry: *Yeah, that's true.*

Dad: *How do you define closeness? My sisters and I didn't play with one another when we were growing up, and Mom didn't do much with Uncle Jim, I guess. You guys are doing something together every day.*

Mom: *I thought about that a lot, too, and wonder where everybody will end up living.*

Les: *I'm going to end up selling jewelry in Arizona. Come and visit me.*

Dad: *So, either we're going to be close or not, but we can't tell at this stage.*

Asking questions is a double-edged sword. On the positive side, it clarifies what is going on and avoids misunderstanding, thereby enhancing contact among family members. Generally, questions prevent projections and introjections. The dark side of feeling free to ask anything at any time is that it may be an invasion of privacy, an intrusive act, and, if that is so, contact among family members is interrupted and undermined.

The therapist scans the family for stuck places. For example, do the questions come from the adults only? Are they interrogating the kids or the other way around? Are there members who do not ask anything, not giving themselves the freedom of inquiry because they are scared? At the other extreme, the therapist may consider the notion of vulnerability. Is everyone willing to ask anybody anything no matter how personal or intrusive it may be? Does the family respect personal privacy?

Therapist: *I'd like to interrupt for a moment now and tell you what I'm watching, as I said I would do if I saw anything that might interest you. I was paying attention to who could ask questions of whom, and who says things about themselves just to give information. And every time I thought I saw a pattern—for instance, that most of the questions were coming from one direction—then it seemed to switch so that the questions came from another direction. Or, when I thought I saw most of the information coming from one place, suddenly it started coming from another place. It seemed amazing that you all seem to be able to ask questions of each other. I'm not sure, because it hasn't completely happened yet, but it looks like each of you feels free to ask for and give information. I don't know if that's exactly true, but that's what it looks like to me. So, I'd like it if you would think for a moment, each one of you, about whether you feel free to ask anybody anything, or if you don't. Or if you feel free to say whatever you're thinking about to anybody, or if you don't. I wonder if you'd be willing to check it out, and whether that interests you, too.*

How do the therapist's language and intention keep resistance down and the interactive process up? Let's look at what was really being said. "I'd like to interrupt," says the practitioner to the family, "I have respect for what you are doing. I know this is your arena and your struggle, and I respect and appreciate this struggle of yours." In pointing out things that might be of interest to the family members, the therapist is reminding them that "this is your work. Your curiosity and energy about how you operate as a family matters a lot to me. I will continue supporting the energy that drives your curiosity and self-examination and your capacity to observe yourselves, so that eventually you will not need me to see what you do and how you get stuck."

The therapist develops the theme of how, and how much, information is exchanged in the family? How easily is it exchanged? How carelessly (a distinct possibility)? And, on the other hand, how hard is it to share sensitive things, and is this related to the danger of "low blows?" The therapist tells them, "It's amazing that *everyone* seems to be able to ask questions and inform each other!" The next step is to pose the possibility of an experiment at the awareness level, namely, to find out whether they can ask or tell "anything to anyone." The clinician develops the theme by stretching its limits, seeing how loose the family is, and exploring the kinks and tight spots, the potential fears and hurts among them.

Matt: *I have an easier time asking Les and Jerry personal questions than I have asking Mom and Dad personal questions.*

Mom: *I was trying to think who I can ask questions. I tried asking Les a lot of questions this summer, and I also told him a lot about me. I'm more careful about asking Matt questions, but I don't think I have much trouble. Do you think so?*

Matt: *Not really.*

Dad: *I think that, for a long time, we weren't able to ask each other questions. I feel hesitant in asking questions of you guys. I think it's got to do with your growing up and exerting yourselves, but sometimes an innocent question gets into a debate real quick.*

Mom: *Do you guys feel that you ask me questions? I can't remember.*

Matt: *I think questions come up when we're looking at photo albums and stuff. I think you're looking for a major question.*

Dad: *I think it's hard to say when it's yourself—I can see you guys asking Mom questions all the time, but I can't see you asking me.*

Matt: *Sometimes you both want to help, but then you'll go on and on. Sometimes I just need an answer.*

Holding onto a question or not revealing feelings is a way of isolating oneself from others by bounding oneself apart. On the other hand, "spilling the beans" all the time can be a way of punishing. To hold a question in and not answer it can be thought of as a "healthy" retroflection, especially if the question may provoke criticism, anger, or punishment. To hold something in creates a sense of privacy. Feeling free to ask questions promotes discussion and contact. Yet asking something that should remain private can feel intrusive to another and may provoke retaliation. The healthy family seeks a balance between curiosity on the one hand and intrusiveness on the other. Also, we may inform to feel known *or* inform as a way of hurting. This family and therapist are exploring these issues.

Therapist: *Let me follow up on what I'm saying. I'm not sure exactly where I'm going, but I did notice that you all seem pretty free talking back and forth, either questioning or giving information. And I think I'm hearing you say, "Yeah, we're free but . . . but . . . but." And there are a lot of guesses about what the "buts" are. So let me suggest something to you, and tell me if you think you'll get anything out of it.*

Each of you think of either asking a question that you don't want to ask or saying something to the others that you don't want to say. Just think of something you won't ask or say here. I guarantee you're not going to have to ask or say it; you're not going to have to say it at all, ever, even when you're out of here. Think of a question that you would want to ask anybody here but you wouldn't ask it, or think of something you would want to say about yourself in relation to the other person but you wouldn't say it. Then see if you can put into words why you wouldn't do it. Then tell the person why you would or would not do it. Don't say what it is. For example, you might say, "I have a question that I'm not going to ask you, and the reason I won't ask you is . . . "

Maybe this will give us some idea of the small things that get in the way—and it sounds like it's small things here. Is this okay? Does it make sense to you? Am I being clear enough? Try to think of how many questions or statements you wouldn't say. Maybe each one of you, the five of you, can think of two with two different people. With some luck, maybe we can get something from everybody.

This third intervention, after much listening and reestablishing of what is going on, is the firming up of the experiment. By saying, "I'm not exactly sure where I'm going" and "You tell me if you think you'll get anything out of it," the therapist enters the family's cautious hearts. It is as if the practitioner is saying, "I'm on a trip with you, and I'm groping along with you, and it's only a possibility that this could be useful to you." All resistances, doubts, and questions are acceptable. Then the experiment is posed in a new, bold form, one that addresses and supports individual boundaries as well as the exploration of what the family members may want to ask or inform that is too painful or difficult, and what that is all about.

The experiment itself is a bold statement: it is okay to have secrets, and it is okay not to reveal them, and it is probably quite valid in such-and-such cases not to tell something because people may tease, call each other names, or otherwise administer "low blows" that hurt. There is nothing terrible about that; it simply happens to people in families. There is also room for "safety realizations" like: "Well, I could ask this and he or she could (would) tell me with pleasure." The experiment gives the family the freedom to not deal with difficult content while pushing them to struggle with difficult feelings.

Dad: *You want us to articulate why it is that we can't say it, and it can be either a question or an exposure of ourselves.*

Mom: *Why we keep it a secret. But then we're going to have to guess why that person can't say that—or, "Oh, my goodness, I never knew that."*

Matt: *If I bring something up and say I can't tell you because of this and that, then your trust isn't there because the other person could say, "Why can't he say that to me?" I think somebody might get hurt.*

Dad: *It opens a can of worms and, all of a sudden, you're exposing that maybe somebody should be disappointed in you, or would be disappointed in you—which is damage done without saying what the specific thing is.*

If you do not share something that is upsetting, no one will be disappointed or get angry with you for having "unreasonable" or "crazy" feelings. If you do not raise a difficult question, you will not upset anyone. But you will also isolate your pain from others and feel out of contact and lonely in the family. So, in *not* retroflecting one's feelings and letting go, you may pay the price of possible disapproval and "low blows." Retroflecting feelings allows for a sense of internal safety, of internal soothing, but entails the price of possible isolation from your family.

Therapist: *I'm sure that, in your family, one of the things that gets in the way is that people would be hurt or disappointed. It isn't in every family, but it is in yours. Set it up so that somebody might feel disappointed already, and that gets in the way. That is a good example. Okay?*

This intervention supports the previous one. The therapist implies that "in your family it may not feel safe to ask a particular question or make a given statement. So this experiment gives you an opportunity not to ask the question itself but only to share the difficult feeling if the question *were* to be asked or if the statement were to be made: 'If I were to say this (statement) to you, you might get hurt. . . .'"

Dad: *So, you wouldn't ask a question for fear that you'd get an answer you didn't want.*

Matt: *And I might get laughed at. Some questions that I think about are just too stupid to ask, and I can usually figure out the answer myself.*

Dad: *When you said they're stupid and you fear being laughed at, are you thinking someone else would think you're stupid? So, rather than ask me a question, you say, "Hmmm, what would Dad answer?"*

Matt: *Well, you might think, "I don't sit there and act as stupid as you."*

Dad: *Was that a low blow?*

Mom: *I have this feeling that if I say anything, everybody's going to laugh.*

Les: *Everybody does!*

Mom: *One of two things will happen. Everyone's going to laugh and say, "Mom!" Or people aren't going to listen, and I'm going to get interrupted. It's a pretty effective way of shutting me up. What I do is that I let it go as a joke. So I try and stay involved by joking, but I let go of what I really wanted to say.*

Dad: *I feel that way. It's difficult to share some things for fear of having your feelings hurt, of being made fun of. But you guys rebound faster. Sometimes I interrupt you, then I'm really impressed when you go back and get into it again. That's hard for me to do when I've been telling you something I'm serious about and you think it's corny; then I get interrupted and the conversation goes elsewhere. And I sort of curl up and say, "Ah, the hell with you." So I am hesitant about sharing things.*

Resistance is paradoxical in this way: the exchange of information generally enhances contact and, therefore, reduces resistance, but overly easy and frequent parting with information painful to others results in repeated hurting; contact is avoided by pushing each other away with the act of hurting, or, to use the family's own language, administering "low blows." The sharing of information, an apparent virtue, can get in the way of contact when it is overdone.

In the above exchange, almost everyone feels like a potential victim of ridicule or of some other way of being invalidated, and no one volunteers to reassure anyone else. When Dad gets close to figuring out what Matt's pain is about, Mom interrupts with her own complaint and so everyone remains hung up. What they share is that sense that all are vulnerable.

Therapist: *Let me tell you what stands out in listening and see if it matches what you're hearing and saying. Again, I want to tell you that I am so impressed with you. I doubt if most families could talk as freely to each other as you do. You say things. You ask things. You give what I once or twice thought might be low blows; you call it kidding each other. You know it's not easy to tell kidding from "too low." But it seems to move with an amazing ease. So I guess that, if you do it here, at home you can also do it with each other. And I think that moves your family along, keeps things going in a very nice way.*

However, in addition, what I'm hearing is that that very nice style hurts almost everybody sometimes, and you may or may not have talked enough about that—how to signal each other when it hurts.

So, those are the things that stand out when I listen to you: you really don't stop each other very much from saying or asking things that can hurt. It's amazingly true. But maybe you want to talk to each other about the times when it doesn't work.

Les: *Mom, I think you want our family to be perfect. I think you're reaching for the ultimate goal, which is difficult for any family to reach. And I think if you stop pushing so hard that maybe it will level out. But you're always trying to work it up to another level and, instead of sticking there, you blow up. You say, "I'm not part of this family . . . blah, blah, blah." You know there might be four guys in the family and only one girl, but you're still 20 percent of the family.*

Mom: *I've heard that message before.*

Les: *That's not intended as cutting you up. I'm just saying that maybe you need to look at that. Maybe that's a problem of not being able to communicate when we get hurt. Sometimes I feel pressure that we have to be able to communicate all the time. And some-*

times it seems like that's not respecting our space. You gave me space when I needed to make decisions and do everything about all the pressure on me, but you still wanted me to be strong in the family. So I really wasn't given space because there was no possible way I could do all that and still give as much.

Mom: *Let me see if I understand. It feels to you like I'm trying to get everything perfect for the family and not paying attention to your needs. Is that part of it?*

Matt: *No. I think you want to take a step more, get deeper into each other's personal feelings when it's not time. I think you just push too much.*

The primary resistance takes place by hurting another person—then pushing that person away. The secondary resistance to contact is not sharing that one feels hurt by what was said. One remains safe by retroflecting the hurt and hiding it but pays the price of not connecting with another family member. There is some taunting of Mom, but Mom does not protest or ask for support and the attack continues.

Therapist: *Let me interrupt a moment. This is the time. How would you know if your mother was hurt? Or how would you show if you were hurt?*

Here, the therapist is gently pushing for clearer awareness: "How would you know Mom is hurt?" and "Mom, how come you don't tell them: 'Hey, I don't like how you're talking to me with the blah-blah. That hurts.'" Where is Dad? Did he fade out? Can he tell Mom is being hurt? How about little Jerry? All the family members continue feeling supported by the therapist and, at the same time, become more thoughtful about how they create hurt and how they may not have the skill to stop hurts from flying around the room. They may even ponder, "Is there a price we pay for being so open with each other?"

Matt: *Mom would probably tell us if she felt hurt. And she gets this look on her face. It's hard for her to accept some of the things we say. Maybe I overemphasize what she's doing a little bit. To an extent, I think I'm right, and to an extent, wrong. I think she sees that, but maybe I go too far.*

Mom: *Sometimes, when I'm hurt, I'll become quiet for a while. And I feel like I'm not even 20 percent. Then I sort of pop out of that and throw my arms in the air and say, "Let' have a family meeting." And then I show it with fireworks.*

Les: *But then you come to the family meetings and you try to rule, and you say, "This is the way it's going to be." That doesn't do any good because then people just leave there saying, "Oh yeah, no problem," go to their room and say, "Oh my God, what did she say?" It's so stupid.*

Mom: *I'm confused. Not by what you're saying, because I hear what you're saying. I guess I'm afraid to give up doing that because 20 percent in a vote doesn't go very far when everybody has such different interests than I have.*

Matt: *It's not your vote so much. It's the way you address the thing. It's like, "Oh, I'm feeling terrible." And your say is more than 20 percent if you want something and the three of us don't; it's not like we'll overrule you. In big decisions, you usually rule closer to 90 percent.*

Mom: *Ninety—wow!*

Jerry: *Yeah, we all see that.*

One way they keep apart and do not become close is that they tell each other what needs to be said but act heroically (stoically) and do not share the stings of the impact of what the sharing does, what effect it has on each individual. It is a kind of perverse sharing of everything and telling the truth at any cost. The result, or the danger, is that wounded family members clench down on their pains and secretly withdraw from each other. This poses a potential difficulty, to say the least.

Therapist: *The reason I'm interrupting is that you've gone back to being able to talk very easily, freely, saying things back and forth, and that's the way I think you're terrific as a family. There's no doubt how much work has gone into all of you to bring it to this.*

However, we started to talk a little bit about the dark side of that, when you go over the line. You call it "low blows" or "hurts." We're going to meet again next week, and I suggest that during this week you pay attention to when you feel hurt. You don't have to do anything with it or change it. I don't think that's important at this point. But pay attention. And then, maybe, we can get some sense of how often—or maybe never—you go over the line with each other. We can take a look at that and it might interest you to learn something. I don't know what you'll find. So, each of you pay attention to when that low blow or hurt happens, and pay attention to how it happens and what you do with it. Focus on that within yourself. Whether you do anything with it or not doesn't matter. And then we can take a look at it here. Okay?

The therapist is meticulous about talking to all the family members and not hinting at any wrongdoing or "bad person." The practitioner stays away from their family meetings and does not give advice to Mom or anyone else. The therapy sessions are aimed at preserving the phenomenological reality of their daily lives and rely heavily on stimulating their curiosity. It has to be, even if we do not have hard data, that they leave the session feeling that somehow they hurt each other and do not connect fully with one another about the hurt they all carry. In our vernacular, it is a kind of retroflection and desensitization. Perhaps that's what "heroic" interchanges require.

Resistances are avoidance of contact. But are they self-destructive blockages to family contact, or do they serve multiple functions?

When you are an adolescent in a family that values questioning, discussion, sharing of information, and working out various issues, what happens if you want to keep a secret or if you are not enthusiastic about hearing your mother's or father's opinion about your goals or daydreams? What if, as that same adolescent, you may have some fears of ridicule or of low blows—even if they may not have been experienced at home but, say, in school? How do you act if your mom and dad want you to be a doctor and you want to sell jewelry in a flea market? And, as a parent, how do you protect your sensitive adolescent child from being too pressured about carrying certain values or protect the child from your possibly grandiose ideas about his or her future profession? How do you say to your growing child-adult, "Please, you are hurting me when you say I'm doing something dumb?"

Conclusion

In the last half of this chapter, we examined how resistances to contact operate at different levels of a given family. Is retroflection always "bad"? No, retroflection is a basic value of a civilized society, and a family is a carrier of these values. Retroflection prevents attacking and hurting others or revealing painful "truths" to others. When we anticipate parental criticism (or that of siblings or teachers), are we out of touch with reality? Are we *projecting* our own punitiveness in this case?

The therapist in the above session leisurely explored questions of this sort with the family. Perhaps feeling free to ask anything of anyone at any time in a family is a mixed blessing. Perhaps the Franklins need to learn when and how to ask as well as when and how not to ask. And the same question applies to giving out information. Each person needs to ask, "Do I want to tell this about myself or what I see about the other? Suppose the other will be disappointed or hurt and experience my telling something as an insult or betrayal or a 'low blow.'"

The therapist began by helping the Franklins explore their mutual concern or apprehension about disappointing or letting one another down. So, as we work with this family, we begin to realize that resistances can be ways of filtering and regulating contact between family members so as not to be too harsh, too critical, too transparent, or too bold with one another. And the Franklins are just beginning to explore how exquisitely sensitive they can be around issues of offending each other, disappointing each other, or delivering the "wrong goods."

I have presented formal definitions of resistances in couples and families as well as examples of some subtleties of contact regulation in a given family. I have demonstrated how the therapist can carefully and respectfully explore the phenomenology of a given family and hone an emerging group theme into a possible experiment. This kind of detailed analysis of a specific session should be useful to therapists in working with resistances. Since all resistances are experienced as interruptions at the contact boundary, it is only natural for the discussion to turn now to working with and managing personal and system boundaries.

Notes to Chapter Six

1. This is akin to the Sartrean freedom-responsibility-anguish triad. See the following passage from J.-P. Sartre (1957), *Existentialism and human emotions* (New York: Philosophical Library): "That is the idea I shall try to convey when I say that man is condemned to be free. Condemned, because he did not create himself, yet, in other respects he is free; because, once thrown into the world, he is responsible for everything he does" (p. 23). Here is a related observation: "The essential consequence of our earlier remarks is that man being condemned to be free carries the weight of the whole world on his shoulders; he is responsible for the world and for himself as a way of being" (p. 52).
2. Some Gestalt theorists argue that resistances are not negative, dysfunctional blockages that need to be removed before contact can occur but are different forms of contact in and of themselves. The idea of resistance as the client's "stance" in the world was first brought to my attention in 1981 by Edwin S. Harris of St. Louis, Missouri, in an unpublished manuscript titled "A new revised Gestalt theory of resistance" and in personal communication. The notion of resistances as contact functions is based on the assumption that conscious awareness cannot *not* be out of contact—that is, one is always in contact with something. This position was first formally elaborated by G. Wheeler (1991), *Gestalt reconsidered: A new approach to contact and resistance* (New York: Gardner Press). Wheeler states that

   > what we are saying here is that there is no such thing as "contact" in some ideal, platonic form, pure and theoretical, which then in the "real" case becomes unfortunately sullied with "resistances"—confluence, projection, introjection, deflection, and all the rest. Rather, the exercise of all these modes, all these variables at the

boundary, which we will call "contact functions," *is* the contact, which can then be described, analyzed, and possibly even categorized by its particular mix of such modes or functions—but does not exist at all without them. Take away all resistance . . . and what is left is not "contact" at all, pure or otherwise, but only a complete merging, or possibly a dead body, pending decomposition, which is finally, completely, and for the first time "out of contact" [p. 113].

While I, to a degree, subscribe to this view, I base my discusion in the present work on the traditional view of resistances as interruptions to contact functioning.

3. J. Kepner (1987), *Body process: A Gestalt approach to working with the body in psychotherapy* (New York: Gestalt Institute of Cleveland Press); L. Wyman, lectures and personal communication with the author, Gestalt Institute of Cleveland, 1980–1989.
4. The descriptions of the Madiar family in Chapters Five and Seven illustrate a typically retroflected family.
5. In Chapter Eight, I give an example of a therapy session with a deflecting couple—Jim and Loretta.

7

Boundaries and Boundary Management

A boundary defines a thing.
—Fritz Perls

In Chapter Three, we discussed the boundaries of the systems and subsystems of couples and families. Forming boundaries gives meaning to a set of events or experiences and differentiates the couple or family from their environment, just as the boundaries within the system give meaning to and differentiate subsystems.

At all times, when you are looking at a couple or family, one of your tasks is to see the boundaries. You ought to be able to pull back at any time and identify the boundaries. Gestalt therapy states that the boundary is where you experience the difference—where there is a "me" and a "you" or a "we" and a "they"—and that growth takes place when there is contact at the boundary.[1] Differences must be heightened before you can make contact: I have to know that you and I are different before we can be together.

Boundaries are not only concepts, they exist. Although we do not see boundaries, we can experience them as "actual" and "real." Just because our sensory equipment does not directly see them does not mean that they are not there. They are, indeed, energy fields.[2] You experience a boundary when people stand too close while talking to you: they seem to impinge on your personal space. You want to send your thoughts at your own pace and rhythm. If the other person is too close when you send out a thought, it touches the other's boundary before you are ready.

As I pointed out in Chapter Three, the qualities of boundaries can differ. Retroflection keeps the energy field small and contained by maintaining a "thick" boundary. Projection throws energy far out and away, making boundaries confusingly "thin." When you begin to visualize the phenomena of boundaries, the exchange within a couple or family begins to make more sense. As you learn to experience boundaries, you will notice their varying existence and nature: where they are, which ones are missing, which ones never form, who becomes stuck where they do not belong, and who or what is never allowed inside.

The Madiars: Discerning and Attending to Boundaries

Let us examine the Madiar family in terms of boundaries. As we saw in Chapter Five, the family consists of the father, Gregor—an industrial worker who was later promoted into management—and the mother, Dotty, who is a homemaker; in addition, there are two teenage children, Theresa (sixteen) and Mike (fourteen). We also noted earlier that the family has constructed a safe haven, a fortress in an unsafe world; it has turned its collective energy inward, so that little energy is projected into the world. The family boundary is thick and rigid. Contact with the world is minimal—primarily to carry out the bare, functional necessities of work and school.

In line with this turning away from the world, the Madiars rarely allow exposure of themselves to the therapist. They tend to stay to themselves and not let themselves be influenced by the therapist. Instructed to talk to each other, they first struggle with accepting the notion that they *have* to address each other as part of this kind of therapy. They will then do it with rigid determination, even when there is an impasse and the going gets rough.

Before we proceed with a discussion of the boundary relationship of the therapist to this family, it will be helpful to look at the internal boundaries within the Madiar enclave. Basically, they are divided into two poorly bounded groups: parents and children. Figure 7.1 shows the tentative boundaries between the four family members as well as the thicker boundary separating them from the therapist. Gregor and Dotty, the parents, talk to each other in telegraphic language, usually in private, about basic issues like money. Theresa and Mike, the siblings, tend to support each other and secretly discuss their tactics for

Figure 7.1. The Madiar Family: Initial Boundaries.

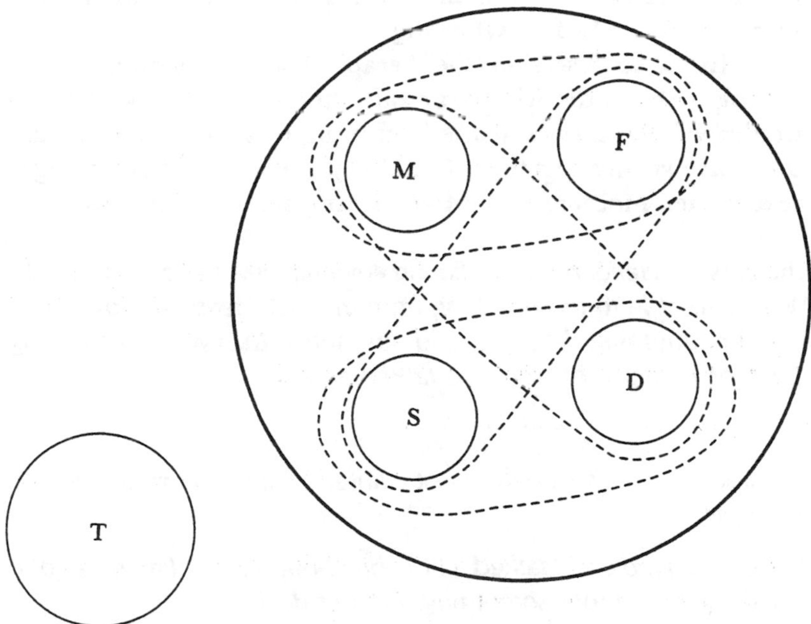

breaking out of the family stronghold. However, because their parents stress role differences between men and women, there is a pull for Theresa to team up with her mother and Mike with his father. The latter happens infrequently because the two males do not know how to talk or what to talk about without the presence and encouragement of the females. The women's talks are usually superficial—about housework, clothing, and so on—and rarely concern intimate matters such as boyfriends or sexual development. Theresa gets a sense of shame about a woman's body from her mother and tends to turn to a favorite female literature teacher to ask questions about men and sex. Father occasionally teases Theresa in a fond way about her boy "callers," much as his son might. Mother tends to boss Mike around (as father does); neither parent talks with him much about feelings, problems, schoolwork, or relationships.

As you may surmise, little subsystem fluidity exists within the family. There are few easy exchanges between father and daughter or mother and son; most contacts tend to be formal, determined by tasks to be executed and fueled by the parents taking an authoritarian stance. Communication is often role-bound and rarely free-wheeling.

In the sixth session, the therapist begins by sitting quietly, waiting to have the Madiars's full attention.[3] The boundaries are drawn like pistols at the beginning of a duel. Gregor and Dotty are sitting together. On Dotty's side are Theresa, right next to her mother, and Mike, sitting next to Theresa.

Therapist: *Hello, hello . . . So did anything new happen this week? Were you able to use anything from our last meeting? How about it, Mike, anything different? Did you notice that you did anything different because of what we talked about?*

(Mikes shakes his head "no.")

Therapist: *That's all right. I just wanted to know. How about you, Theresa?*

Theresa: *Dad and I talked a little bit about school. I made a point of asking him about something. No big deal.*

Therapist: *Okay, thank you for sharing that with me. I'm glad you worked a little bit harder at just making ordinary talk with your dad. Good for you.*

This is the beginning of an important boundary formation between the daughter and father, one of the weaker subsystems in this family. The therapist takes note of it in moving from person to person.

Therapist: *How about you, Gregor, did you do anything different because of our last session? Did you remember our talk during the week?*

Gregor: *Nothing much, really.*

Therapist: *That's fine. I just wanted to know how things went.*

Gregor: *I was satisfied. Things were pretty quiet.*

Therapist: *How about you, Dotty?*

Dotty: *Yeah, I noticed something. I noticed that when the kids wanted to go out, I really didn't want them to go. I did let them go, reluctantly. I remembered what happened here so I said okay. I let them go. (She raises her chin proudly and glances briefly at Gregor.)*

Therapist: *I am delighted that you were able to do that. I know how hard it is for you, and I appreciate you remembering to tell me about it.*

Dotty is showing that she is loosening her tight grip on her children—a potentially major accomplishment in loosening the boundary between the parents and the children—and therefore making the family more open to the community. As the therapist scans their faces, Gregor looks serious, Dotty is quiet, and the children are smiling at each other.

Therapist: *Then if there isn't anything else, I'd like you all to turn to each other and talk to each other again—the same way we've done in the last session. Remember, if you need help or get stuck, please ask me. I'll be glad to help out. I'll watch you and listen and tell you what I see when something stands out for me.*

The therapist has in mind successive images of how the family has formed boundaries in the previous sessions: which boundaries are fixed (as between mother and father) and which have changed (as between father and daughter). The therapist is interested in seeing what the Madiars are going to do in this session and is watching for change—especially whether the internal family boundaries are becoming more varied and more flexible.

Now the therapist leans back and is ready to watch how the Madiars form subgroups. The family members are allowed to "reunite" and re-form their boundary. Until now, the therapist has been meeting the family at its boundary; now, in withdrawing, the practitioner forms a separate entity. This is done so as not to distract the family members from the work they are doing. Once the therapist has given clear, crisp instructions, it is appropriate to let the individuals know, perhaps nonverbally, that he or she is ready to be separate and to watch dispassionately. One way to achieve this is by looking down, looking out the window, or otherwise becoming disengaged.

Theresa: *(Turning to her father) Did you hear what Mama said about letting us go? You know, she really is learning to let us go. I don't know if you are.*

Here is an unexpected shift that immediately excites the therapist, because until this week, daughter and father were the least bounded system within the family. They seldom discussed serious things. When they tried, the mother would become protective of Theresa and interrupt to explain things to Gregor. This attempted contact represents a significant change in the internal boundaries of the family.

The safest and easiest conversation would be between Theresa and her mother. The next safest coming together would be between Theresa and her brother within earshot of the parents. Theresa might say to her brother, "I've noticed that she lets us go more easily. Have you noticed that too?" The most difficult connection is the one now attempted between Theresa and her father.

(Gregor is thinking about his daughter's challenging remark. He looks at her but a little past her, as if focusing on a spot in space.)

He may be tempted to become defensive and reestablish a strong, unyielding position in the family by saying to Theresa, "You are now going to tell me what to learn, Theresa? You've got a lot of nerve!" But he doesn't speak. He may be aware of a kind of ache in his chest, a pain, a hurt—perhaps a sense of betrayal that his wife did not get his okay before getting all of this started.

Gregor: *(Shifting his gaze from the space next to Theresa and addressing Dotty) How could you do this without talking it over with me?*

This is probably the first time Gregor has shown his hurt—any hurt—to his whole family. He feels safe enough, somehow, to show his vulnerability in front of his children.

Dotty: *Gregor! We spent a couple of sessions talking about how the kids need a little more freedom to socialize with other kids. Remember?*

The therapist intervenes here to emphasize the importance of this open exchange between husband and wife and how this new boundary is valuable. Indeed, in the Gestalt approach, we always tend to support and strengthen the primary adult relationship first, before future work with other subsystems.

Therapist: *Stop a moment, the two of you. I just want you to know that this issue of what the children should or shouldn't do is very important to both of you. The fact that you want to talk about it together is wonderful. I'm going to make sure these kids stay out of the way and give you all the room in the world to do it.*

The parents bounded themselves by talking to each other despite the others' presence, and it is important to maintain that boundary long enough for them to have a conversation. Anticipating that Gregor might not respond and that would be the end of the contact, the therapist leans heavily on the couple to practice actually discussing the matter. The goal is to "stretch" what might be a momentary, rather impoverished confrontation—the kind that has occurred in past sessions—into something deeper, fuller, and more contactful. The children seem to have gotten the therapist's message, and the whole family falls into a somewhat tense silence waiting for Gregor to respond to Dotty.

Gregor: *I know, I know. You're right. We did discuss it before. I'm just awfully worried that these kids are gonna get themselves in trouble with that guy, Markus, who's been pushing dope in the neighborhood.*

Dotty: *I'm just as nervous as you are about that, Greg, but sooner or later we're gonna have to take a chance with them and count on their good sense.*

The children are somewhat awed by this reasonable discussion between their parents and are managing not to interfere, respecting the boundary around their parents. This passive, silent act is symbolic of *their* ability to be together as a subsystem, enjoying the quiet glow of being a real force in the family.

The silence continues. The therapist watches Mike and Theresa, who are getting somewhat restless and preparing to speak up. Sensing this, the therapist turns to them.

Therapist: *I know it is hard for you because they're talking about you. Nevertheless, by staying out of this and letting your parents struggle, you are giving them respect. A first-class job!*

Mike: *Thanks.*

(Theresa shows nonverbally, primarily with her eyes, that she understands. Gregor and Dotty talk for a short time and then stop. They appear united in their silence.)

Therapist: *Do you need help to keep talking or do you want me to wait for a while?*

Dotty: *I think we've taken it as far as we can. What else is there to say?*

Knowing that this is typical of the abbreviated, staccato exchange between mother and father in the presence of the children—a retroflected subsystem boundary—the therapist attempts to extend their contact by pointing out that Dotty has not acknowledged Gregor's having shown her his hurt feelings, nor has Gregor acknowledged Dotty's courage in allowing the children to go out despite her fears. The couple now seize that opportunity and exchange their appreciation. The therapist has not forgotten that Gregor never answered his daughter's challenge about Dotty "letting go" of the children. He made a tactical decision to support an open struggle between the parents in front of the children, and that goal has been temporarily fulfilled. This may be a good time to help them shift boundaries to the father-daughter subsystem and to finish what was started.

Therapist: *As I remember it, Gregor, you didn't have a chance to respond to Theresa's question. I think it would be nice if the two of you could finish your conversation.*

Theresa: *It's okay, Dad.*

Gregor: *No, Theresa, the doctor is right. I never answered you and I want to. Now that your mother and I had our little discussion, I can tell you how I feel about you and Mike going out to visit friends. I don't mind telling you that I'm nervous about it. But your mom is gonna hold my hand if I get too nervous and we'll see what happens.*

Theresa: *That makes me feel good. I'm glad you are showing more confidence in us. And I'm happy for you and Mom talking like that right in front of us.*

Gregor: *Well, Terri, I'm glad to please you.*

Mike: *I'm glad when you and Mom talk in front of us, too.*

A criterion of good family functioning is the ability to form, destructure, and re-form clearly delineated subgroups. Members of the family know if they are players or bystanders in any given situation and if they are satisfied with either position. They have faith that the boundaries of the various roles or subgroups can shift again and again, yet that, as family members they will always be included in the different roles or subgroups. In healthy, functioning families, this process is graceful. It is "good form."

In this session with the Madiar family, we see that the parents are forming a stronger bond with each other, a bond visible to the children. This stronger parental bond allows the children, now high school students, to feel more secure and freer to consider breaking the powerful bond with their parents. In a subsequent session, the parents are again able to stretch their brief encounters into more comprehensive discussions. They lose themselves in conversation and the children show signs of boredom. During a brief pause, the children ask their parents and the therapist if they can "go out and get a soda." This, in a sense, is a symbolic test of how loose the family boundaries have become. The parents and the therapist exchange glances.

Gregor: *Okay, go ahead if it's okay with the doctor.*

Therapist: *This is just fine with me. You've got your business to do and they have theirs. There is a machine down the street from here.*

After Theresa and Mike leave, another dramatic breakthrough occurs. The parents turn to the therapist and ask a question.

Dotty: *Well, what should we do? What would you do about these kids? We're worried about them.*

Therapist: *Well, the kids need to explore the world and that's important. I realize how hard it is for both of you and that you are worried. Of course it's scary. There are few parents on earth that don't worry. Nevertheless, the two of you have to help each other through this. Of course you want to know where they're going, what they plan to do, and when they come home. I understand how you feel.*

When Gregor and Dotty turn to the therapist, they form a new subsystem that, for the first time, includes an outsider. The therapist is part of the outside world, and the Madiars are freely inviting this "outsider" to help them. For four or five sessions, they spoke only to each other and politely responded to the therapist's observations. Now they are incorporating an agent of the outer environment into a family transaction. This means they are getting ready to form new boundaries with the outside world and are practicing on the therapist. They can now call the school and ask about how their children are doing, or they can call the library or other neighborhood institutions to find out about after-school programs. The outer boundary of this family is slowly becoming more fluid and permeable.

Let us back up a moment and return to the point in the session when Theresa and Mike left to get a soft drink. They returned with their drinks, sat and listened, and later participated in a discussion regarding the "outer limits" of their adventures: what they were allowed to do and not do, when they had to be home, when homework had to be done before leaving, and so on. The parents treated their children with dignity signifying a mutual respect, and all seemed to be satisfied with the outcome. The therapist makes a final intervention:

Therapist: *Excuse me, may I interrupt you? The session is coming to a close and I would like to share with you what I observed. Is that okay? Good. I think from what I saw today you're all ready to try out new things, new ways—even though it's somewhat scary to all of you. You, Gregor and Dotty, you'll help each other to let the kids go and to figure out when to say yes and when to say no. I think you need to ask other people how they do it, what the school recommends for hours, and what other parents do and how it's done—the same way you asked me. Theresa and Mike, I think it's clear from what I saw today that you are ready to go out into the world and to come back. And you'll continue to do that. You are all ready for some good, constructive change, and I'm pleased.*

Figure 7.2 shows the Madiar family's boundaries after this therapy session. The outer family boundary is more permeable,

Figure 7.2. The Madiar Family: Boundaries After Therapy.

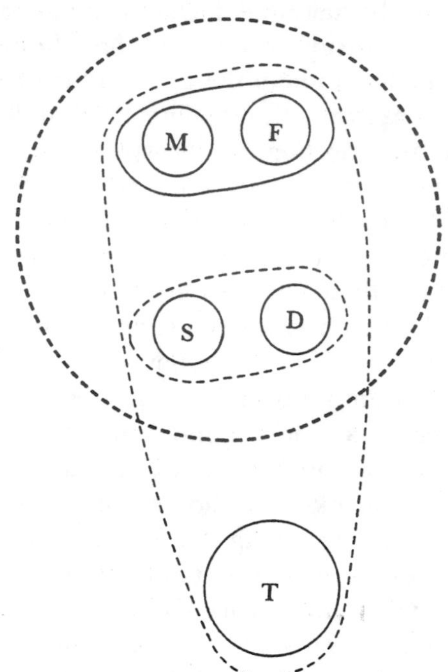

and the family is able to make itself more available to the therapist and to the outside world in general. Mother and dad feel like they can talk things over without interference from the children. The boundary around them is stronger. Developmentally, they are ready to recommit to their couple relationship more fully as their children make appropriate moves to eventually leave home, go to college, or get jobs and become more independent. The parents will feel more comfortable in turning to other adults for help, company, and entertainment. The children will feel good about each other most of the time and begin to feel comfortable about moving in and out of the house.

What challenges does the therapist anticipate in future sessions? Theresa and Mike might discover that they are more frightened of the dangers of the world than they had anticipated. They thought they were the ones ready to go and their parents were the ones holding them back, but they may find conflicts within themselves (perhaps introjected fears as well as real dangers) that worry them about their weekend excursions into the homes of neighborhood friends. Gregor and Dotty may find themselves fighting about what they should or should not allow the children to do and forget to get help in resolving their conflicts. They may find themselves giving mixed messages to the children about what is acceptable and what is not, and then being angry with Theresa and Mike because they did not anticipate certain outcomes or complications in their dealings with the world. In short, as the family boundaries become more fluid, problems and challenges will have to be confronted and negotiated, but these will hopefully be experienced as opportunities for deeper contact and creative adaptation to one another and with the outside world.

In discussing boundaries, we are not talking about anything magical, but *something that will make life clearer.* Therapists should work to get clearly defined boundaries around subgroups so that they can put all their energy into what they are doing without any of it leaking out.

Therapists' Boundaries: Creating a Presence and Managing Boundaries

When therapists sit down with a couple or family, there is a moment when they switch from being bystanders to being a presence for the others.[4] The therapists' presence creates an aura and reinforces a clear boundary around the couple or family. At that moment, they know they are doing couple or family therapy. Without presence, therapists are witnesses who are making comments.

The dictionary mentions "spirit or ghost" in connection with *presence.* Although this is far from an adequate definition of *presence,* it hints at that special state of being fully here with all of oneself, one's body and soul. It is a way of *being with,* without *doing to.* Presence implies being here fully—being open to all possibilities, when the therapists' intrinsic being-here stimulates stirrings in the deeper parts of people's selves. The therapists' presence is ground against which the figure of another self or selves can flourish, brighten, and stand out fully and clearly.

When I experience another's presence, I feel free to express myself, to be myself, to reveal any tender, vulnerable parts, to trust that I will be received without judgment or evaluation. My therapist's presence allows me to struggle with my own inner conflicts, contradictions, problematic questions, and paradoxes without feeling distracted by leading statements or overly determined questioning. My therapist's presence allows me to confront myself, knowing that I have a wise witness.

Perhaps the term *presence* can be better described by what it is not.

- Presence is not posturing or self-conscious posing or strutting before another; there's nothing flamboyant, dramatic, or theatrical about it.
- Presence is not style.
- Presence is not charisma. Charisma asks for attention, admiration. Charisma calls to itself, while presence calls to the other. Charisma is a figure competing with another figure, while presence is ground "asking to be written on."
- Presence is not affected religious humility (which is really a form of secret pridefulness).
- Presence is not polemic. It does not take sides. It sees wholes.

Therapists who simply have presence are rare. Those gifted few seem to have been born that way. Most of us acquire presence through the continual pounding of time—time that reminds us again and again how much there is to learn and how little we know. Presence is the acquired state of awe in the face of an infinitely complex and wondrous universe. Presence comes easier when we have already received approval and affirmation—when our cup is full and we no longer need undue acceptance from anyone. Presence is easier to experience when we learn to live with other people's pain and disappointments without having to save or rescue them. Presence often comes when we are seasoned and older, when our hot longing has cooled down to a kind of warm, mellow glow.

When we speak of the presence of therapists, we mean that they communicate another dimension of self beyond verbal interventions—as seen, for example, in the sessions with the Madiars. The vision of therapists in a state of presence is peripheral and diffuse. In a silent and subtle way, they are grounded and slow rather than light-headed and rushed. In this state, our breathing is deep, full, even. Our sense of time is slow and measured. Our body-self is supported and aware. We do not "care" in the sense that we are not overly attached to the content of the clients' stories. In a moment when the family is stuck, for example, the therapist rides the silence until the tension in the room is ripened for a strong, clear entry. The family is relieved and does not feel abandoned. In the beginning, these well-timed, cognitively clear, and well-crafted entries enhance the clients' confidence in the therapist's role and personal power.

In stepping forward at the right moment to articulate an idea and connect with everyone in the room, therapists also leave plenty of psychological space for family interaction. The clients feel validated and supported, with each individual feeling fully heard and seen. The therapists' silence as they listen and attend is as important to the total impact of the session as the words they speak. The silence of presence evokes liveliness in the system.

This means that once a session is underway, therapists do not make small talk or otherwise distract the family from its main task of becoming more fully aware of its own process. While each intervention is strong and bold, the space between interventions belongs fully to the family, and therapists neither hang on nor linger to draw further attention to themselves. Presence and timing frame the power of each intervention, while supporting the role of the therapists as important figures in the process. At the same time, the clients feel respected (seen) and cradled (encircled) by the practitioners.

When therapists are distracted by a headache, an unanticipated life event, or a "special" thought that they feel compelled to grind into the family, their presence and effect on the family are diminished. This happens occasionally to all of us simply because we are human.

Like the couple or family system, you, the therapist, also have a field of energy that must be managed. You must establish the rhythm of awareness. This is done by leaning forward and entering the system to begin the session or make an intervention; then the point is to pull back, sitting quietly and free associating. To withdraw from the system and make a clean boundary, you must be able to manage your own energy to establish a state of creative indifference: an alert, open, nonmobilized state.[5]

The amount of intrapsychic energy is the same when you are making an intervention or simply attending. The difference is in how you use the energy. Staying calm and "uninteresting" means withdrawing the energy level from the contact boundary of the couple or family system. The energy level is still high, but it is not being directed anywhere. You are in a state of creative indifference. There will be moments when you experience the difference between yourself and the couple or family while considering the boundary of the system; then the difference recedes and you daydream in order to become interested in something new happening before you.

Therapists should be aware of when they are breaking into the clients' boundary to become part of their awareness. It is important to know when to be part of the couple's or family's field in order to influence and when to just watch. In watching, you do not want to pull energy toward you, whether it be concern, interest, or simply looking. You should only pull energy toward you when you want the clients' full attention . . . then you move away again.

Suppose a family is talking, as the Madiars were at the beginning of their session. The family is within their boundary; the therapist is within a different boundary. The therapist is separate in the sense of not sending any energy toward the family.

Now the practitioner wants to influence the family. The therapist has to bring the family to his or her boundary, at the same time moving toward theirs. The family members first have to become disengaged from each other, then to turn toward the therapist, alert and attentive. The clinician and the family must meet at the boundary before the therapist says anything. There must be a tension at the boundary: the family ready to hear, and the therapist ready to say something. If that is not done, the family's attention and concern are elsewhere, and there is no meeting point.

There are other times when you may not want to intervene in this way. Perhaps you have already made an intervention but want to remind the family of it or reinforce the "goodness" of what they are attempting. You do not want to disengage them but instead should be a disembodied voice that says quietly, "You're doing it now." The clients should continue to be more interested in what is going on among them than in what you are saying.

Each of these examples is a form of boundary management. The first example—meeting the family's boundary and getting their attention—is an intervention. The most powerful intervention is always made right at the boundary. In the second example, the therapist temporarily steps inside the family's boundary. It is like lobbing something in over the boundary. Often, just a different tone of voice will allow momentary entry into the family's field. The second example simply involves reinforcement, a reminder. This is a very important distinction, for when the therapist is managing the boundary from *outside* the system, attention remains *within* the family.

The same process operates when working with self-awareness. The attention remains within different parts of the self. As the therapist, I do not want to say, "Pay attention to what's going on inside your stomach," because then you have to shift from attending to yourself to listening to me. But if I can toss it in, without coming right up to the boundary, you can stay within your own boundary.

That is boundary management, and we do it when working with an individual, couple, or a family. The therapist must always decide whether to meet the couple or family at the boundary and contactfully engage them, or to keep their energy within their system without disturbing their ongoing energy field. The therapist must be able to withdraw from their boundary and not draw attention away from the couple or family. Some therapists do this by closing their eyes. Once clear instructions have been given and people are still hesitant about what to do, you can close your eyes. This simple, conscious withdrawal still maintains presence as well as the supportive field that you have created around the clients.

I have a fond memory of working with a couple who had a new baby. While they were working, a member of our staff picked up the baby and left. When the baby was returned twenty minutes later, the couple had finished their piece of work and were surprised to learn that the baby had not been in the room. They had been so clearly "within" that anything happening "outside" was irrelevant.

The initial boundary is disrupted and re-forms when therapists make contact with it by talking to the entire family and drawing attention and energy to themselves. This is the point of intervention: talking about what has been occurring within the family and setting up an experiment. Then before the family proceeds, therapists must leave the field by breaking contact with the boundary.

The only time something can be lobbed in, in the sense of the family members paying minimal attention, is when their attention is already engaged fully. The information cannot be brand new because that would be too interesting. The information must be familiar, a reinforcement or reminder; not enough to grab attention, yet enough to wake them up a little. If new information is lobbed in, it will be ignored totally because it is too difficult, or the couple or family will come to a stop so as to pay attention to it. Either would be disruptive.

The "lob" raises awareness another notch. Because the information is already present in the system, it does not take a lot of energy to raise awareness about it. When awareness drops, you raise it a little bit more, then when it drops again, you raise it once more, and so on. You say softly, "There it is, that's it." You provide necessary support and keep the awareness up just a little bit. "Terrific" could be uttered quietly. If you really want to say "Terrific!" emphatically, you would have to stop and say, "I need to tell you something. What you just did is really terrific! Why don't you do it again?" That is a strong intervention. Each method is appropriate to different times and situations, and both are essential to a therapist's repertoire. It is simply a matter of choosing how to manage the boundary.

Conclusion

In the preceding chapters, I have devoted a great deal of discussion to the idea of "good form" and basic systems theory and have shown how these two conceptual stances help focus our vision when looking at couples and families. The interactive cycle was presented, along with its many uses. Awareness, as the cornerstone of our work, was discussed at length; I showed how a simple, even minuscule, shift can precipitate change in human systems. I also pointed strongly at the end of Chapter Five to the elegance and power of the three-step intervention formula. I then reviewed the various key resistances and showed how they are at once symptomatic of illness and strength in the system. The identification and management of boundaries was covered, and a brief interlude detailing the concept of the therapist's presence was included. Having established this theoretical framework, we are ready to turn to practical applications—the subject of Part Two.

Notes to Chapter Seven

1. See F. S. Perls, R. F. Hefferline, & P. Goodman (1951), *Gestalt therapy: Excitement and growth in the human personality* (New York: Julian Press). Perls, Hefferline, and Goodman state that "growth is the function of the contact-boundary in the organism/environment field; it is by means of creative adjustment, change, and growth that the complicated organic unities live on in the larger unity of the field. We may then define: *psychology is the study of creative adjustments*. Its theme is the ever-renewed transition between novelty and routine, resulting in assimilation and growth" (p. 230, original emphasis).
2. Here, of course, I am referring to human energy fields as well as personal and psychological space. See I. Bentov (1988), *Stalking the wild pendulum: On the mechanics of consciousness* (Rochester, VT: Destiny Books); B. A. Brennan (1988), *Hands of light: A guide to healing through the human energy field* (New York: Bantam Books); F. Capra (1991), *The Tao of physics: An exploration of the parallels between modern physics and Eastern mysticism* (Boston: Shambhala).
3. The therapist's task in creating a presence will be discussed later in this chapter.
4. Donna Rumenik first introduced me to the notion of presence as an important aspect of "self-as-instrument" in Gestalt therapy. Rumenik

discusses presence in her unpublished manuscript, "Gestalt principles for working with dysfunctional couples and families" (1983). We have had many profound conversations about the meaning and importance of a therapist's presence and its healing effect on those with whom we work. Rumenik's work stimulated my thinking about presence, which contributed significantly to my writing "Presence as evocative power in therapy," *Gestalt Review, 1*(2), 1–2, 1987, and the section on presence in this chapter.

5. For a discussion of "creative indifference," see F. S. Perls (1969), *Ego, hunger, and aggression: The beginning of Gestalt therapy* (New York: Vintage Books). Perls says that "S. Friedlaender differentiates between the uninterested detachment—the 'I-don't-care' attitude—and the 'creative indifference.' Creative indifference is full of interest, extending toward both sides of the differentiation. It is by no means identical with an absolute zero-point, but will always have an aspect of balance" (p. 19). Also see G. Wheeler (1991), *Gestalt reconsidered: A new approach to contact and resistance* (New York: Gardner Press). Wheeler makes the following comments about this concept:

   Salamo Friedlaender (1871–1946) was a relatively obscure, now almost totally forgotten critic, poet, Nietzsche scholar, and sometime satirical novelist (under the pen name Mynona) of the late Second Empire period in Germany. In his 1918 work *Schoepferische Indifferenz* (never translated, but better rendered in English as "creative undifferentiation," or perhaps "predifference," not "indifference," with its English connotation of lack of investment), he argued, *à la* Nietzsche, for a relativization of descriptive or evaluative terms on the basis of an essentially Aristotelian notion of polar continua in perception . . . . Thus the quality of "good," say, is not fixed or absolute in value, but rather depends for its meaning on an implicit presumption of "better" than something else—which is itself relative to some corresponding polar term, in this case "bad." This is in explicit contrast, of course, to the Judeo/Christian model criticized by Nietzsche (1886)—or for that matter the Platonic model—under which the notions of "good" and "bad," while possibly relative in application, each derive from separate absolutes, to which they refer, and which are given from some source outside the perceptual process itself [pp. 47–48, original emphasis].

PART TWO

Practice

8

Intervening in Couple Systems

The primary word I-Thou *establishes the world of relation.*
—Martin Buber

Increased awareness promises change at every level of our lives. In Gestalt couple therapy, *awareness of process* is the foundation for meaningful change.

As a rule, couples are not aware of their own process: its flow, its cognitive solidity, its energy, its potential contactfulness. They attend to the content of what they do, and that is what they are most passionately attached to. When their process goes well, they should not be aware of it. A couple's process goes smoothly when each can start at a different place, draw together, do something, then feel finished and satisfied. Any interruption in that process will result in leftover energy, which is experienced as dissatisfaction or malfunction—a "something not right." When their process is poor, they experience pain, and that is when they ask a therapist for relief.

A couple that functions well does not have to pay attention to its process. It is only when function is interrupted or stuck that examining the process is truly helpful. When driving a car, for example, you do not pay attention to your process of driving; you simply attend to getting where you are going. If you are a poor driver and constantly strip the clutch, you must bring your process of shifting out of the background and into your awareness. You must pay attention to how and when you shift. The minute you have relearned the right way to shift, your process returns to the background. You simply drive without thinking about how you shift.

As long as the process works well, it remains background. When the process malfunctions and becomes foreground, you are forced to examine it. When a couple goes to therapy, they stop just living and shift their attention from the *content* of living to the *process* of living. They shift from the content of what they are living to the process of how their living takes place. When life is smooth again and leads to satisfaction, process again becomes background.

What must a couple do to correct its process? They need to talk about what is going on with them, their thoughts, feelings, and experiences. They must stay with that process until they tap into something that has interest, caring, or energy attached to it. They need to arrive at a "figure" that each of them is attached to and cares about. Then they live it through, digest it, finish it, and pull apart.[1]

As therapists, we go through the same process as our clients. We watch the couple, not yet knowing what we care about, what interests us, or what matters to us. We allow something to become figural in that process, then tell the couple about it.[2] We call this sharing an *intervention.* The intervention widens the couple's awareness, drawing something from the background to make it figural. If the couple can chew over the awareness, get something out of it, and choose to change their behavior, we are satisfied.

If the couple cannot do as I have described, we create experiments that provide a structure for playing with this new awareness in a concrete framework. The experiment exposes the couple to a new behavior, experience, or insight; then they can choose whether or not to incorporate the new experience into their repertoire of living. Having introduced the couple to a novel way of seeing themselves, we close the session.

This chapter applies the theories and principles of Part One to couple therapy. It outlines the ground rules of a therapy session and describes how to create and present interventions that lead a couple to fuller awareness of its process and the opportunities to change it.[3]

How to Set Up a Couple Therapy Situation

As therapists, we must watch long enough, listen long enough, and experience what is occurring with the couple so that we can get enough data about its process to create interventions appropriate to their dilemma. To do this, we must establish our presence in the system and elicit the couple's participation in an examination of its process.[4]

The first thing we do is to engage in a certain amount of small talk. This establishes our presence as therapists and initiates contact among all participants. This is the ordinary social talk of welcoming. We make sure we make contact with everyone and provide the warmth that enables talk about intimate matters.

Next, we discuss the therapeutic ground rules. We tell the participants that the best way we can help them is to watch them, that we are going to ask them to talk to each other about anything that is important to them, and that we will act as witnesses who will interrupt when anything stands out for us that we believe will be of interest or use to them.

I have never given these instructions without meeting with resistance. These are the comments that I hear time and time again:

> "But we've already talked about it at home, so it won't be of any use to us here."
>
> "There's no point in talking about it because they won't listen anyway, and that's why we're here."

"I didn't expect this."

"I want to tell you . . . don't you want to know anything about us? Don't you want to know our history or how we got to this place?"

"What we came for is some advice from you, not to talk to each other about the same old thing."

"That would be too embarrassing to do. I don't know if I could just talk in front of you while you just sit and listen."

"That feels contrived and theatrical. It's a faked situation, and I don't see what good it would do if we just fake it."

At this point, we highlight the resistance (as we do in all good therapeutic work) by staying with it until we get each person to express all of his or her resistance to the situation.[5] For example, if the clients say it feels very contrived and phony and they feel uncomfortable "acting" for you, your response might be:

Therapist: *I appreciate that you can tell me that you're uncomfortable. You're right, it is contrived. The therapeutic situation is not natural. However, it is very important to me to be able to watch you so I can see how you communicate. I know it's contrived and uncomfortable, but I hope you'll be able to do it anyway because I believe that's the best way I can be useful to you.*

We also explain that, just as we can interrupt them when we see something that we want to tell them, they can turn to us at any time they need help or get stuck, or when they want to inform or question us.

As soon as our instructions are clear, we lean back out of the system and draw a boundary.[6] As they talk to each other, we watch their process and wait for something to become figural. When there is something that stands out for us, we interrupt them to make an intervention.

As it is set up, the therapeutic situation with the couple is, in itself, an experiment. We start the situation with an experiment. All experiments are contrived, dramatic, or artificial situations. Nevertheless, they are a slice of life where you can see what is happening and lay it bare.

Once we have a good intervention, we work from there. Either the couple can move with it or we can create an experiment in which to chew it over and learn something from it.

We end the session by reverting to small talk. We change from an artificial, structured situation back to a more social, easy, and natural human contact. We wish them well and say good-bye. The session is like an airplane ride: we take off, reach a certain altitude, travel for a while, and then land.

How to Choose an Intervention

A novice might ask, "What do I do with all this talk? What can stand out? What do I pay attention to?"

Let us imagine that you are sitting in front of a couple and the number of things going on are beyond count. Without a theory that describes human behavior, you are simply not going to see anything. It is going to be too confusing. Only when you use a "cognitive map" will information be organized, stand out, and lead to an intervention. All the things that we talk about in Gestalt therapy are the "screens," the "eyes," through which we see the world. There are four major "screens" that you can superimpose on what you see and hear.

1. *Strengths and weaknesses in the couple's process.* First is the interactive cycle described in Chapter Three. How does the couple move through the cycle? How do they join with each other? How don't they? How do they stay with something to achieve a good resolution? How don't they? If the couple has a good cycle, they will have a good psychological experience.

Therapists should watch not only for interruptions in the process but also for strengths in the couple's interaction. Most couples are not aware of their own competence. Statements of their competence are powerful interventions. Sometimes they are even more powerful than statements of how they interrupt themselves. The reason they are powerful is that people do not know what they do well any more than what they do poorly.

Jim and Loretta: A Couple's Process

Here is an example of a couple's process when it goes well. Jim and Loretta are talking about their twenty-two-year-old daughter, Marilyn.

Jim: *How do you feel about helping Marilyn pay for her apartment?*

Loretta: *That would be nice, but if we're going to put money into our retirement fund this year, we can't afford it.*

Jim: *But she may not be able to swing it at first. I worry about her.*

Loretta: *Me too, but we must let her struggle with it so she can learn.*

Jim: *How I wish we were rich.*

Loretta: *That's not the point, Jim. Marilyn is not a child; she's a competent young woman.*

Jim: *I guess we just have to let her learn to support herself. How about this: if she gets into hot water with her rent and comes to us, we'll try to help her examine her finances to see what she can do.*

Loretta: *And if it looks like she needs our help, we'll help. She should be okay with her present salary.*

Jim: *Agreed! Aren't you pleased that she's finally on her own?*

Loretta: *Yes! She's wonderful. I'm very proud of her.*

By pointing out the strengths that you see in your clients, by bringing them into awareness, you remind them to use their strengths when they become stuck. When they are confronted with a dilemma, they can draw on their knowledge of what they do well and choose to use those strengths in resolving their problem. What might we want to tell our couple about their competence?

Therapist: *I want to tell you how impressed I am by your ability to stay with your problem and not become distracted by general issues of wealth. You really care enough about Marilyn's situation to hang in there and reach agreement. When you both felt relief and satisfaction, you were able to let go of the matter. Well done!*

In terms of the interactive cycle, Jim and Loretta were able to invest their energy fully so as to maintain a clear figure and achieve resolution. A malfunction in a couple is a disturbance in the process by which it functions. Specifically, it is a disturbance in the interactional cycle. Let's look at Loretta and Jim again. This is how they would sound if they were stuck.

Jim: *How do you feel about helping Marilyn pay for her apartment?*

Loretta: *That would be nice, but if we're going to put money into our retirement fund this year, we can't afford it.*

Jim: *But she may not be able to swing it at first. I worry about her.*

Loretta: *Me too, but we must let her struggle with it so she can learn.*

Jim: *How I wish we were rich.*

Loretta: *That's not the point. You're daydreaming again. We have to look at the realities as they are.*

Jim: *What are the realities?*

Loretta: *You should know by now.*

Jim: *Tell me again.*

Loretta: *She needs $1,000 a month to survive, and that's what she makes right now.*

Jim: *What if she goes on a trip?*

Loretta: *She'll have to sacrifice something else to save money for it.*

Jim: *What are our actual responsibilities to a grown child?*

Loretta: *Different people handle it differently. The Donoghues gave Mark a lump sum at graduation time.*

Jim: *Well, that's amazing! Their income isn't even as high as ours.*

Loretta: *Maybe we should get together with them and ask their opinion about this.*

Jim: *We should be able to figure this out by ourselves.*

Loretta: *I saw Les Donoghue the other day at the supermarket. He looked great.*

Jim: *We haven't seen them for weeks.*

Loretta: *I'm getting a headache . . .*

In the second dialogue, Jim and Loretta are not able to finish what they started. There is no sense of completion and satisfaction. The moment they start talking about the Donoghue's income, they veer off, deflecting from their principal goal, which is to agree about dealing with their daughter's newly found independence.

In terms of the cycle, we can say that they are stuck in *awareness*. They feel the need to gather more data to know that they are doing the right thing, but they are not able to gather enough energy between them to decide on the best course of action. Good, solid contact is not possible, and one of them is already beginning to hurt. They have not even been able to make an interim decision to get together with their friends; they are stuck. Nevertheless, they can still be told what they did well because, even here, we see competence. It is always nice to hear what one did well before being informed about one's difficulty. The therapist might say:

Therapist: *I like how patient you are with each other and how you try to answer each other's questions. I like your curiosity and your sense of the philosophical.*

Later, they can be told:

Therapist: *Because you take so much time to discuss all the possibilities and contingencies involved, you have trouble coming to an agreement and feeling fully finished with this.*

If you see a couple sharing information, asking and answering questions, trying to influence one another, and allowing the energy to build and the excitement to flow and hook the other person, they are doing well. If you see any interruptions in that process—questions asked but not answered, information given stingily or not at all, long pauses, discussions trailing off, one person speaking and the other losing interest but not saying anything about it, one person saying he or she wants to do something about a problem but investing no energy and not attempting to reach the other person—the couple has a problem.

Any situation that stands out for you can become a powerful intervention. Even if you have only this one screen to watch through, you will see many things your clients need to learn. The Gestalt cycle model gives you a language by which you can comprehend the process of human interactions. And it gives you a way to convey to the couple what you see and what is of interest to you.

2. *Content issues.* So far, we are assuming that you are process oriented. How do you not succumb to the temptation of getting into what the couple is talking about when it is so inviting and seductive to comment on the content of the couple's conversation? Is there something you do with your body, or in your head, or with your environment as a way of not getting caught up in content? My answer is that it is not our job to pay attention to content. Our job is to see the process—*how* clients say what they say and not *what* they say. This is a real challenge. It is only when we are lazy that we float along with content. Think of all the potential content issues in the second dialogue that could trap a therapist without being helpful to our couple in the least.

> "At twenty-two, Marilyn is old enough to look after herself, don't you think?"
>
> "A thousand dollars isn't much money to survive on these days."
>
> "A thousand dollars is a lot of money for a young person to dispose of every month. She needs your guidance."
>
> "Why not encourage Marilyn to find a roommate? She'd have more money that way."

We cease "working" the moment we become entangled in the content. Our work is to see the couple's process and to help them change it. Their work is to get on with their content. If we simply join the couple in their content, we are no longer adequate consultants to the process.

Our assumption is that malfunctioning of the system occurs over and over again, independent of what the couple is talking about. They could be dealing with sex, money, or moving to another city, but the areas of interruption will tend to be the same. And that is process. It is not the content they get stuck on. This is not to say that some content will not be more problematic than other content, but it is in the process that trouble most often occurs.

A couple might be stuck with processing too much through their awareness and not being aroused enough to make a strong contact. For example, if they are trying to solve a financial problem, they can talk about the money for a long time, but as long as they do not invest their energy in making something happen, their efforts will go flat. Or they can talk about moving to another city, but if they do not generate arousal or excitement, their conversation will not carry them to resolution.

Getting stuck in awareness without excitement flattens our experience of things, no matter what the content. In awareness, the energy investment is relatively low. It is not exciting yet. We are not attempting to hook anybody with it. We are just laying things out. Awareness itself is a low-energy modality. And it is important that it remain low because it is experimental. We want to be able to throw away half of our ideas because, if we do not, everything becomes important and we will be stuck in place forever.

What if the couple achieves a smooth cycle and then asks for information from us? How do we handle this? Because our opinion on some things is more informed than the general population, people who come to us have a right to expect that we will give them an option about certain issues. For example, a couple may ask us what we think about sending a child away to a private school: What is its effect? How old should the child be? What should they watch for? Or we may be asked what we think about a primary parent working: What age should the child be when the primary parent returns to work, and is the effect good or bad? Another couple might ask our opinion about having one of their in-laws live with them: Do we think it is a good idea, or do we think it would be too stressful for the family?

These are tricky moments, because no matter what we know as a result of our expertise, no matter what we believe, we really do not know what is best for someone else. At times it is our job, however, to take the risk of saying what we believe would be best. What makes this a particularly treacherous area is that it is usually in the more retroflective systems, the systems with tighter boundaries, the systems that do not ask us anything, that we want to give our opinion because there are so many obvious things they do not know. It is hard to counsel a couple that asks you nothing yet has content information that seems wildly incorrect to you. For example, you may believe that children do very well in situations where both parents work, yet your clients say that it would be bad because the child will feel unloved or become delinquent. You will feel an enormous temptation at that moment because you badly want to correct their opinion.

At such times, we urge therapists not to intervene. You should always wait to be asked. If you are not asked, the chance of your being heard is minimal. It will not be useful to jump over working on the process by giving them content information. However, as professionals, when we are asked (even though we know we do not necessarily know what is best), we can give an informed opinion, and it should be prefaced as such.

There are times when we do intervene with content issues without being asked. But the contract we lay out at the beginning is that we will watch the couple's process and tell them about that rather than give them content information. With content information, we wait to be asked more often than we do with process information. The reason for this is that we feel much freer with process information and more certain that our values are clear. We believe it will be useful for them to learn these things, so we are more willing to intervene. Also, in the process intervention, we are much more clearly anchored to the data that emerge during the therapy hour.

3. *Polarities askew or other imbalances.* Any time we see a polarity that is askew, that is out of balance, it can be a potential intervention. If the system is healthy, each part develops many potentials. If one person is too heavily invested in a function while the other is not, they encourage skewed polarities and run into intrapsychic and interpersonal difficulties. They will feel either less than or more than the other person, either too admiring or too contemptuous of the other. If this lopsided condition exists for too long, it will result in psychological stasis and deadening or psychological agitation, anger, and irritability.

How does polarization occur in our development? And what happens when we get together with another? There will be parts of the self that remain undeveloped for a long time simply because, for whatever reason, we are developing other parts in ourselves. The result is that all of us develop certain psychological traits at the expense of others. For example, taking care of others may be well developed but taking care of myself may not have received enough attention. Or perhaps seriousness is well developed but humor is underdeveloped.

Seeing in someone else a quality that is underdeveloped in you can look enticing. It is easy to obtain that undeveloped part simply by joining the other person; suddenly you have humor or self-caring, a sense of being lively or well organized. It is an instant self-realization and a wonderful sensation. We call it "falling in love." You feel complete and, indeed, you are complete in that moment. And the other person, who has different things to develop, will also find the beloved attractive. So you join together and become a unit and you love it for a while. Together you, as a couple, make a whole, new person.

Often, however, things start going wrong after several years and, ironically, it is due to your underdeveloped side. Part of the reason is that you do not value that characteristic in the same way you value what you did develop. At the same time, however, you think it is important and very good. You have ambivalent feelings toward the characteristic. You stay with your partner and live through the positives of that particular characteristic. With humor, for example, you may have lived through such positive results as liveliness, a good time, and good feelings. However, it is not long until you start to get in touch with the shadow side of that pleasure: humor has its deflective quality, its touch of cruelty, its capacity to shut off seriousness when seriousness is required. And the very thing you liked before, you now do not like. You are irritated with your partner's humor.

This is the most difficult time that every relationship must transcend: to detach your eyes from what your partner does well and badly and to re-own what you do well and badly. You must acknowledge what you have learned from your partner about a certain characteristic and from living with that characteristic in yourself that you have projected onto your partner.[7] You must stop the process of gluing your eyes to your partner. You must neither love your partner's humor once you develop your own nor hate it—you can live with both. You can like it and not like it knowing it is your partner's responsibility to handle it. You can detach your eyes from your partner because humor is no longer underdeveloped in you. Once you develop your humor, you know the complexities of it and are no longer attached positively or negatively to it in the other person.

What can you, as a therapist, do when you see skewed polarities? For example, you see that he keeps making jokes while she looks like she is in a lot of pain and wants to tell the story of their difficulties. Here is a potential intervention:

Therapist: *Okay, I want to stop for a minute. I'd like to tell you something I notice. I notice that there is both seriousness and humor in your interaction. For whatever reason, one of you is the serious one and one of you is the funny one, and you seem to keep it that way. Have you ever noticed that? Do you do that at home as well as here?*

After they answer, you could ask:

Therapist: *Why don't you tell each other how you feel about this? Would you like to do that? Or would you like to see if you can make some changes in it?*

If they are interested and want some changes, you could suggest experiments, such as reversing roles, that would lead them to greater awareness of their polarities.

In Jim and Loretta's second dialogue, we notice that Jim poses dilemmas and asks questions, while Loretta gives answers. Here is how an intervention might be formulated for them.

Therapist: *I want to tell you my observation of your problem-solving process. I notice that, generally, Jim inquires, asks questions, and provokes, while you, Loretta, take responsibility for explaining, justifying, and coming up with possibilities. Are you aware that you divide your tasks that way?*

After they discuss their reactions to this phenomenon of polarities askew, you can formulate an experiment.

Therapist: *I would like for you to try a little experiment. It might be useful for you to reverse roles: for you, Jim, to give the solutions to problems while Loretta raises the questions and dilemmas. What do you say? Do you want to see what happens?*

Any polarity that is askew can be used as an intervention to heighten the couple's awareness of something that you believe is a disruptive factor.

When you see polarities askew in a couple, it may be a diagnostic statement that, as individuals, these people are not well developed. No one, however, is completely developed in all possible aspects. Full development of all characteristics is the ideal that none of us ever reaches. Each of us chooses certain characteristics to be our primary definition of self.

At a higher level of development, we are aware of our choices. We know that we are not going to put energy into developing all aspects of the self, simply because we do not want to or need to. We can appreciate what the other person brings to the relationship, not like it, and still live with it. For example, if the husband is more sociable and outgoing than his wife, the wife can choose to let him be the way he is and she can appreciate how much that adds to her life. She can know that she does not value his gregariousness a great deal and cannot understand why he invests so much in it or why it matters so much to him, but if it is okay with him, it is okay with her. It is not a quality that she needs to adore in him, nor does she need to detest it either—it is nothing she needs to do anything about. This balance is akin to the zero point of "creative indifference" mentioned in earlier chapters.

At first, the wife may have felt inferior to her husband: "Isn't he wonderful? Look how friendly he is!" Then she may have felt superior: "How can he waste his time on superficial social things? He's such a shallow person." Where there is a mature complementarity, however, there is a sense of the philosophical about one another, rather than feelings of inferiority or superiority. When a couple achieves complementarity, polarization does not get in the way of their process. Polarizations do not disappear; they are perceived and dealt with differently. They no longer have the energy attachment of projection.

4. *Complementarity and the middle ground. Fusion* with another is a very compelling, ecstatic experience. It is the first principle, the original dream, the first dream of union with the mother. In the beginning of life this fusion was not "love" in the usual sense. This "need," this image, is a kind of undifferentiated longing—before the words are there, before one can utter "I love you" or "I long for something"—it is a psychological sensation without awareness. At that time—the time of physiological sensations—if the need for union is not met in some way, the infant or child may be forever damaged.

Only later does this enormous longing acquire words. These words are different in different cultures. Different societies have developed different ways of meeting this unmet need. Therefore, love has different meanings at different times in one's life, but the experience of falling in love and the need for fusion remains an essential mystery, which, regardless of the words, is a form of psychological alchemy. There is some recognition that somehow without the other one is not whole, one is not fully oneself, but also there is no recognition of the other as a whole person. There is mostly a reading into what the other is—the fantasy overpowers one's sense of curiosity about the actual other. Union is like alchemy in putting things together and creating a new form. In alchemy, our ancestors tried to put opposing metals together in an attempt to make gold. This, in a sense, is what we think the golden ring of engagement and marriage is about. There is also alchemy in the biology of sexuality. The Other is different, and it is the mystery inherent in the difference that is so compelling.

But fusion fails. The fetus dies if it stays in the womb. If a young person stays at home with mother or father, he or she dies spiritually as well as in other ways. What must follow fusion is separation, and separation always involves differentiation. Differentiation means that the couple begins to move away from fusion and must develop their own selves. In Jungian terms this is *individuation,* while in Gestalt therapy it is termed *boundary formation.* We say in Gestalt therapy that the only way you can have adequate contact is by having adequate boundaries. You cannot have contact with mush. You cannot have conflict with mush either. You must evolve from a psychologically homogenized blob into a differentiated, bound organism with your own ideas, feelings, preferences, and buoyancies. Then, when you come together with the other out of your special boundedness, you experience fire. Fire, in this case, not only consumes joyfully, but illuminates as well.

What happens in a two-person system is a rhythm of fusion and separation. We touch each other at different places in our lives and in our rhythms of daily life. We also touch each other with different intensities. Sometimes we touch with ecstasy, other times in rage, but most of the time we touch with just a nice bit of magnetism. After this touching, we move away from one another. Then we come together again. This process of moving toward and away is the dynamic juice pulsing through the relationship.

The theme of fusion and separation is a lifelong experience appearing in different forms that match different times. Couples experience fusion when they first fall in love. They are inseparable. They sit and stare into each other's eyes. They profess love for each other for ever and ever. Later, as they proceed with the tasks of life and as they grow more familiar with each other's ways, a slow and subtle process of separation occurs.

During this period, there is a greater recognition of differences and a return to the task of self-actualization. Fusion becomes more difficult when children are born. It may be sublimated into the system that includes children and the family as a whole. Separation is again experienced as the children grow up and leave. Again the couple is alone, hopefully as more mature and separate adults, who choose once again to become deeply intimate with one another. Later, illness and death confront the couple with separation and with the fantasy (or reality) of fusion with some eternal power beyond themselves in an experience of transcendence.

One is brought into the world only to give oneself away again and again.

The need for asserting the "I"—as between mother and child—follows fusion. After the falling-in-love experience, each stands separately and is once again confronted by the self—its internal needs, conflicts, and special talents. Each partner tailors his or her mode of functioning in the relationship, the partnership, to make it work. Each person needs to gain an awareness of self as a separate entity different from awareness of the other. Each person must learn to differentiate his or her internal experience from the appearance, awareness, and experiences of the other. The therapist supports individual boundaries and so might ask each person to say sentences like "I feel . . . " and "You look like . . . " Introjection, projection, and confluence are favorite resistances to contact at this level: "I feel like you look hungry" or "I feel tense and you look tense" or "You look angry with me."

Before the couple can experience the "we" of the contact between them, they need to articulate the "me" of self-boundaries:

> "I sense . . . "
> "I feel . . . "
> "I want . . . "
> "I don't want . . . "

Each person says these things in turn and not reactively to the other. It is only much later after their separate internal visions become illuminated that each can truly validate and care about the experience of the other. Before this can happen, however, confluence-contact must be replaced by conflict-contact. One cannot have differentiation without conflict. But many couples have been conditioned by Hollywood to feel that conflict means "we are no longer in love" or that "we are not really suited to each other," and they may never have witnessed resolution of conflicts—followed by expression of caring—in their own families of origin. The couple may be scared by their fantasized image of conflict and fear the failure of the relationship.

The Gestalt therapist at this point needs to teach the couple how to fight cleanly and how to resolve and integrate differences in a way that enhances both and does not cause loss of esteem for either one. The therapist validates the experience of each while encouraging both to respect the other's way of seeing a situation. Having supported both partners, the therapist moves on to support the "we" by encouraging them to find a creative integration of their divergent qualities.[8] The heat of resolved conflict leaves the couple drawn to each other with renewed interest and often even passion. Differentiation is followed by fusion. And so this rhythm goes on and Nature follows her course.

Some differences, on the other hand, are not reconcilable and must be accepted as such. One can love and respect one's partner and learn to accept the existential reality that not all problems are solvable. Just as Hollywood sold us the myth about love as fusion, the personal growth movement sold us the myth that all interpersonal problems are resolvable. This introjected ethic forces some couples to fanatically negotiate and renegotiate all differences until both are exhausted, experiencing shame, failure, and disappointment in the relationship.

Differences are essential in a mature relationship. Differences keep the relationship alive. Differences taken to an extreme lead beyond healthy separation to an irreparable rupture in relationship.

Complementarity is the functional aspect of differentiation. It is how differentiation is lived out. From a developmental point of view, one partner chooses another to complement the parts of oneself that are not in awareness, are not accepted, or are aesthetically repugnant. The qualities are seen in the other in a romanticized form. Two half-persons come together to make one whole being to more effectively cope with the world.

The complementary function is accepted and appreciated in the other as long as it is not experienced in oneself. Later, when that disowned quality begins to move to the surface of oneself, the partner's complementary behavior may be experienced with annoyance, anger, irritation, and embarrassment. What was romanticized is now seen in its utmost crudity—the sociable extrovert is seen as a "loudmouth," while the introspective one is seen as "depressed." At this point, the Gestalt therapist can help each partner to experiment with each one's disowned polarity, as discussed in the previous section. Some complementary modes—matters of both character and style—will remain as stable traits in a particular partner no matter how much individual growth takes place. It is here that true (nonneurotic, nonprojected) complementarity can work to lend variety and excitement to the couple's life. The more fully the two partners develop individually, the more their polarities are filled out and stretched and the more they can appreciate the "crazy" or idiosyncratic behavior of the other.

Where complementarity stresses differences, the middle ground attracts similarities. Life takes place in the middle, not at the extremes. Mostly, life is just ordinary. So it is with the life of couples. There are chores, work, paying bills, errands, phone calls, morning showers, meals, and resting in one another's arms at the end of a long day. It is only when we take the time to stop, look, and reflect that the extraordinary aspects of life emerge.

Whereas complementarity increases the excitement of the couple's life, the middle ground provides a place to rest, a place where energy is even rather than peaked—where energy levels synchronize. Whereas complementarity stimulates conflict, the middle ground is the repository of quiet confluence.

The couple's survival and growth are determined by a balance between complementarity and confluence. The figure of differences is only meaningful against a background of agreements, understandings, compromises, and ordinary pleasures. The figure of confluence is viable only against a ground of color, difference, lively discussion, arguments, and emotional explosions. One could say that the survival index of a couple is some ratio between confluence and differentiated contact, or between middle ground and complementarity.

To determine the middle ground and to balance the work, as well as the couple's perception of themselves, the therapist may wish to pose questions like these:

> How did you meet?
> What did you like about each other?
> What are your common beliefs?
> What do you enjoy together when things are all right?

Answers to these questions remind the couple of their common ground: their loyalty, devotion, friendship, and hard work. Or the therapist may readily discover that this couple's middle ground is not stable ground at all, but a sheet of thin ice. The therapist may find, in fact, they did not use their best judgment in moving toward each other. Each may have denied personal feelings and lied to the other, making for an impoverished friendship. Finally, the therapist may discover that loyalty and devotion are strangely absent in this couple.

The therapist can judge in the here and now how much conflict this particular system can tolerate without breaking up. The couple may need to be confronted with these questions—to ask them if they are willing to start building a basic ground of trust in order to sustain the kind of conflict they are engaged in.

5. *Attending to resistances.* Resistances are what happen at the boundary between any two subsystems and so are a form of contact. Resistance can occur within the couple at their contact boundary, or the couple may form a subsystem in resisting the therapist's interventions. People generally have "favorite" resistances; they are ego-syntonic and characterologically true. That is, a couple will use the same resistance in their interactions with their therapist as in relationship with each other. For example, people who retroflect with each other will hold together as a system and avoid contact with the therapist by retroflecting. Their relationship as a couple with their therapist will mirror their relationship with each other.

We often talk about resistance as if it is an exclusively intrapsychic phenomenon: "I am a retroflector" or "I am a projector" or "I am confluent." Resistances, however, originate in interactions. It takes two people to produce a resistance. Resistances become intrapsychic when they become habitual as the same interactions are repeated again and again. The person responds to each new situation as if it is an old situation, not noticing other things that are happening and, therefore, carrying intrapsychically into new situations what they learned interactively.

Since we have already discussed the different resistances in depth in preceding chapters, we will confine ourselves here to the operation of resistance in a system as an opportunity for intervention by the therapist. When the therapist looks at a resistance within an interactive system, it is critical to recognize the collusion within the system to maintain the resistance. No one person can maintain resistance to contact. Every resistance can be converted into a contactful experience by either person. Let us look at Jim and Loretta again.

Loretta: *I saw Les Donoghue the other day at the supermarket. He looked great.*

Jim: *We haven't seen them for weeks . . .*

Loretta: *I'm getting a headache . . .*

Therapist: *I like how patient you are with each other and how you try to answer each other's questions. I like your curiosity and your sense of the philosophical when you talk about Marilyn. So, stay with it.*

Here the therapist points out what they do well before going further with what obviously needs to be done.

Jim: *Yes, we were both philosophy majors in college.*

Loretta: *Thank you. We do talk well. Perhaps we should talk about Kathy while we are at it.*

Jim: *Okay. What do you have in mind? Kathy is about to graduate. What is she going to do with that degree in English Lit?*

Loretta: *Well, we always encouraged the girls to get a liberal arts education. I suppose she can go to grad school and become an English professor. She'd have to get a scholarship or some sort of assistance.*

Jim: *What are we supposed to do? I talked with her the other day and she said she is confused about grad school. She wants to take time off and get away from school and term papers.*

Loretta: *When we were college kids we didn't go on vacations. This generation is spoiled. They want everything.*

Jim: *What's wrong with vacations? Perhaps these kids are smarter than we were: working our asses off and always thinking about the future.*

Loretta: *We had a sense of purpose. You wanted that degree so you could support me while the babies came.*

Jim: *Things have changed. They don't think about babies until they're in their thirties.*

Jim and Loretta have covered a lot of ground in a short time and seem to have lost track of their original intention to discuss their daughter Marilyn and the difficulty she might have in supporting herself. They have veered off into talking about another daughter, then their own experiences in college, and now they are discussing the differences between their generation and that of their daughters. It may be useful for them to look more closely at this pattern in their interactions.

Therapist: *Excuse me. I want to share with you what I am observing. Because you take so much time to discuss all the possibilities and contingencies involved, you have trouble coming to an agreement and feeling fully finished with any one topic. For example, you left the matter of Marilyn's rent up in the air. Then you didn't decide about getting together with the Donoghues. Now you seem to be leaving Kathy up in the air. Each time one of you focuses on something, the other changes the subject. We call this* deflection.

(Loretta looks at the therapist strangely as if she is daydreaming. Jim is impassive and seems to be examining the elm tree outside the window.)

Loretta: *Jim, see that moon watch the therapist is wearing. It's exactly what I want to get for you. Exactly!*

Jim: *I like the watch I have . . .*

Therapist: *The two of you are amazing. I just got through pointing out how you deflect with each other and now you are deflecting with me. You have trouble connecting with each other, and you disconnect from me in the same way.*

Loretta: *(To the therapist) I don't know what you mean.*

Jim: *He was just talking about how we distract each other and we started distracting him with talk about watches.*

Loretta: *Now we have a name for what we do*—digression.

Therapist: Deflection.

Jim: *Deflection! We do that all the time with each other and now we're doing it with you. Drives me crazy.*

Loretta: *Okay, let's see, can we finish our talk about Kathy?*

Another place where interventions are possible is where we point out to the couple the typical resistances that prevent them from having contact with each other. In this case, it was deflection.

Recapitulation

I have suggested a number of things that can stand out from the couple's interaction and provide potential fodder for devising an intervention.

1. *Strengths and weaknesses in the couple's process.* To complete a cycle—that is, to begin, develop, and finish a situation—is healthy for a couple and must be given attention.

2. *Content issues.* True, you, the therapist, are an expert in human behavior. You know how to respond to certain life situations. But be careful because you cannot necessarily know what is best for others. Always remember that content is seductive but that working with process is how change occurs in the couple's system.

3. *Polarities askew or other imbalances.* A system is healthy if each person develops more parts of self rather than habitually

relegating some functions to the partner. These need to be pointed out and explored with awareness and experimentation.

4. *Complementarity and the middle ground.* Fusion with the other makes the "we," while separation from the other makes the "me." This rhythm of coming together and drawing apart is the choreography or dance of the couple, which changes form to match the "music" of different times.

Complementarity is the functional aspect of differentiation. It is how differentiation is expressed within the couple system. While complementarity is based on differences, the middle ground is composed of similarities. Life, as we said before, takes place in the middle, not at the extremes. The middle ground literally provides the stable foundation of trust and mutuality on which the exciting figures—now stormy, now sizzling with excitement—can appear, be expressed, be appreciated, and allow the couple, as individuals and as a system, to grow and mature.

5. *Attending to resistances.* Resistances are a system phenomenon. When the couple becomes aware of ways in which they collude to interrupt contact, their contact skills will gradually improve and they will experience greater satisfaction when being together.

Let us now consider *how* to make interventions.

How to Intervene

To intervene is to make something figural for the couple, to tell them something you see or experience about their behavior that they are not able to sense.

1. *Intervene boldly.* Your own sense of arousal about your observation must stand out if your statement is to be received. Examine your objections to being bold. You may ask yourself, "Suppose they don't find it relevant?" Then you may ask them, "What doesn't fit for you about what I said?" In this way, you will obtain more information about the couple's thoughts and feelings. Never argue your point when meeting with objections to your observation, since you will simply meet with increased resistance. Instead, be curious about the couple's way of experiencing themselves.

You may be worried if the couple does not acknowledge your statement. In that case, chances are you did not make your statement strong enough to make yourself heard. This is especially true if the couple is fully involved in their discussion or if they are too retroflected to invest energy in others. If this is so, you may choose to bring that observation to their attention. Remember that you are always on safe ground *when your intervention is based on material you have observed.*

2. *Provide phenomenological data.* Always give phenomenological data as support when you hear or see something you want to use as an intervention. You will be heard this way. The hard part is to find a way to say to the whole system what you hear and not just to an individual while phrasing it in as useful a way as possible. For example, you may tell the couple:

Therapist: *I would like to share something I have observed in your talk. I notice that every time you speak, Hans, you, Adriana, cut in before his thought is completed. And you, Hans, don't seem to notice or become distracted. You seem to take turns doing this. Then both of you lose clarity about the problem at hand. Did you know that?*

The therapist makes pertinent observations to the couple and describes the role each person plays in creating the loss of clarity. The intervention is more likely to be well received because it is not judgmental. How can Hans and Adriana use this observation? They may even have noticed this and found themselves helplessly repeating the same behavior. If the couple acknowledges the observation, the therapist can follow with a suggestion:

Therapist: *I suggest you watch each other more closely and allow the other to complete a thought. If you feel interrupted, please tell the other you are not finished. There is no danger of one of you not taking your turn. I promise I'll make sure of that.*

Notice that the therapist takes care not to make a villain of one or the other. The therapist gives them a clear sense that they are both attended to equally. Here is an intervention that could raise resistance:

Therapist: *I would like to share something I have observed in your talk. Adriana, you interrupt Hans all the time.*

Hans becomes the "injured child" and feels favored, but without realizing that he allows the interruptions. Adriana naturally feels slighted, almost "slapped on the wrist," and does not become aware that she too allows interruptions from Hans. Change in behavior would seem to have to come only from her and not from him—which is a distortion of what must happen for the system to change. The couple is treated like punished children, rather than like competent adults.

The couple may not notice that they interrupt each other. In that case, the therapist may elect to ask them to continue their discussion, adding:

Therapist: *See if you can spot the moment when you interrupt the other or are interrupted. I will bring it to your attention if you don't seem to notice.*

Thus, a "good" intervention

- Describes what is actually there
- States how all parties contribute to phenomenon
- Implies a potential action that each participant can take to improve the system

3. *Report what is evoked.* Reporting what is evoked in you, the therapist, can be a powerful intervention. This is especially true after you have seen the couple for several sessions and have earned their trust. Imagine saying:

> As I sit here with you, I feel invisible, unseen by anybody.
> I want to tell you how you move me with the care you take responding to each other so gently.
> I feel like a translator at the United Nations.
> Sitting here with you, I feel so helpless. If I only had a magic wand!
> After twenty minutes with you, I started getting so lethargic and sleepy.

It's only been a few minutes into our session and already I feel as if someone is spinning me around. I feel dizzy and disoriented.

You are doing so well that I can feel comfortable enough to make myself a cup of tea.

When you feel something deeply and share it clearly and strongly, people often respond at the same level within themselves from which your message came. This is not a trick or a technique or a matter of just inventing metaphors. It is a heartfelt message that you develop out of your emotional generosity as a witness to a drama you care about.

If, for one reason or another, you cannot bring yourself to care, do not bother sharing your feelings—unless "not caring" is evoked by the couple's way of being with you. Telling them how you turn cold in their presence is yet another powerful way of letting them see themselves.

4. *Teach.* Teaching is another way of intervening. It is a pleasure to teach when a couple directly asks for help. Remember, in the very beginning you offered them the option of turning to you and asking for help. Too often, a couple is so retroflected that the energy is turned inward toward each other and they do not have the impetus to turn toward you. They may not be fully aware of your presence as a significant resource for them. After all, they have been behaving in the same rigidly bounded way with the rest of the world before they came to you.

If they do choose to ask for help, you have the opportunity to teach. Teaching is an art. It is not always giving information, although information often offers great help and relief. You can also talk about books you have read or experiences you have had, or you can tell them a story that is tailored to their dilemma. The goal of teaching is to touch the couple's minds and hearts, to inform, to inspire, and to let them go on their way. Do you remember how your parents or other adults told stories that were beyond your interest level even when you started being interested in their experiences? Keep that in mind as a "parent" figure to the couple.

Sharing experiences or telling stories, however, has the capacity of drawing too much attention to the therapist and can be used as a way of relieving boredom or may reflect egotism. Make your story fairly short and relevant to the couple's question and then establish your boundaries again clearly and send the couple back to work.

5. *Suggest an experiment.* One can always intervene by suggesting an experiment. Experiments are grounded situations in which new behavior can be evoked and practiced.[9] An experiment generally involves the following developmental sequence, although it may vary since it is an organic process evolving over time:

- Laying the groundwork
- Negotiating consensus between therapist and client-system
- Grading the work in terms of experienced difficulty for the client-system
- Surfacing the client-system's group awareness
- Locating the client-system's energy
- Focusing awareness and energy toward the development of a theme
- Generating self-support for both the client-system and therapist
- Choosing a particular experiment
- Enacting the experiment
- Debriefing the client-system—insight and completion

Let us return to our first couple, Jim and Loretta, and look at how as their therapy session unfolds an experiment forms. When we left Jim and Loretta, they were embroiled in deflection and Loretta's headache was returning.

Therapist: *Right. Let's try a little experiment. Choose any of the topics you discussed and practice not changing it, not deflecting from it until both of you feel satisfied that something is finished. Would you be willing to try?*

Jim: *Okay, let's do it.*

Loretta: *Yes, let's. How about getting back to the matter of Marilyn's apartment?*

Jim: *Okay. I think we should decide to help her with the initial security deposit.*

Loretta: *That's okay with me if we also sit down with her and go over her monetary situation or at least offer to do so. And if things look manageable, we should leave her alone.*

Jim: *I suppose she'll have to struggle with it just as we did. Okay, I'm satisfied.*

Loretta: *Me, too. What a relief!*

Therapist: *How does it feel to have finished this one problem? Can you tell the difference when you finish?*

Loretta: *For one thing, my headache is gone!*

Jim: *I feel better, too. I feel closer to you, Loretta. How about going out to dinner tonight?*

6. *Use of individual therapy.* When one part of the system is stuck in some way that does not allow the whole system to move on, you can intervene with just that one part. You can do individual therapy with the immobilized person who is too troubled to join with and work with his or her partner. Let us say that Loretta falls silent, crying quietly. No systemic intervention directed to both Jim and Loretta seems to get her unstuck. Here is how to arrange an individual piece of work with Loretta.

Therapist: *I notice, Loretta, that you're having a hard time. Jim, would you mind if I talk with Loretta for a little while?*

Jim: *No, I don't mind.*

Therapist: *Good. I'll get right back to you, Jim. Just sit in with us for a few minutes.*

Moving into individual therapy with Loretta should involve temporarily extracting her from the pair. Jim can be an onlooker while the therapist works with Loretta. By witnessing the therapist's interaction with Loretta, Jim can maintain a sense of connection as a temporarily "silent" partner.

Therapist: *So, Loretta, this is hard for you, isn't it?*

Loretta: *(After a long pause) All these years (she begins crying softly) I've been trying to please him and he never asks me what I want, what I wish.*

Therapist: *It's easier to tell me right now.*

Loretta: *Yes.*

Therapist: *Do you want to try to say that to Jim now, or is that still too hard?*

Loretta: *(Tears rolling down her cheeks) I'd like to try to tell him.*

Therapist: *Okay, go ahead and try.*

Loretta: *(Turning to Jim) You never ask me for what I want . . . it makes me so sad, because I love you.*

Therapist: *Jim, you can have Loretta back now and you can respond while I listen in, okay?*

Jim: *(To Loretta) I never knew you wanted me to . . . that it mattered to you.*

Loretta: *You never . . .*

Jim: *Please don't say* never. *It makes me feel so bad when you do that!*

Loretta: *(Raising her voice with more passion, more energy) I wish you would for once ask me or surprise me with something that truly matters to me.*

Jim: *I've asked you. Last year, remember, we went to Washington.*

The stuck place in Loretta has been overcome and now they can look at the interactional dynamics that keep her from telling him what she wants and keep him from asking her. We are moving on.

Therapist: *Loretta, you are so busy giving and being so sufficient unto yourself that it's easy for Jim not to ask. And Jim, you are so busy being served and doing your work, you must feel she doesn't really need very much. So, Jim, Loretta is ready for you now, to take you in now.*

Jim: *Loretta, what would you like from me? What would please you, dear? I mean this weekend, what could I do to please you?*

In doing individual work, one must be careful not to make an identified patient out of one person. If you do individual therapy with one, make sure you do it with the consent, and in the presence, of the other partner. Also, notice the careful delineation of the newly formed boundaries for the work: forming a new boundary around Loretta and the therapist and, later, recreating the boundary around the couple with the therapist clearly outside once again. The couple is always the major figure in the drama that the therapist enhances and supports.

7. *Provide for reentry.* Finally, remember to finish a therapy session by returning the couple to the ordinary world. As in flying, reentry is the lowering of the altitude and the landing back on earth. This way, the couple can leave the office feeling grounded again. The landing is accomplished just by ordinary talk, which does the following:

- It maintains the therapist's presence and relationship to the couple on a human, compassionate level.
- It defines clear boundaries for what is therapy and what is not therapy, what is the couple and what is not. The therapist "borrows" the system for the therapy hour, then returns it to itself.
- It reinforces learning by reminding the couple to follow through with new behaviors or insights. For example, the therapist suggests "homework": "Jim, I'd like you to practice asking Loretta what she wants. And Loretta, I'd like you to practice telling Jim what you want. Do you want to try that during the week?"
- It balances the tone of the session by making things either lighter or more serious: "Loretta, when you're telling Jim what you want, don't ask him for that Mercedes you saw in the parking lot—he might panic!"
- It gives support so the couple leaves knowing that the therapist cares for them and their welfare.

Working a Couple's Issue in Individual Therapy

Great care must be taken when seeing an individual for marital therapy because the therapist may become the love object and may then be perceived as colluding with the client to split up the relationship with the partner who is not attending therapy. The client may look at the therapist and say, "My spouse is mean to me and you are so nice." This threat of separation or alienation, whether it comes from the environment as a catastrophic situation, from psychotherapy, or from some other internal experience, clearly throws off the balance of the system and may throw the couple into a potential crisis.

Transference can become a substitute for dealing with the marriage. As psychoanalysts well know, the client's statements about the therapist should be considered not only as simple compliments or criticisms but as possible statements about the client's parents, siblings, or spouse. Such statements should prompt the therapist to raise questions about the client's significant relationships and to stimulate the client's awareness of problems in these relationships.

Our point is that the therapist may unwittingly support problems in a marriage by not bringing to the client's awareness the implications of his or her growing attachment to, or sentiment about, the therapist. Even though we have an individual sitting in our office, we are constantly aware and mindful of the impact of our work on the client's "outer circles": family, spouse, children, employer, friends. It is naive to assume that our impact and responsibility are limited only to the individual sitting in front of us.

In general, it may be easier to work with a same-gender client (if it is a heterosexual system)—to love and care for the client—without endangering the system. Keep in mind that if the couple is homosexual, you become just as much a potential rival or threat if you and the client are the same gender.

Is it possible to see only one of the marital partners but to "pay attention to the system?" In a time of crisis, it is not enough to just pay attention. You must invite the other person into the office and work with them both. Just being mindful of the absent partner and understanding the system may not be sufficient. The therapist's ethical dilemma is the desire to include the partner and expand into more ambitious work on the one hand and, on the other, to honor the client's wish to be seen individually. When individual therapy is chosen, the therapist must learn how to carry any anxiety about the couple's future without projecting that anxiety onto the client.

You cannot work on the development of one partner without affecting the development of the other. If one partner is working on the dark, undeveloped side—the "shadow" in Jungian terms—the other partner also must be working on the dark, undeveloped side. Problems are likely to occur if one is working on that darkness within while the other is not.

Gabriel (and Sue): Individual Therapy for a Conflict

Let us consider intrapsychic work on a conflict with a partner.[10] Individual therapy for a conflict may allow the client to return to the partner with a greater appreciation of the other person's point of view. One can only appreciate that other person's point of view when it is more fully integrated within the self.

Therapist: *Gabriel, name some of the conflicts you and your wife, Sue, have.*

Gabriel: *I don't like that she's so blah—that she fades out at eight at night.*

Therapist: *And how are you when she fades out?*

Gabriel: *I'm sort of torn. If she goes to sleep, I'll have the house to myself and can do whatever I want, but I also want to be close and play around with her.*

Therapist: *So you have some energy when she is pooped?*

Gabriel: *Yes.*

Therapist: *What are some of the other conflicts?*

Gabriel: *I would like more sexual excitement in us as a couple. It isn't as exciting as I would like it to be. That's nitty-gritty. I'd like her to be able to be more with me and for us to be able to put the kids aside. I feel like that doesn't happen. When I walk into the house, I feel drudgery is awaiting me, so I manage to spend long hours away.*

Therapist: *What's the drudgery?*

Gabriel: *Oh, the basic things, like preparing meals, cleaning up.*

Therapist: *I'm interested in the excitement conflict and the sexual conflict. Which one of those two would you like to work on?*

Gabriel: *Well, they're related—they're kissing cousins.*

Therapist: *Yes, they are. I'll tell you what I have in mind. I would like you to imagine that this conflict you have with Sue is also a conflict inside of you. That inside of you there is a Sue part, and that you sought out Sue to play this out with her, to externalize it with her because it feels easier at first glance to work it out that way. I propose that you put "your" Sue part in that chair and that you put the sexually dissatisfied Gabe part in this chair, and have a dialogue. But remember that you're talking to that part of yourself, rather than to Sue. Is that clear?*

Gabriel: *I took in some of what you said and I'm willing to try it.*

Therapist: *At the moment, the polarization is not yet clear, so spend at least a few minutes as you talk searching for the polarization.*

Gabriel: *As I was listening, some of it seemed to flesh out. I can start.*

Therapist: *I'll be right here.*

Gabriel 1: *I'm really excited. I'm so excited, I just had five new ideas. Am I talking to myself?*

Therapist: *Yes, you're talking to yourself.*

Gabriel 2: *Five new ideas? What about the 101 other new ideas?*

Gabriel 1: *These new ideas are so exciting. This first idea is so wonderful that I just thought it up on my way here, and I want to tell you about it.*

Gabriel 2: *In a couple of minutes, I'm going to have to go and check the bank statements.*

Gabriel 1: *I just got this idea about the book I've been working on and these are really good ideas.*

Gabriel realizes that in the last interchange he was speaking as Sue, his wife, would speak rather than as a part of himself. He says that he would not have made the comments about the bank statements but that Sue would have. The therapist encourages Gabriel to answer as himself.

Gabriel 2: *(Much slower in pace) There are a lot of other new ideas, so is that what you need, some new ones? There are still a lot of old ones unfinished.*

Therapist: *Pay attention to how, in this second chair, you are slowing down.*

Gabriel: *And I feel more grounded.*

Therapist: *That's nice. Let yourself feel what you're missing here (gesturing to the first chair).*

Gabriel 2: *(Slowly) You know, there is such a thing as gravity. I feel it. It holds me down in my seat and makes my two feet work. I feel it on both feet while I'm sitting in the chair. As I sit in this chair and look at you in the other seat, you don't seem to be paying much attention to gravity. You seem to go off in one direction, then in another direction.*

Gabriel 1: *(Smiling) It's fun, isn't it?*

Gabriel 2: *There you are, fluttering like a butterfly. I feel a great sadness. (A quiet tearfulness comes across his face; there is a long silence.)*

Therapist: *Do you know what that sadness is?*

(After another long silence, Gabriel nods.)

Therapist: *How do you feel now?*

Gabriel: *Calm.*

Therapist: *I'd like to bridge this work, although I know we're not by any means finished. What would you like to say to the excited*

Gabriel about him and Sue, to teach him something that he can take home? What can you teach him from this part of yourself so that the next time he gets bored and needs more excitement he'll know how to deal with that?

Gabriel: *As you walk in the door, there is something lovely about the drudgery that you could walk into. It is rooted and has a purpose.*

Therapist: *Substitute* she *for* it.

Gabriel: *You are rooted. Who am I talking to?*

Therapist: *You are talking to Gabriel about Sue. When you walk into that house and all of this is going on, you are his counselor.*

Gabriel: *When you walk into that house, there is something lovely about what you call "drudgery." These are the basic living tasks that permit you to fly around. You have some place to come home to. You have Sue to come home to. When you are home, Sue can fly and come back to you. She needs to do that, too. There is excitement as well as rootedness. Don't take for granted that you have a home, because without it all of your flying around would have no center.*

Therapist: *Tell him what you would like him to appreciate in Sue that he winds up criticizing. You see, there are parts of her that he (gesturing to the first chair) is really critical of. What could he begin to savor in Sue that he is being critical of?*

Gabriel: *I'm not sure what I'm critical of in Sue, except that of "why aren't you more . . . "*

Therapist: *"Why aren't you more exciting?" So what would you like to say to him? He's the one who needs so much stimulation. What could you say to him that would make it easier to deal with the criticism that he puts on Sue about having to be more exciting for him? What can you say to him out of your groundedness, your sense of gravity?*

Gabriel: *This part of me is stupid . . . which is good. I don't try to jump out at every word you're saying. I don't try to understand every piece.*

Therapist: *I think that's the answer. Why don't you make that into something that's good and use that idea to help you?*

Gabriel: *(To the first chair) I want you to understand that the times that you are here (in the second chair)—the time that you think is shallow, dull, recuperating, time passing doing nothing—is essential. (To the therapist) That's probably more intrapsychic and I'm not sure how Sue participates in this.*

Therapist: *It's hard for you to make that bridge.*

Gabriel: *She is always interested in my excitement.*

Therapist: *Sure, and then she can be grounded and dull and maintain everything. Let me try to make a bridge for you here. If I were playing you, I would say, using your ideas: "Gabe, let yourself be dumb. It's okay to let yourself be dumb. Allow yourself that pleasure." Try to say that now out of your dumbness.*

Gabriel: *What it feels like is that out of my dumbness I stay within my skin and I don't jump into yours. Out of my dumbness I have my own territory. You have yours. Out of my dumbness, I give you room.*

Therapist: *Who's the "you" here?*

Gabriel: *Sue.*

Therapist: *So now we've changed—we've put Sue in that chair. Do you now have a better sense of what you need to do to be with her and to deal with that conflict?*

Gabriel: *There's a lot of richness here. I don't feel dissatisfied.*

Therapist: *(In a light fashion) Oh, you've got a lot of new ideas?*

Gabriel: *No, and I don't feel like I'm jumping out with all of these new ideas. I feel like the ideas I've gotten from this experience are within me—they're not out there—they're here in me.*

Therapist: *Thank you.*

What was just demonstrated was not couple therapy, but it did allow Gabriel to explore a conflict with his partner. This same intervention can be used in couple therapy by having one person give you one or two conflicts experienced with a partner. Take fifteen minutes to let one partner work that conflict as if it is an intrapsychic conflict, then switch roles and do the same thing with the other partner. This gives each a taste of owning whatever is seen in the other as opposing his or her nature.

This is what Gabriel was groping with. Instead of being critical of the mundane, quiet, grounded ways Sue functions, he came to grips with these qualities within himself and found more inner union. Chances are, if you call your partner names, what you are doing is struggling with a part of yourself that you do not like, a part you are ashamed of or embarrassed by, or simply a part that is as yet unknown to you. You can pick up what seem like the most awful characteristics in another and learn something. In fact, you can learn more from your enemy than from your friend, although we do not necessarily recommend associating too closely with one's enemies.

Conclusion

In this chapter, I have given you an idea of how to use my theory of the interactive cycle and systems theory in doing therapy with couples. Among other things, I have provided suggestions on how to set up the therapy situations, how to choose the interventions to be made, how to attend to resistances, and how to create experiments.

Now that you are fairly well grounded in this systemic, Gestalt approach and have just read about two-person systems, it is important to be reminded that a couple, as noted in Chapter Three, is actually composed of three subunits: the two individuals and the relationship or relational space between them. A couple, when standing alone as a unit, is a system unto itself. Locating that same independent system within the larger system of the family now makes it a subsystem within a greater whole. And, naturally, it takes no great stretch of the imagination to continue up the social hierarchy and include the family within the community, the community within the state, the state within the country, and so on. As we will see in the next chapter, much of what has already been said about working with couples can be applied to working with families. But there is a caveat. A family is necessarily more complex than a couple, and so a larger, more encompassing view must be taken in order to understand the phenomena. To provide the reader with this larger perspective, my presentation is based on a series of basic assumptions and orienting principles.

Notes to Chapter Eight

1. I conceptualize this as the Interactive Cycle of Experience, as described in Chapter Four.
2. See Chapter Seven for a discussion of the "presence" of the therapist.
3. The basic structure of how to set up a therapy session and how and when to intervene in a couple system is based on notes by Sonia M. Nevis as presented to our students at the Gestalt Institute of Cleveland.
4. In Chapter Three, I discuss couples as a system; in Chapter Four, I explain the Interactive Cycle of Experience.
5. Chapter Six discusses resistances to change.
6. See Chapter Seven for more on creating boundaries.
7. The discussion in this section is drawn from J. Zinker (1992), "Gestalt approach to couple therapy," in E. C. Nevis (Ed.), *Gestalt therapy: Perspectives and applications* (New York: Gestalt Institute of Cleveland Press). I also recommend the following: "On stimulation: A conversation with Dr. Wes Jackson" (1981, Winter), *News* (Center for the Study of Intimate Systems, Gestalt Institute of Cleveland), *1*(3), 1-2; "Couples: How they develop and change: An interview with Barbara DeFrank Lynch, Ph.D." (1982, Fall), *News* (Center for the Study of Intimate Systems, Gestalt Institute of Cleveland), *2*(1), 1-2; "Intimacy and sexuality: An interview with Sol Gordon, Ph.D." (1984, Fall), *News* (Center for the Study of Intimate Systems, Gestalt Institute of Cleveland), *4*(2), 1-2; "Marriage: The impossible relationship: A conversation with Sonia March Nevis, Ph.D., and Joseph Chaim Zinker, Ph.D." (1985, Fall), *News* (Center for the Study of Intimate Systems, Gestalt Institute of Cleveland), *5*(1), 1-2; "What do you think?" (1987, Spring), *News* (Center for the Study of Intimate Systems, Gestalt Institute of Cleveland), *7*(1), 1-2.
8. One model of such work with couples—a model requiring them to

hear one another, to own projections, and to move toward a compromise without losing face—is presented in J. Zinker (1977), *Creative process in Gestalt therapy* (New York: Vintage Books).

9. For a detailed discussion of the use of experiment, see J. Zinker (1977), *Creative process in Gestalt therapy* (New York: Vintage Books, esp. chaps. 6 and 7).
10. This particular demonstration is drawn, in edited form, from J. Zinker (1981), *Complementarity and the middle ground: Two forces for couples' binding* (Cleveland, OH: Gestalt Institute of Cleveland). It was originally performed during a presentation to the Conference on the Gestalt Approach to Intimate Systems, Gestalt Institute of Cleveland, Apr. 1980. (I gratefully acknowledge the original transcription and careful editorial work by Philip Rosenthal.)

9

Intervening in Family Systems

The "family" is not an introjected object, but an introjected set of relations.

—R. D. Laing

The principles we apply when working with couples also apply when working with families. When a family comes to you for therapy, the first step is to have the family members make initial contact by talking with one another. Your task is to sit back and allow yourself to attend to what you see, hear, and experience with them. When something becomes figural, you then have to decide how to build on this awareness. There are several choices: you can have the family talk about some aspect of what you observe about them; you can introduce an experiment to expand on your observation, or you can teach some new be-

Note: The core of this chapter was conceived, outlined, and written by Sonia Nevis.

havior related to your observation. The final step is to bring the unit of work—the family learning—to a close.

However, some significant differences between couple and family therapy exist that must be taken into account.

Unique Aspects of Family Therapy

The greater number of people involved in family therapy than in couple therapy makes all arrangements more complex and requires the therapist to pay more attention to the structure of interventions. The mechanics and format associated with family therapy are apt to be significantly different than for couples, simply because there are more people involved. For example, your work space needs to be larger to accommodate a family, and it is important to pay attention to the seating arrangements so that everyone does not have to sit in the same place each session or throughout a session.

Typically, it is harder to schedule a whole family, especially during the daytime, due to school and work conflicts and a greater number of activities that the family must coordinate on a daily basis. The therapist and family are often faced with the problem of someone being absent from the session for this reason. Because of inevitable complications, a therapist will often work with parts of families, and both the therapist and the family may feel rushed or "crowded." We can try to minimize difficulties by paying attention to these issues and the accompanying dynamics.

It is often helpful for a session to be longer than one hour, and three-hour sessions are not unusual, depending on the size of the family and ages of the children. The duration of therapy—that is, the number of sessions—is apt to be shorter; often there will be only one, two, or three sessions in family therapy. Description of the family process may be a goal in and of itself, such that when a family has a fix on itself, it will leave therapy prepared to work toward change.

Process work in families is more complicated than with couples simply because of the increase in data. No matter how complex a system is, the process is discernible, and so the work remains essentially the same. However, family work presents many more aspects of figure formation because of the potential for the formation of different subsystems together with the issue of greater or lesser power.

Adult subsystems have more power than those of the children, or at least they should as an ideal. How power is used among subsystems is something we must attend to, since the sheer number of people makes for many potential interactional combinations. Watching these shifts can feel complicated, even though the basic principles are the same.

When there are more people, there is more action, and events tend to move faster. Content is different than with couples, but the basic process of identifying how a system is strong, as well as where and how it interrupts the basic process of gestalt formation, can still be seen as it is with couples. The family will not join together on any project or goal if the awareness is meager, if little information flows, if the parents do not volunteer feelings and thoughts, if questions are discouraged.

Co-therapists often mirror the systems with which they work, and this aspect of co-therapy is especially useful when working with complex systems. Part of watching a couple or family is allowing oneself to be confluent with the system—to imitate by sitting in the same ways, matching their voices, assuming the same feelings (anguish, anger, sadness, excitement, and so on). When co-therapists each become confluent with a different person in the couple or family, the interactions between the two therapies will often be similar to the interactions of clients. This source of data, gathered without awareness and later noticed, reflected on, and taken into account, is most useful when a couple or family appears confusing to the therapists. No clear pattern emerges until the co-therapists examine their own behavior and become aware that they are unconsciously mirroring the system they are counseling. For example, when therapists who generally speak easily to each other notice that they are hesitating or holding back, they must consider this mirroring phenomenon.

Basic Assumptions and Orienting Principles

Obviously, therapists use many different theoretical stances and value bases in making choices for intervening in family systems. These provide principles that guide the therapists' choices. I refer to the principles I follow as *orienting principles.* This term is useful because it suggests that the principles provide a perspective, yet are not "etched in stone," immutable, and monolithic. Different therapists will naturally have somewhat different orienting principles based on their own values.

Beneath each orienting principle for therapeutic intervention there lies a core value, a *basic assumption,* concerning satisfactory family life, which defines the criteria of health held by the therapist. This section delineates the major orienting principles that guide my work, together with the underlying basic assumption for each. I present these in no special order, since they all seem equally important.

1. Celebrating Good Functioning

Good functioning is a logical starting point.

1a. Basic Assumption: *A healthy family system supports itself by knowing what it does well.*

1a. Orienting Principle: *Families are often unaware of what they do well: helping the family see what it does well has a great impact on family behavior.*

When you accentuate what a family does well, members of the family become interested in discovering what they are doing, are less frightened of the therapeutic process, and are more accepting of their potential for change. On the face of it, telling people who come to family therapy that they do something well may be seen as a denial of, or a deflection from, their problems. However, we find that acknowledging good functioning supports the task of facing up to the negative or dysfunctional aspects of the family process. In fact, it frequently mobilizes energy to deal with problems by adding an aura of hope that things can and will improve.

1b. Basic Assumption: *Living in families is difficult; no family can constantly maintain an ideal level of functioning.*
1b. Orienting Principle: *The therapist should recognize and celebrate "good enough" and not demand perfection.*

Theories of good functioning are just theories. Rich awareness, easy joining, actions full of life, and clean endings are not always present. Accepting "messy" living that manages to move along is often more important than holding to an ideal. Therapists, as models for the family, need to notice and applaud any process that shows creativity or liveliness.

The Coleman family is an example of these assumptions and principles. Harry, Bess, and their teenage daughters, Leslie and Miriam, came to see us when Leslie had just started college and Miriam was a junior in high school. In the first session, Harry tentatively mentioned that he had been feeling "blue" since Leslie had been away (she was home this particular weekend). Miriam wanted to know what it was like for her father: Did it affect his work? What was it that he missed exactly? Bess interjected, saying to her husband, "You have been feeling restless lately, Harry. I thought it was pressure at work."

The temptation for us was to focus on the pathology of the family's overinvestment in what each member was feeling—a moving inward, rather than looking outward to the world where the children's lives were moving. Instead, I decided to focus the intervention on what they did well: when a member of the family expressed a giving feeling, everyone showed interest in that person's feelings.

The intervention gave concrete examples of how each person responded to the father's sense of loss. This had an encouraging effect on everyone. The responsive sentiment in the family was, "We are good people. Whatever the problem is, we do care about each other. We know how to investigate each other's experience and to show we care by asking questions." This sense of goodness laid the ground for more critical interventions later in the session.

2. Defining the Family

The boundaries of a family are fluid.

> 2a. Basic Assumption: *The definition of who is included in a family continually changes, and boundaries vary for different life events.*
>
> 2a. Orienting Principle: *Phenomenological awareness, rather than structural givens, informs the therapist's "daily" definition of the family.*

This assumption and principle focus on determining who and what constitute the family. It implies a creative rather than a static definition of the family, which may include friends, distant relatives, and "bystanders" at any given moment. "Bystanders" are people who look like they are not part of that particular system but who actually play an important role in the family. It is not necessary to be a very active participant or to do or say something that is either helpful or causes trouble to have an impact. In some cases, a person may have impact simply by existing: an abusive boss, for example, or an ex-spouse. Thus, a bystander becomes an important member of the family system through being part of the phenomenological field.

It follows from this that there is no easy answer to the question of who is the family. Boundaries can be drawn in any way that makes sense for the particular session or interaction within a session. Perhaps there is a neighbor who is with a family member every day. Is that neighbor a part of the family or not? Is an absent, distant grandparent part of the family? It is important to make a choice and draw a boundary for some specific piece of work that needs to be done, if not for all of the family functions. At any time you can deal with any unit or configuration. You can define a larger or smaller unit for given intervention purposes. I have often worked with families where a visiting grandparent or aunt attended sessions to deal either with a specific issue or to promote better communication in general.

Paying attention to where the boundaries of a family are drawn reveals that they change with changing events. The child who marries or leaves home to go to school may be truly outside the field of work for some family issues. Likewise, to whom a family tells things, or to whom things need to be told, does not remain constant. Different people are selected for inclusion in different family events, although families often do this selection without conscious awareness. I often see tension develop in a family when it plans a celebration such as a wedding: Who will be invited and who will not be? Some boundary has to be drawn around who will be included in the family circle. Those who are invited define the boundary of the family at that time. At a later time, another circle could be formed to define the family.

By learning to constantly redefine the family, the therapist expands the field of observation and intervention beyond the structurally driven work of the nuclear family and to include definitions of extended families that change with time.

2b. Basic Assumption: *Families have life cycles.*
2b. Orienting Principle: *Intervention should take into account the needs of adults and children at each stage of development.*

A family's ability to change with time is critical to good family health. Most change does not take place in therapy. Change takes place because situations are new and, therefore, new solutions are needed. Yesterday's solutions do not work today because today's events are novel. Change takes place day by day. When the fluid process of family living gets stuck because new solutions do not emerge, families fall into serious difficulties. For example, trouble is brewing when rules for an eleven-year-old are rigidly adhered to when the same child is sixteen. At this juncture, families usually ask for help.

Change is natural in the course of living and expected in every open system. The therapist should be familiar with developmental stages of families and the changes that are expected with each stage. Interventions should be "stage appropriate."

2c. Basic Assumption: *Each family is as unique as each individual member.*

2c. Orienting Principle: *Intervention should take into account that each family has its own particular experiential and structural configuration and that the family's increased awareness of its dynamics can be a stimulus for change.*

Each family has its own specific configuration. It has its unique ways of handling life tasks, with some subsystems pulling together more often and some less often, and some individuals more important to one another and some less important. Each family has its own way of living in the world.

The range of what is "good enough" in families is enormous. That is one of the reasons we emphasize countertransference as much as we do. Countertransference is the phenomenon in which therapists' perceptions and behaviors with a given family are heavily influenced by their personal experiences in their own couple, immediate family circle, or family of origin. Interventions based on countertransference are often related not so much to what the family in treatment needs, but on unfinished business in the therapists' own lives. If, for example, a therapist has managed to survive a difficult family situation by moving far away from mom, dad, and brother and having very sparse contact with them, this therapist may be tempted to suggest a similar solution to an adolescent who is having problems at home. Or a therapist who comes from a family in which rigid boundaries were kept between children and adults may prefer to rigidify the separation between these two subsystems in a client family—even though the family may, in fact, need more loosening of such boundaries. It is only too easy to see through the screen of the few families that we know well, and to look at the therapeutic family as the same family that we came from—which means that we view the family as a "good" or "bad" family depending on how we evaluated our own family system.

Countertransference phenomena come from the whole range of the therapists' past experiences, not just from unfinished or biased situations in our own family. Certain ideological or religious notions—about what men and women should be like or how children should be treated or what constitutes sexual aberration or what a good education is or what a proper family diet should be—may heavily bias therapists' views or opinions of a family in treatment. We must constantly confront what is or was "good" or "bad" for us and what is truly suitable and realistic for a particular family in treatment.

For this reason, we should try to "supervise" each other's work as colleagues, take workshops on developing as therapists, and return to personal therapy at times when events in clients' lives trigger difficult, painful, or irrational feelings in us. I also believe that well-rounded therapists must be aware of the nature of various families who live side by side in their towns and cities—that, for example, Italian Catholics are different from Irish Catholics, that religious Jews are different from Reform Jews, that upper-middle-class blacks are different from inner-city blacks. A good family therapist, a competent one, is part sociologist, part cultural anthropologist, part philosopher, and, most important, a *reliable observer* who is truly interested in how *this* family works within its own neighborhood and social milieu.

We should always be aware of our reactions to a family when we

- React *too quickly* with a comment or opinion
- Strongly "love" or "hate" a family, couple, or member
- Are *convinced* as to "what is good" for a given family without taking much time to observe them, ask them questions, and find out about their competence, shortcomings, and past history
- Get into arguments with a member of the family and cannot back off, or take a particularly rigid stance with a family
- "Take sides" with one member or subsystem of a family against another part of the family
- Feel that a family is "just great" and does not need to be examined critically
- Tolerate excessively abusive behavior or any extreme behavior because it is reminiscent of our own past and we assume that "all families tend to do this"

I am certain you can add more items to this countertransference "danger list" and invite you to make up one for yourself. It will help you to make stronger boundaries between what is good and bad for you and what data in the family lead to a "good" intervention tailored especially to its needs.

Our intent as therapists is not to change the configuration or patterns of a particular family: how they like to be together or how they like to solve their problems. What we are looking for is if anyone is being harmed by the particular pattern or if a family cannot accomplish what it wants to and cannot function as a work unit. Therapists are encouraged to be fascinated with the particular configuration of a specific family and to respect each configuration. Respecting "what is" enhances change.[1]

2d. BASIC ASSUMPTION: *The family is a work unit.*
2d. ORIENTING PRINCIPLE: *The therapist must evaluate how well a family or a subunit of its system carries out its daily tasks.*

The family has to run a household, raise children, clothe and feed them, and conduct all the daily tasks of living. They have to be a good work unit to accomplish this. If the work cannot get done, the therapist has to find out why. What is getting in the way? Are the patterns set in such a way that one person bears the brunt if things are not working well? If that is so, many times that person becomes the scapegoat or "identified patient." Often, one person, or one place in the system, feels the pain. There is either too much energy or not enough energy concentrated there. That spot is either "too hot" or "too cold."

It is the therapist's task to fully evaluate the family system. As stated previously, families need to know what they do well and how they are competent. Most families know more about their faults and failures than about their talents and successes. Awareness of its own strength propels the family into repeated competent behavior. On the other hand, emphasis on shortcomings and failures does not necessarily stimulate positive change. A good therapist can find ways to use the family's strengths to overcome its weaknesses.

2e. Basic Assumption: *Cultural influences are likely to be more prominent in family therapy than in couple therapy.*

2e. Orienting Principle: *Families are the transmitters of culture and, therefore, clearly articulated religious, social, cultural, and community values are important.*

When a couple has children and becomes a family, the views, habits, and values of the larger community become important. Religious, ethnic, social class, and extended family influences are more evident in families than in couples. Families transmit values through teaching the children. These values are less salient to a couple without children.

The desire to "look good" to the therapist may be more of an issue in family therapy because parents feel responsible for how their children behave. The therapist represents the outside world.

The children's culture is often at odds with the parents' culture, since each generation has its own behaviors, play, language, music, art, and goals.

Often, parents and children defend their actions on the grounds that "they" do it. "They" is usually some poorly defined entity that sets the rules and represents the extended family, the neighborhood, or the social or religious community: Johnny has to go to nursery school because all the three-year-olds on the street do.

By being aware that both family and community goals need to be articulated and respected, the therapist will provide a model and support for the family to examine, discuss, and appreciate the larger picture. The therapist is often the mediator in conflicts regarding family and community values.

3. Family Subsystems

If you think in terms of systems when you are working with a couple, you should also think of each individual as a system in its own right.[2] When we talk about putting a part of ourselves in "the empty chair,"[3] we are taking advantage of the fact that, as an individual, we are intrapsychically part of a system that needs to work as a coherent whole. When a person does not operate as a coherent whole, that person feels like his or her parts do not have a way of finally coming together into a single figure, a clear thought or gesture.

When you are working with a family, the number of potential subsystems necessarily increases. If a family has no way of coming together to a single figure, they are left with the same feeling of fragmentation that an individual is. Because a family has more subsystems, the subsystems shift frequently: first, you have one parent and a child; then another child enters and a whole new subsystem forms; then there is another subsystem if one person leaves the room and another enters.

The boundaries around each subsystem form a figure, and this figure keeps changing. Every combination of interactions is important because each has the potential for either enriching the life of the family or for disabling it. Within a family, you will see some subsystems that work well and in which the people feel good and other subsystems in which people do not feel as good.

> 3a. Basic Assumption: *A family is best seen as an organization of numerous, flexible, and frequently changing subsystems. The more subsystems that work well, the healthier the family.*
>
> 3a. Orienting Principle: *The job of the therapist includes helping the family see the structure and dynamic qualities of these subsystems.*

When you attend to a family, what you are looking at is the shifting of subsystems: How are these systems organized? Which subsystems work well and enable people to feel good in them? Which ones are avoided when possible? Which ones are painful because the people do not know how to be together?

If you see fluid movement of a clear boundary, and then a letting go to form another boundary made up of another subsystem, you are witnessing a good process. In looking for this moment you become alert to which subsystems never form, which individuals hardly ever talk to each other in a clear way so that other members of the family remain disconnected, and which ones are always stuck together. If a parent cannot be with one child, *and* with each child, *and* with two children, *and* with all the children, you see a potential trouble spot exacting the price of less-than-optimal family functioning.

> 3b. BASIC ASSUMPTION: *The subsystems of family organization are as important to the well-being of the family as is the total family system.*
>
> 3b. ORIENTING PRINCIPLE: *The therapist does not always work with the total family system; at times the choice will be to work with the subsystems.*

In any session or group of sessions, you are either working with the whole system or a subsystem. Wherever anything suddenly "pops out" at you and becomes figural, that is the system you want to work with, whether it includes the entire family or not. Frequently, work must be done with part of the family or with a particular relationship in order to prepare for total family learning.

In this process, it is crucial that the therapist not make an identified patient out of a specific subsystem, and that he or she avoid picking one or two members of the family as the location of all the familial problems. This is accomplished by working with many or all of the subsystems. First you will work with one subsystem, and then with another, and then another. Do not be deceived into perceiving a single subsystem as the problem, because everyone in the family contributes to the family process. While it may seem apparent that one person is the focus of the difficulty, you must assume that everyone is contributing.

This perspective is also useful for other reasons. Sometimes there is just too much occurring to deal with the complexity of the total family dynamic. Even more critical, working with subsystems follows from our strongly held assumption that a change in any one part of the system will change the whole system. Energy is redistributed when a subsystem improves its functioning. Often, energy is focused in a small part of the family and little is available to other parts, or others have little room to make a contribution. It is as though the "left out" subsystems are flattened against a wall. As you loosen the more powerful subsystem and teach its members to see their process, energy becomes available for unfinished business, other connections, other people, new events.

A small change in one subsystem allows other subsystems to re-form in new ways. The nature of the change is less relevant than the fact that it took place. When a resolution is achieved in one set of relationships—between mother and father, daughter and mother, sister and brother—relief runs through the entire family, as though everyone had exhaled after a long period of holding their breath. A change in one subsystem is powerful and rewarding for everyone and opens the possibility for change in other areas of the family system.

Interlude: Accessing Transgenerational Themes Through Dreamwork

It is also possible to affect the relationship across generations by working with a single system member in relation to another member who is either not present or deceased, even extending back several generations.[4] I have found much success in accessing transgenerational themes with the Gestalt dreamwork technique combined with family systems therapies. This is an unusual and unique approach in that it is an existential-experiential method that can readily be used to unearth and explore multigenerational themes.

While couple and family therapists do not usually embrace individual dreamwork as a standard technique, they do have considerable interest in transgenerational themes. Applying the ideas of the family systems model to varieties of dreamwork, we can address the recurrence of patterns over varying periods of time. These patterns—which on the surface can be resolved in a brief period of time—usually indicate the presence of deeper processes that take longer periods of time to complete. In the following session, the therapist uses the traditional "empty chair" method as a path for accessing transgenerational themes. "Samuel's Dream"—related below—is long and complicated. The work involves dialogue with intrapsychic parts of Samuel as well as with his introjected father. The depth of the work is surprising and quite moving. A theme develops, becoming the thread connecting Samuel's great-grandfather with himself. Attention is paid to both content and process as the theme of the dream is carefully followed and teased out in a supportive and caring manner.

Samuel's Dream

Samuel: *I had a dream last night. The dream felt like what I'm doing right now. Rushing. In the dream, I was rushing around from one room to another. They were small rooms; it was like at a conference. And I found a man I was looking for, and the next day he was to be televised and to present to the whole world. The moon was going to be right, everything was going to be right for him to bring out this big gem. He was going to set it out and he was going to crack it with a special hammer, and it was going to break into six pieces. One of the pieces was to be mine, and I didn't want to wait for it to happen then. I knew somehow that there were FBI people there that I couldn't trust. There were lots of people there that I couldn't trust. My colleague, Jane, was there. I coaxed the man to come out and he did break it. I grabbed my piece and I began running, and the whole dream continues on, one struggle after another to keep my piece. I even had a seductive encounter with Jane in a washroom. She grabbed my piece and stuck it under her skirt.*

Therapist: *She wanted a piece of the action. So, what was the end of it? You succeeded in keeping your piece?*

Samuel: *Yes, I succeeded in keeping it, but I was interrupted.*

Therapist: *So, talk to us about your ambition. How would you like to set it up? This could be a presidential address. You talk about it with ambition or you could just tell about it.*

Samuel: *I started to think about telling my parents this dream, how I might be telling it to them. That's not as big as a presidential address, or it might be.*

Therapist: *Okay, so can you imagine your father sitting in front of you. You're telling your father his biography, as well as you know it. Just start with that and I'll help you go with it.*

Samuel: *(To his father) Okay. A lot of things I know about you, I've gotten from you directly, and a lot of things I know about you, I've gotten from my grandmother. Those have been my two sources and my sense is that you wanted to be very special for your own father and to be wanted on your terms. He was never there for you, though he offered you many things, such as being in charge of his hotel and sending you to the best schools and many other kinds of things. According to you, you always ran away. Or else, you would tell him you didn't want that. You even married some woman who you knew that your father and your mother would not approve of and they paid her off to get a divorce and go away. And you met my mother and . . .*

Therapist: *Excuse me, Samuel, each time you say a unit of information, say something to him about his ambitiousness. "You went to all these schools . . . " and say something about his level of ambition. "You were married . . . "*

Samuel: *You're asking something I know nothing about.*

Therapist: *Just make it up, don't worry about it. Is he still alive?*

Samuel: *Yes.*

Therapist: *And you have some idea about his level of ambition?*

Samuel: *I know about his lack of ambition.*

Therapist: *Right! I didn't say how much or how little, just that category, that's very important. "You had an opportunity to go to all these schools . . . "*

Samuel: *You had an opportunity to go to many schools, to even marry someone else your father wanted you to marry. You had the opportunity to go into what seemed to be a thriving business. You had an opportunity to be . . . You've been given a lot of opportunities and didn't want any of them. When I've talked to you in the last few months . . . (starts crying and sobbing) . . . you've said that your life is done, that your whole life . . . is done . . . (choking and sobbing). But, I still need you . . . I experience your dying . . . and I'm getting on with my own life . . .*

Therapist: *Tell him what you think he did with his life.*

Samuel: *He had help. You have shown me how to love, how to care for other people. I think you have been successful . . .*

Therapist: *What are you interrupting? You started crying and you got into some feeling and then you stopped it.*

Samuel: *I'm interrupting my anger.*

Therapist: *Tell him that.*

Samuel: *You are seventy-five, seventy-six years old now and I really don't want to let you know how angry I've been at you. What I just put aside was, "Let him die in peace."*

Therapist: *I'd like him to die in peace and I'd like you to be born in peace. You have the right to give him your anger for both of those things to happen. See, it's an interactional thing.*

Samuel: *In your lack of showing me how to do things I went out and learned how to do it on my own. And then despised you for it. For your neglect, for your selfishness, for your continued adolescence, for your whining, for being a spoiled brat. Your mother would always take care of you and then you got a wife to take care of you. You don't have any friends. You have no friends. No male friends, no female friends. You say what you had was your family. How you dealt with your wife, my mother, and her craziness, was to go deaf and not get a hearing aid. You're disgusting.*

Therapist: *Tell him how he wasted his life.*

Samuel: *Your whole family are bright and creative people. Artists, politicians, nurses, and you were the favorite son, the baby. And you, when things didn't continue to come as easy as they should, you got angry, because what you were used to was for things to come in an easy way. And you weren't going to kiss anyone's ass, which meant you weren't going to cooperate with anyone to get ahead.*

Therapist: *"And I'm your son." Begin to say, "And I'm your son."*

Samuel: *You refused to cooperate with anyone in order to get ahead, and I'm your son. You are used to being spoiled and getting everything you wanted, and not having to work for it, and I'm your son . . .*

Therapist: *What is it that's stopping you now?*

Samuel: *There are things that don't fit.*

Therapist: *Whether things fit or don't fit well will come out with the dream, because you are going to tell him the dream. "And I, your son, am going to tell you a dream I had, because only your son could have this dream. You left me holding your bag." And you can tell him how he left you holding his bag. How are you like him and how are you trying to get away from being like him? Okay? Make more sense?*

Samuel: *I'm going to tell you this dream that I believe is going to help me get a better sense of how I'm holding your bag.*

Therapist: *Right.*

Samuel: *In the dream, I'm in this place that is kind of like a hotel. There's a conference going on with a lot of superstars around. I knew what was going to happen, and that I was going to get what was coming to me as a special gift. Not out of the clear, blue sky, but something that I had worked for, and it was mine.*

Therapist: *Okay, stop right there. Say that again. Pay attention to what you are saying. How you are his son and how you are not his son. Just in that initial introduction.*

Samuel: *Being around a lot of people . . .*

Therapist: *Okay. How are you like him or unlike him being around a lot of people?*

Samuel: *It seems to me that what I know about you when you were younger is that you were well liked and that you did have a lot of friends, and that was when you drank a lot. And you were a lot like your father, my grandfather, in that you were very free with your money, and you enjoyed excitement and dancing and these are things I've been told. I've enjoyed dancing and drinking and being around with a lot of people and excitement. Unlike you, I didn't go to a place or retreat away from people. Unlike you, I like to stay in the background, and I like to serve. Unlike you, I think I've worked hard for a lot of things, some of which I've gotten and some of which haven't come yet. I believe they will. I haven't given up yet.*

Therapist: *What does that mean—"I haven't given up yet"?*

Samuel: *I always feel that that's possible.*

Therapist: *He's leaving you that inheritance, for you to give up? Tell him that: "According to your script, according to your Karma . . . "*

Samuel: *According to what I've experienced with you, you've progressively over the years given up more and more, and your own father did too. He and your mother, according to other people, during the Crash, just gave away lands and money and everything in a crazy manner. So, he gave up. And I've seen you give up. And I have a fear that I'd give up, that I'm burning out. That's scary. I was pretty alone in the dream. I was alone, except for this very special man, this person, but he was in the beginning of the dream.*

Therapist: *And then what happened?*

Samuel: *It's pretty frantic. I'm going running from place to place . . .*

Therapist: *You're going running from place to place and some woman grabs something off of you and puts it under her skirt. What kind of feeling is that?*

Samuel: *Rage. How dare you? That's mine!*

Therapist: *If it's yours, why do you have to run?*

Samuel: *I broke the rules of the agenda. If I were to get mine, it would have to have taken place on stage with the cameras and the pomp and circumstance.*

Therapist: *So why did you have to run?*

Samuel: *I have to take it. I don't trust that I'd get mine.*

Therapist: *He, your son (speaking to the father in the empty chair) can't trust that what he has is really his. Are you having trouble with that?*

Samuel: *As your son, Dad, I can't trust that what I have is really mine. That I really deserve it and that I will be able to keep it.*

Therapist: *"And that I'm entitled to it." Samuel, let's go to the dream. Your vision is that you know exactly how to take this thing and hit it so perfectly at just the right moment that it will crack into six even pieces. In your dream you are that person. You are also another person who is going to grab one of the six pieces and run with it. How is that like your family? How is that like where you come from? How does that tell the story of your family? Does it tell the story in any way?*

Samuel: *My father's side of the family was wealthy, not only materially and with prestige but also in creativity. More so than other families. There were five children in my father's family, of which my father is the second youngest, actually. Youngest boy. And things were divided among them when my grandfather died.*

Therapist: *What did you get from your father, Samuel?*

Samuel: *What comes to mind, what first comes to mind, is arrogance.*

Therapist: *He gave you your arrogance?*

Samuel: *Arrogance and a sort of pride. I was going to say humility and then I think of wimpiness. Sometimes it's humility and sometimes it's wimpiness.*

Therapist: *Yeah. But there are those two aspects in your dream. There's the arrogance of the guy who has the gift. Okay? He knows exactly what he can do . . . how it will work and at just the right moment, he will do it. And then there's the wimpy guy. He has to grab and run. They are both you. The you that you inherited from your father. So, do you feel like you are fully grounded to split that thing in six pieces? And that you can support your arrogance, so that it is fully supported by your skill? You are arrogant in your dream. Is your arrogance supported by your skill?*

Samuel: *Yes.*

Therapist: *Your father was arrogant. Was his arrogance supported by his skill?*

Samuel: *No.*

Therapist: *Well, do you understand that?*

Samuel: *Yes.*

Therapist: *So, I want you to get into the guy that splits that thing. Let someone else grab the sixth piece and run. See what that feels like. You see somebody get five pieces.*

Samuel: *The FBI got a little.*

Therapist: *But see, you're also the FBI. You see, your power is projected on them. The arrogance that is supported by skill is projected on this magical man.*

Samuel: *It's true.*

Therapist: *I want you to close your eyes and meditate on the angle of the moon. Get your feet on the ground, and in front of you will be this gem. This is what your father failed to give you, to support you, to love you. This man who doesn't have a foundation can't give it to his son. I want you to own this. Get into being this man who is fully grounded. Maybe you need to go back to before 1928, to whoever made the original wealth. Get in touch with his groundedness. Is it a he? (Samuel nods.) His groundedness, and his sense of the power and the manliness. What was his name?*

Samuel: *Samuel.*

Therapist: *His name was Samuel? Was that your great grandfather? (Samuel nods.) The original Samuel comes back in your dreams and you skip over all the wienies between the original Samuel and you, and get in contact with him. And this stone that is in front of you belongs to you and the stage belongs to you and the audience belongs to you and the power belongs to you. The knowledge belongs to you. So, are you ready? Imagine yourself standing on a stage and the lights are hitting the sword and you can feel the power and the beauty and the clarity of the whole moment. Enjoy the moment.*

The power is from your great-grandfather to his great-grandson. And when you are ready to make the symbolic move to split that thing, you will do so with ease and with very little strain and don't run because it's your show. Let somebody else run. I'll just be quiet for a while and you just experiment with your sense of readiness and power and the move that you want to make.

(Samuel wields the sword and cleaves the gem.)

Therapist: *How was that?*

Samuel: *There's something natural . . .*

Therapist: *Now look around the room. You see, you can't just stay in your head. Now look around you. (Samuel looks at each person.) Talk with the Samuel that grabbed a piece and ran. You are the master gemcutter. You had an agreement with him. Talk to him. Get the sense of these two different parts of yourself. Did you have to run just now, when you were looking at their faces? Talk back and forth.*

Samuel: *Sam, you really bought . . . you've bought a story that you can settle for less. And the little bit that you think you have, you're afraid that will be taken away . . . at the end of the story . . . I don't know what to do with you . . . (wipes his eyes).*

Therapist: *You know what to do with him. That's what your father would say, "I don't know what to do with you . . . "* Bullshit.

Samuel: *My father wouldn't dare say that.*

Therapist: *You know what I mean. Let him answer, let him answer first, and then you can respond. (Motioning to the empty chair) This is the part of you that grabbed and ran.*

Samuel: *(Switches seats) I really don't have any control, I . . . I was frantic, and what I think, if the dream had gone on, I would have lost it. I would have lost my piece.*

Therapist: *Right. Now you're the master stonecutter over here, great-grandfather Samuel.*

Well, first of all, it's not yours to lose . . . and it's something that in order to have . . . in order to keep it, you have to continue to do something about it. And, it's not running, it's showing it, it's polishing it, it's adding something to it. The way you lose it, is by running with it. And your reward is not in the hereafter.

Therapist: *So say a little more to the group . . . "The way I will do it is not by . . . " Put yourself here (motioning to the chair), "The way I will do it is not by . . . "*

Samuel: *The way I'll do it is not by running away, running with it, not by clutching it so tightly and holding on to it. That's the way I'll lose it. What I need to do is to hold it up, in front of those who can see it, and continue doing some things, to polish it, to continue to keep it, and it's mine.*

Therapist: *How does it feel? Now you can hold it, now you look a little more like you don't have to tremble with it.*

Samuel: *Thank you.*

"Samuel's Dream" is an example of how dreamwork can be used to access intergenerational themes—in this case, how the theme of competence and power are transmitted in varying form from one generation to the next. What is important to note is that even though Samuel's father and great-grandfather were not physically present in the therapy session, the client worked with their *introjected presences* to resolve the struggle within himself.

3c. BASIC ASSUMPTION: *Some subsystems create a lot of energy, and other subsystems have little energy.*
3c. ORIENTING PRINCIPLE: *It is tempting to direct one's attention to the subsystem creating the most energy. Do not be seduced away from subsystems that show little energy. A system is stuck when little energy flows; therefore, attention is needed there.*

In some ways, a family therapist must attend to that which does not appear figural. The parents may be having a loud argument while the teenage children listen respectfully. The natural tendency would be to attend to the parent couple, but what are the children feeling and thinking? At the right moment, the therapist turns to the quieter subsystems to explore the whole family. You might ask the children, "Do you see your parents arguing frequently? What is it like for you when they have a heated argument?" Or you might ask them, "Can you help me understand why your parents are so upset with each other?"

In the above example, no energy flows between the two subsystems. It is apparent to the therapist that the children have been conditioned to stay out of disputes between their parents, which is basically a healthy attitude. But this session is a family affair, and the children's ideas and feelings should be used to understand the larger system. If neglected, the children may lose interest in the family session, and the therapist may not get the opportunity to use them as potential consultants.

Here are some answers the children might give to the therapist's inquiries: "Usually, they don't argue in front of us. They're *so* polite. This is very exciting—Mom and Dad are real!" or "When they get going like this, I get real scared; I think of the worst, like maybe Dad will hurt Mom" or "They go at it like this all the time and nothing ever comes of it—they just get stuck in the same place."

By involving the "silent subsystem," the therapist helps spread the energy, awareness, action, and potential direction of behavior within the whole family.

3d. BASIC ASSUMPTION: *The health of a family is directly related to its capacity to move in and out of its numerous subsystems.*

3d. ORIENTING PRINCIPLE: *The therapist must be alert to fixed gestalten within family subsystems. Triangulations are the most commonly fixed gestalten within families.*[5]

The health of a family is reflected in its ability to shift from adult-adult, adult-child, and child-child interactions, and to freely use every possible combination. Any "fixed" combination that occurs more often than other groupings should be noted and assessed as to its nourishing or poisonous aspects. The most common fixed grouping is of the parents and one child. This can be dysfunctional, preventing the adults from interacting with each other and preventing the child from freely leaving.

Therapists who notice which combinations form and interact easily, and which combinations either never interact or do so with pain, will be cued into the work that needs to be done to enable families to move smoothly into and out of interactions. Here is where experiment is most useful and people can experience new behaviors and feelings.

> 3e. BASIC ASSUMPTION: *The children in a family form a powerful subsystem of their own. The degree of health in their subsystem has a strong impact of family functioning.*
>
> 3e. ORIENTING PRINCIPLE: *An important task of the family therapist is to recognize and support the children's subsystem.*

Children need to interact with each other, not only with the adults. There is power in children forming a society of their own. In addition to bonding, the sheer presence of models from whom to observe and learn teaches children how to cope. This does not mean that children must relate smoothly or that their relationships are free of difficulty; at times siblings can be very mean to each other. Nevertheless, a lot of learning about living takes place with their peers. Children may be frightened by unpleasant moments, but when they have a group they belong to and feel attached to, they can overcome these potentially traumatic experiences.

I have known and worked with numerous families where the parental system was in poor shape, including some with severely disturbed parents, and the children's society proved to be the source of support for the growth of the children into accomplishing and reasonably happy adults. This is particularly true where there are at least three or four children in the family.

Now that families are smaller, with many single-child families, I hear numerous wistful comments from parents that they wish their only child had brothers and sisters to "bounce things off of." This shows recognition of the need for sibling or peer interactions, including the sharing of feelings and complaints about the parents. If a child does not have a sibling with whom to do this, it can work equally well with a friend. Whatever the interchild combination, the formation of a children's society appears to be a natural wish or need of children. This is especially obvious at the adolescent age level, where peer-group issues are all-powerful, but it is equally critical at earlier ages.

Teachers and other educators show they understand this in focusing on the social development of students. Today, it is interesting to see the formation of single-parent groups, indicating the need to compensate for gaps in the parental society. Thus, we assume the healthy pattern at all age levels is for people to create and take part in a society with its own special language, communication patterns, and norms, and that the children in any family need to be able to do this as part of their healthy development.

4. Parent-Child Dynamics

Parent-child dynamics include a wide range of interactions.

> 4a. Basic Assumption: *The dosage of protection used by parents with children is an indicator of family health.*
> 4a. Orienting Principle: *To develop a healthy family, it is important to do "parent therapy" as part of family interventions.*

An infant will die if it is not fed and protected.[6] When children are little, the amount of protection has to be total. As families grow, the protection should diminish. The amount of protection must change with the age of the children. Both too much and too little protection are damaging. For example, if you ask a question of a three- or four-year-old and the parent steps in and answers because the child is shy, that is appropriate protection. The small child who is shy with a stranger should not have to answer. However, we have a totally different response if we ask a question of a shy eleven- or twelve-year-old and the parent steps in to answer.

As a child grows, parents must let go of their inclination always to step in to protect the child. An eleven- or twelve-year-old child has to be able to deal with people outside the family, including the therapist. With a child of that age, the parents should know that a therapy session is a comparatively safe situation. What are they protecting in a child of this age who understands the situation? On the other hand, a three- or four-year-old does not understand the therapy situation and cannot perceive the therapist as potentially safe, because there is no prior context for understanding. A parent who would say, "Go ahead, talk!" to a child of this age clearly has no sense of the needs and resources of a very young child.

This particular dimension, where we see too much or too little protection, is one of the most critical in dysfunctional families. Every family makes mistakes. Every family protects too much or too little in particular instances. This is not damaging. There is a middle range in which we can all grow up healthy. Nobody ever gets it quite right because there is no perfection. However, most healthy people who protect too much will notice it and move back a bit, and if they protect too little they'll increase it. Healthy parents are always moving in that wide middle range, and there is a general aesthetic sense in their trying to get it right.

When you see a problem in this area, it probably means that a lot of work has to be done on the adult system. The most obvious thing is to heighten the parents' awareness of what they are modeling, because children learn what it is like to be adults from their parents. It is also critical because the children's fear is crippling without a healthy adult system. There is no way they can sustain the amount of fear they have without the security of healthy parents.

School phobia is a good example of a dysfunction in this family dynamic. The child simply cannot leave home, and the parents cannot let the child go to school. What it takes to separate them is pure, brute strength because that six-year-old has to go to school. The point is, you *know* you have trouble if the child is already six and cannot leave. If a three-year-old is still hanging on in a strange situation and the parents say, "Stay here, it's okay," the therapist need not be concerned as long as the child begins to move away as it gets more comfortable.

Children start out by holding on tightly and looking out in the world. If they feel safe enough, they let go and wander out a small distance. Then they get scared and run back, hide behind parents, and peek out again. As soon as their fear subsides, out again they go. Children need to have a place to run back to, where no one is scaring them with "Be careful, be careful" and increasing the sense of danger. So long as they are able to return to safety and wait for the fear to fade away and as long as nobody minds if they let go to venture out further, that distance slowly increases as the years go by.

> 4b. Basic Assumption: *Children should be watching and listening to the adults' process. It is not healthy for them to be participants in, or "enablers" of, this process.*
>
> 4b. Orienting Principle: *The family therapist works toward having the adults take full responsibility for adult roles and toward eliminating "enablement" on the part of the children.*

Children should be the bystanders to the adults' process. They should be watching; they should be listening. In a healthy family, the children wander off to play with each other when the therapist is talking to the parents. This adult segment of the session is not interesting to the children and should not be. The children will stay within earshot and eyesight and, if it gets interesting, they will be back. The parents are comfortable enough to let the children go so long as they see it is to a safe place and they are protected. But they do not need to have an eye on them or to be listening keenly all the time. They can hold on lightly to that boundary.

On the practical side, it is important to have crayons, paper, and a few toys or books around so that the children can come and go. The therapist can show them how they can leave the room and come back at any time. The children will usually test this once or twice to see that it is so, and then they are fine.

Dysfunction occurs when children are constantly drawn into the parenting function. This is perhaps most commonly seen in families with an alcoholic parent (or parents). The parents no longer function as adults. In such families, having the children act as enablers of the parenting functions is sometimes the best possible solution. It is not wonderful, but somebody has to be an adult in the family.

I treated a single-parent family in which the mother was almost completely dysfunctional. The eleven-year-old boy had to say, "Mom, it's time to get dinner on the table," or "Mom, make sure you sign the report cards so we can get them back to school on time." This child assumed an enabling role for the adult. Was it good for this child? No, it wasn't. But it was a lot better than if nobody had done it. Therapeutic interventions focused on getting the mother to resume her parenting role, so that the child could release the enabling role.

It is tragic when children cannot behave as children. The level of enabling is a clue to how frightened they are and the degree to which they have retroflected that fear.

> 4c. Basic Assumption: *In healthy families, it is clear where the power lies; it is firmly in the hands of the adults.*
> 4c. Orienting Principle: *Whenever there is unequal power, it needs to be managed well.*

Power issues are likely in a family, since there are built-in inequities among individual family members and subsystems. In healthy families, the adults have more power and use it in a manner appropriate to the age of the children. They use more power with young children and less power with older children. There are two major difficulties in an unhealthy family:

1. There is no clear focus of power, no leader-follower principle, so family life is chaotic.
2. The power is abused in that it is applied inappropriately in relation to the age of the children involved. For example, young children are beaten and older children are inappropriately overcontrolled.

Therapists provide a model for the use of power. By virtue of their role in the family, therapists can be more or less powerful in terms of approving or disapproving and prescribing solutions, viewpoints, and values about family life. This power has to be managed well; the healthier the family, the less power therapists need to use. Disorganized families require therapists to take more power and stronger leadership to nudge the family into more adaptive behavior that encourages the family to act more cohesively.

The Millers: A Case Study

The Miller family consists of the parents, Arthur and Jean, who are in their forties, their eighteen-year-old son, Rick, and their fifteen-year-old daughter, Gail. The father is vice president of human resources in a small publishing company, and the mother is a nurse. Rick is in his first year of college, and Gail is a high school student.

This family came into therapy because the daughter was withdrawing, staying in her room, and not socializing. Her friends had expressed concern about her. Recently, when her father called Gail to come downstairs to dinner, she did not respond. He knocked on her door and called her name, but she did not answer. When he knocked louder and tried to get in, she finally responded. When she opened the door, she looked ill. Also, the parents received a call from Gail's teacher, who felt that the girl's work was going downhill and that she was not taking care of her appearance. Her hair was not clean and she had lost a lot of weight.

The daughter in this family is known in our kind of work as the "IP," the identified patient. In family work, we do not focus on the IP. We focus on the family as a group of people who get together to create difficulty or success. The IP, then, is the family member who "volunteers" to express the pain that exists in the family.

Our first assumption is that a healthy family supports itself, and the first thing the therapist wants to do is to help the family see what they do well as a family.

In the first session, the parents were forthright in talking to each other about Gail's problems and their feelings of helplessness in not knowing what to do to change her behavior. Gail talked when her brother asked her about her weight loss and dropping out of her after-school activities, but she only spoke to reassure everyone that she was okay.

At the end of the first session, we tell the Millers what they do well. We comment on the great amount of concern expressed and about how the parents are particularly good at talking to each other about what is wrong. The children also seem to be able to say things to each other to express some of their concerns. The goodness is that the family does express internal concern; especially within these two subsystems, they do it very well.

In subsequent sessions, the flip side became apparent. The parents do not engage the children, nor do the children engage the parents, with questions and with confrontations. There is a kind of confluence within each system and no free interaction between the parents and the children. The son and daughter are good friends with each other, making a strong, collaborative team. Mom and dad are a strong subsystem. The weak link is the interaction between the children and the parents. There is almost a fearfulness in the children's faces when it comes to expressing their feelings. They usually glance at their parents to see if it is okay to speak.

In the past, the parents were concerned with their own careers and taking care of each other. They did not focus as much on the needs of the children, so the children were forced to be more or less on their own. The children became playmates and learned to take care of each other. This was because the emphasis of mom and dad was on the children learning to entertain themselves rather than be "entertained" by the parents.

In the last year, the family's life cycle changed when Rick started college. Although he chose a local college so that he could live at home and be near Gail, most of his time is spent studying or being with friends. Arthur and Jean are at the height of their careers, enjoying the success that comes from years of hard work. Gail, being the shyer of the two children, did not use the other girls in the high school to rally support for herself in the absence of direct support, coaching, and encouragement from her parents. She feels alone, lonely, and pseudoindependent: she does not really want to be independent, but that is the situation she finds herself in.

To encourage a stronger subsystem between parents and children, we would make the following comments to the family.

Therapist: *Rick and Gail, you are very strong when you're talking to each other. You're really expressive. And Jean and Arthur, you're consulting each other very well. But I notice that you kids don't say much to your parents, and Mom and Dad, you don't say much to your kids. We encourage you to ask each other questions and to challenge each other and to talk more directly to each other. Let's see if you can do that.*

We would start with a general invitation and see how well they do. If they have difficulty, we can create experiments. For example:

Therapist: *I've given you encouragement to talk to your parents and for you parents to talk to your kids, but you seem to be stymied, and you always turn back to each other. So here's what I'd like you to do: I'd like both parents to talk to each other, while Rick and Gail listen.*

What we are doing here is isolating a particular subsystem and giving the other subsystem directions to listen in. That first subsystem will be used as an example of how to talk with each other. And we might say:

Therapist: *You can talk about anything that matters to both of you, as the males in the family, and I'll just listen in. If you get stuck, I'll help you out.*

At first, father and son falter. Arthur has trouble asking Rick about what is happening at school because he does not have enough information to ask meaningful questions. And then, eventually, Rick starts talking about how he has always missed his dad getting involved in soccer when he played in high school. Rick begins to cry and tells his dad how sad he always was that his dad was always too busy to come to the games. And Arthur becomes emotional, too; he puts his hand on his son's shoulder and tells him that he is sorry—he was so busy working and trying to make a living that it did not even occur to him that being at his son's game would be a good idea. Jean then tries to interrupt:

Jean: *Yes, your dad used to have a very hard time at work.*

Therapist: *(Interrupting her) Excuse me, but would you please stay out of this interaction. Arthur and Rick are talking now. You'll have your chance to talk with your daughter.*

The Millers are protective of themselves as a family in that they do not let a lot of outsiders into the family. It is not a very gregarious family. But they are not protective of each individual child. In fact, in that sense, they are overly permissive. In allowing the children a certain degree of independence, they do not always check out what is going on with them and, therefore, have no sense when they are in pain vis-à-vis a broken relationship with a boyfriend or girlfriend or anything like that. So, in some ways, this family is paradoxical. They stay isolated as a total family. But they allow their children to move into the world, and that creates a sense of loneliness in the children, who are missing satisfying contacts with their parents.

The boundaries—along with the definition of the family—have been changing since the son entered college. Now that the children are trying to be more autonomous, the parents are becoming a couple. The daughter, with her symptoms of depression, is forcing them to be a family again. In a sense, they all rally to help her. While Gail may be the IP, the family dysfunction is the lack of interaction and energy between certain subsystems. The low-energy subsystems are mother and son, father and son, and father and daughter.

One way to redistribute the family's energy is to encourage family members to cross old boundaries and create new subsystems. The therapist might make an intervention like the following.

Therapist: *Well, Rick, how do you feel about what your mother is saying? Do you want to tell your parents how you feel about it?*

That is, if they are not biting on the bait of doing it spontaneously, you can set up a situation where the father is asked to talk with his son, or the mother is asked to talk with her son, or whatever combination you want to play with.

As you saw in the previous example, energy is increased

and the interactions are enlivened. The son did not have to feel sad. For example, he could have expressed anger: "*Now* you're asking me questions? For four years in high school I had a rough time on the team and sat on the bench all the time. Where were you then?" And then they have a big fight. In terms of energy mobilization, it does not matter to the therapist whether they cry together or fight together. What matters is that energy is heightened in that subsystem and, therefore, contact becomes stronger and more vibrant. This happened when mother and daughter were asked to talk together. Jean was trying to cajole Gail into talking about her friends at school, when Rick broke in:

Rick: *You know, you're being very sweet with Gail, but she's been depressed for a long time while you've been working extra hours at the hospital and didn't give a damn about her breaking up with her boyfriend and how upset she was about that. Now you're sweet and wonderful to her!*

After this is over, the therapist is able to say:

Therapist: *I'm so glad that you're able to talk to each other in this new way. I trust you all much more when you're able to mind each other's business for a change. Sometimes in good families you have to mind somebody's business when they're in pain.*

In this family, the retroflective quality is such that when someone is in pain he or she does not ask for help, and someone else in the family who sees the pain does not offer help. The retroflection in this family was not immediately apparent because one of the strongest cultural assumptions for Jean and Arthur is a sense of responsibility to others. Both chose "caretaking" professions, and both have been very successful. But after long days at the office and hospital, they had only minimal energy left for each other and almost none for supporting their children. When they first entered therapy, the parents presented one image: now that we are in therapy, we must show concern and caring for our daughter in the presence of the therapist, because that is the image we want to project as loving parents.

When Rick and Gail began to talk about their own experiences and feelings, a different picture emerged.

The last basic assumption is that even though no family is going to operate perfectly, and there are some families that will not ever achieve optimal functioning, as a therapist you want to acknowledge that there are some things that are simply "good enough" for this family. You want to find a way to celebrate with them the good process they have achieved, even if everything is not resolved.

Therapist: *In an intimate relationship, one of your freedoms is to complain to somebody you love if you're feeling bad, or sick, or whatever.*

So the Millers begin to practice complaining to each other about ordinary things. For the first time, Gail starts telling her mother about how hard it has been in school and how, ever since her breakup with her boyfriend, it has been difficult for her to concentrate on her work. And Jean then is able to tell her daughter stories about when she was in high school and had trouble with a boyfriend. Now, for the first time, Jean and Gail are starting to share things with each other.

The "good enough" quality is that the daughter is less and less isolated and does not have to carry the problem of feeling bad about her boyfriend and her schoolwork on her own shoulders. Her mom, dad, and brother are able to carry some of the pain for themselves and, therefore, she loses her status as the IP. The IP problems are literally spread around among the other members of the family. When dad comes home from work and Gail is studying, he goes up to her room and asks her how her day has been, and Gail allows him to do that now that she is no longer so private.

There is more normal interaction in the family. The paradox here is that teenagers should be more independent and should be allowed to move away from home. So the temptation for this couple might be to pull the kids back in while in the process of fixing this problem. And what they will find challenging is to make good contact with the kids and eventually let go of them. When Gail finds a new boyfriend, hopefully her parents will support her to enjoy her new relationship. When adolescents feel closer to their parents and more secure, they can move away more easily because they feel grounded in their home. Looking at it from that point of view, they should be able to have more courage to move into the world, because they feel loved and cared for in a more concrete way by their parents.

Conclusion

This chapter has presented basic assumptions and orienting principles that can guide therapists in conducting Gestalt psychotherapy with families. Again, I have emphasized the importance of recognizing a family's competence and what constitutes "good enough" functioning. The chapter stressed the arrangement of boundaries in a given family that is fitting to its particular developmental tasks. I showed how the "heat" of being an identified patient can be redistributed in the whole family, thus relieving one member from carrying the pain for everybody else. The work, as I hopefully made evident, focuses a family's attention and awareness on itself and emphasizes the family's capacity and courage to heal.

Achieving therapeutic change within a family system is a complex and challenging task, even with the assistance of the theory, lenses, and techniques such as the ones this book provides. And this is as it should be, since the addition of a single person into a system increases the complexity of the possible interactions geometrically. Nowhere is this more true than when the couple or family is dealing with such complex transactional issues as lying and truthfulness, or traumatic life events such as the loss of a member, which will be taken up in the next two chapters. But, as has been hopefully made clear throughout the book, your task, while arduous, is not impossible as long as you are grounded in the fundamentals of seeing, thinking, and experiencing human systems. We now turn to the impact of truth and falsity within intimate systems.

Notes to Chapter Nine

1. See Chapter Five.
2. See Chapter Three.
3. This is a technique in Gestalt therapy in which an alienated part of the self is put into an empty chair so that the person can engage in a dialogue with that part to achieve reintegration. This technique was popularized by Fritz Perls to such an extent that it eventually became synonymous with Gestalt therapy in the mind of the public, much to our collective misfortune.
4. Excerpted with permission from J. Andrews, D. Clark, & J. Zinker (1988), "Accessing transgenerational themes through dreamwork," *Journal of Marital and Family Therapy, 14*(1), 15–27. The coauthors of this paper are Gestalt therapists trained at different, long-established Gestalt Institutes in Los Angeles, Chicago, and Cleveland, Ohio. All have moved in the direction of systems thinking in their clinical practice, whether it be the Intimate Systems of Couples (J. Zinker and S. Nevis) or the Gestalt Integrated Family Therapy (GIFT) model (J. Andrews and D. Clark).
5. According to H. J. Aponte & J. M. VanDeusen (1991), "Structural family therapy," in A. S. Gurman & D. P. Kniskern (Eds.), *Handbook of family therapy* (Vol. 1) (New York: Brunner/Mazel, p. 314), triangulation is a form of "coalition" in which "each of two opposing parties seeks to join with the same person against the other, with the third party finding it necessary, for whatever reasons, to cooperate now with one and now with another of these opposing parties" (p. 314).
6. For more information on parent-child dynamics, see "Why Children? A conversation with Edwin Nevis, Sonia Nevis, and Joseph Zinker" (1984, Spring), *News* (Center for the Study of Intimate Systems, Gestalt Institute of Cleveland), *4*(1), 1–3. For an informative videotape on Gestalt family therapy, see C. O. Harris & S. M. Nevis, *Gestalt family therapy,* produced by the Center for the Study of Intimate Systems of the Gestalt Institute of Cleveland in collaboration with Harriet Harvey Enterprises and Herbert Wolf, producer.

10

Lying and Truthfulness in Intimate Systems

One lie can kill a thousand truths.
—West African proverb

Our parents taught us, categorically, not to lie. Were they right? They were right that it is important not to lie *to them.* The parent-child relationship is an intimate one, and lying to an intimate is damaging. However, what most parents did not tell us is that not all of life is an intimate situation. Intimacy is where we get our emotional nourishment and, without intimacy, our lives become barren. But most relationships *are not* intimate.

Note: The basic material for this chapter appeared in the form of a conversation between Sonia Nevis and Joseph Zinker. See "Lies in intimate systems" (1981, Spring), *News* (Center for the Study of Intimate Systems, Gestalt Institute of Cleveland), *1*(2), 1–2.

Lying or truth-telling has no meaning without a context. The statement, "I am a Jew," means different things to different people. What does this statement mean to a person with a gun who is controlling the piloting of a transatlantic airliner? What does it mean to a gentle priest studying the Talmud? What does it mean when spoken to one's child? What does it mean when uttered by a newly converted woman to her Catholic mother? What does it mean to an immigration officer in Tel Aviv, in Egypt, in Moscow? How was it understood by an SS doctor in Buchenwald? How is it experienced by a close friend?

The worth or awfulness of lying and truth-telling is discussed here not so much with a concern for defining lying and truth-telling, not with a concern for ethics or morality, but with a particular interest in *relationships* between people.

The essence of intimacy is knowing another and being known by another. To be known for one's Jewishness by a close friend may be very different from being known as a Jew by a stranger on a plane. In this context, we are not talking about lies and truths in the epistemological or moral sense—let philosophers do that.[1] Lying and telling it as it is are examined here as phenomena affecting the solidity or looseness of intimacy. They are seen not as monolithic concepts but as complex processes—as vehicles that carry one toward or away from intimacy. To tell the truth is to struggle.

Learning to Lie

It is important for us to know that we do not have to be known, that we do not have to tell the truth to everybody who asks it of us.

Sometimes, at a party, perhaps while drinking too much, we "spill our guts" to an acquaintance, only to feel uncomfortable after we sober up the next morning. The reason for this is that each of us has a psychological boundary within which we feel safe and contained. We feel fully ourselves within this border. Internal dialogues (which are perfectly normal) go on within this boundary for those of us who have some deep knowledge of ourselves, our needs, motives, and conflicts. We make continual judgments about what "stays inside" and what feels comfortable to share "outside." Even with close friends, some things feel like "better form" to keep inside. We always operate with boundaries, the permeability of which is controlled by who and how we wish to be with different people under different circumstances.

Lying has to do with an old tenet of survival, and we practice this skill in many innocent ways. Here is a survival experience of a sixteen-year-old boy found in a tent in a girls' camp at night: "The director of the camp, who looked like he was eight feet tall, walked in and barked, 'What are you doing here?' I could not offer a reason that would not get me into big trouble, so I started talking Yiddish. I talked Yiddish a mile-a-minute until he finally threw me out. To have told the director why I was there would have involved a total stranger in intimate content. He couldn't know me in that moment in the context of an intimate."[2]

A close friend is having a love affair with a married woman. Another friend asks if this is so. What do you do? How can you be truthful with one friend and not betray another's confidence? It is hard to be discreet gracefully. You may answer, "I'd like to tell you what I know, but I'm not at liberty to talk to you about something that doesn't belong to me" and thereby thread the eye of the needle.

Truth-telling is a leap of trust. I have to trust it will be received gently. If I tell a stranger on the airplane, "I am a psychologist. I've worked very hard all weekend and I'm tired. I would rather not talk right now," will that truth be received as gently as it is offered? If not, if the person feels offended and tightens up, we will both have to suffer the tension between us for the length of the flight. Sometimes it is simpler, and often wiser, to lie or to avoid telling the truth by being silent.

Lying to an Intimate

What happens when one lies to an intimate?[3] A lie immediately creates a distance between the sender and the receiver. It says,

"I don't want to be known by you." Often people say, "I lied so as not to hurt him." This is probably a projection, since what is actually being expressed is the fear of *being hurt* in retaliation by the person who was deceived or betrayed. So we protect ourselves from the hurt of our own truth.

If you are having a love affair while committed to a spouse, to keep the affair from your spouse is to create distance between yourself and that person. The third person is now like a wedge between the two of you. Problems that drove you to the affair are not confronted in the primary relationship and, instead, are dealt with indirectly with the new partner.

To lie is to decide not to know another and not to become known in some special way by one's intimate. There are all kinds of complex reasons why we may decide not to be known, but the other person will generally experience it as a loss. When we "protect" someone we love, we also lose a part of the relationship that is potentially precious, powerful, or enriching. It is regrettable; it is a loss.

The lie not only separates and alienates, it also takes away another's choice to experience and act on a shared reality. The lie takes away another's freedom to react and respond to the "actuality" of the relationship and leaves him or her in a limbo of responding to what "appears" to exist in the relationship.

If, for example, you were driven to another because of a sexual problem with your partner, your partner does not get to talk about his or her side of the problem, to confront you with your side of the difficulty, or to offer help to resolve it. In addition, your partner does not get to experience the anger, dismay, or disappointment of your betrayal or to act in response to those feelings.

The most common falsehoods or distortions of truth in couples have to do with money and sexual relations with third parties.

Lies, or lack of disclosure, about money have to do with maintaining control or power over another. In some traditional marriages, husbands do not reveal their financial holdings to their wives and simply deposit prearranged sums into their wives' accounts. In more contemporary marriages, the situation is not as simple, since many women work outside the home and contribute financially to the running of the household.

Secretiveness about sexual encounters outside of the relationship has similar characteristics. The "acting out" partner maintains control and power over the other by not sharing. The "unknowing" partner is not given a choice to respond, to threaten, to carry on, to cry and stomp around, to leave the relationship, or to take similar liberties outside of the relationship. The lie maintains a status quo within the couple.

Some therapists believe that the *couple* unwittingly colludes to invite a third person (triangulation)—a kind of "sexual therapist"—to aid them in maintaining the stability of a weak or failing intimate relationship. I have seen evidence of this in some cases where the *whole community* is aware of one partner's indiscretions, but, since the spouse never asks revealing questions, the affair is reinforced and perpetuated. Husband and wife live in silent agony and alienation, often for years and years.

Systems theory appears to hold that the "lied-to" unwittingly colludes with the liar by, for example, not confronting the spouse about various matters. People may not always push their spouses about their income or other financial matters. But if the "lied-to" spouse is simply not able to frame a situation as deceptive, how is he or she able to formulate a confrontation without feeling "crazy" or "paranoid"? Yet there is an expression: "If you feel paranoid, perhaps someone *is* trying to get you!"[4]

Spouses rarely confront each other because they appear not to want to know. The knowledge is denied, pushed away, and repressed because it is so painful. Whether truth is withheld about sexual encounters, money, or anything else of significance to the couple, the result is almost always a loss of closeness and intimacy.

Choosing Between the Truth and the Lie

When you withhold something important from a loved one, you must carry it by yourself, along with your guilt and self-reproach. This withholding focuses you on yourself and feels weighty and solitary. The lie or the withholding keeps you isolated. A great sadness and a sense of emptiness envelop you and, because you have turned away from your loved one, you have no one to comfort you.

The difficult truth has its own consequences. If shared in a close relationship, it can be discussed and examined from every vantage point. It is carried by at least two persons. You become known by the other in a new way. This new knowledge may make you appear more complex or more difficult by the other and, consequently, your intimate may be deeply moved or deeply disappointed. Your partner may possibly show you a different part of his or her nature stimulated by this new knowledge of you. In the space between the two of you a new form is born. This relational work may be filled with feelings, thoughts, and sentiments not previously encountered between you.

The lie isolates. The truth may also isolate, depending on what response is evoked, but truth-telling does have the potential for unifying, for bringing people together, for forming deeper sharing.

When it comes to intimate relationships, life does not promise us simple outcomes; it offers no guaranteed successes. There are no linear formulas for what happens between people. But we must go on trying to be the best people we can become, for as Epictetus said: "But what says Socrates?—'One man finds pleasure in improving his land, another his horses. My pleasure lies in seeing that I myself grow better day by day.'"[5]

Trusting the Truth

We begin relationships with lies or "little truths" by simplifying what we know of ourselves and the other. We say things like, "You have beautiful eyes" or "I am a psychologist." These are lies because we do not tell the other all that we see, nor do we tell much about what we think and feel.

Trust grows when we have repeated experiences of successful interaction, when we share something, develop a theme, and have a sense of satisfaction and resolution at the end. As intimacy grows, we are able to tell more and more of the truth, more than the bare bones of our feelings and thoughts.

Truth is fat, full, complex. If someone you care about asks you, "Do you love me?," to really answer might take an afternoon to say all that you feel. When you tell the truth, you have to push yourself to articulate just how you feel and what you think. It is hard to tell the truth because you do not always like what you feel or know what you think until you say it; nor do you know how it will be received until it is said. Telling the truth is painting the entire picture:

> Well, I love your mind—how it simplifies important things. Yet, sometimes, I find it difficult when you are righteous about what you know. It's the righteous part that puts me off. I suppose that's because I don't like my own righteousness.
>
> And I love how you teach: loud and clear and bold—a student can feel secure with you.
>
> Your passion is special for me. Sometimes you surprise me with your matter-of-factness. You say, "I have two things to get done tonight: to review a manuscript with you and then to make love with you—how would that be for you"? You take me aback, then you warm me up. You charm me.
>
> You have a way of objectifying sentiment.
>
> You are graceful most of the time. Actually, I have never seen you move heavily. You walk and dance gracefully. You swim gracefully. Only once, when you were teaching some advanced students and one of them asked a provocative question, you became defensive and lost your grace.
>
> I love your confrontations and your complaints. They mobilize and enliven me. But when I travel, I have trouble taking your complaints on the phone. I can't take it when I can't see your face and when my energy is low.

This is just a snippet of the work of truth-telling to an intimate. Even with the greatest effort of truth-telling, there is editing and minimal "lying"—leaving out things that are too painful to say aloud or that break good form, or emphasizing the strong side of love to fit a special event like a birthday or anniversary. Modulation of what and how something is communicated is part of the work of truth-telling.

We can dismiss someone with a quick lie, but to tell the truth implies telling the whole story, searching for the fitting words that represent our actual experience. It takes *time* to share the actual experience. Intimacy is hard to come by.

When something is revealed and suddenly we feel too well known, exposed, hurt, or betrayed, if there is not time spent repairing the tear—the rent in the emotional fabric—lies reappear to help cushion the contact. We pull back by telling lies, by not saying something, by simplifying something, by avoiding or changing the subject. We have to attend to both the telling and the receiving of truth—it cannot be done on the run.

How can we receive truth well? It depends on how well grounded, how anchored, one is in oneself, in one's center, and how strong one feels, as opposed to being vulnerable and caught off guard. Under ideal conditions, let the other's statement wash over you without jumping in and responding prematurely. Let the other speak fully. Let yourself enjoy the goodness of the words and the phrases that fit, and let the things that do not fit, or that feel painful, stand without swallowing them. Put them aside to think about at a future time when you may feel sober and uninvolved; try the fit then and see what happens. If, at that time, the statements still do not make sense, you have two choices:

1. Ask questions for greater clarification.
2. Throw the material in a psychological garbage bin for things that feel "indigestible" and not worth pursuing even with an intimate friend.

The Truth as "Poison"

We always suspect the person who begins a sentence with, "To tell you the truth . . . " This throwaway line is sometimes an arrow meant to hurt your pride or your sense of being a good person. Such "truths" are often used to hurt and abuse others.

"To tell you the truth, I don't care *what* you do . . . "
"To tell you the truth, I don't care about you very much . . . "
"To tell you the truth, I don't care if you stay or go . . . "
"To tell you the truth, you have been less on my mind than the daily newspaper . . . "
"To tell you the truth, people have been saying that you always compromise yourself . . . "

Telling the truth can be mean and hurtful when the intention is to hurt. This intention may not even be in our awareness. To tell a painful truth in an atmosphere of tenderness, caring, or regret can have an effect totally different from the pain brought by the intention to hurt. It is not that the kindly telling hurts less, but rather that the gentle sharing may have a better chance of transforming the hurt into a richer knowing, a sadness, a wisdom about the way things are versus a *freezing out,* a protection, a defense. In a fully intimate situation, difficult truths can be told if their full complexity can be acknowledged. It is not inevitable that we close off from each other; we may grow sadder and wiser from it.

Lying and Truthfulness in a Therapeutic Relationship

Therapy is a one-way intimate relationship. The therapist makes himself or herself known only in small ways to the client. This is done to keep the client free of interference from any parentlike influences of the therapist. The therapist keeps a clear field (tabula rasa) for the phenomena of the couple or family to write on.

This is not a formal principle of psychotherapy. It is simply a practical matter that ensures that the couple or family uses the therapy hour to work on *its* problems, *its* places of stuckness. Therefore, the degrees of truth-telling or lying belong to the couple or family. It is the couple's or family's truth, their way of conducting their lives and their way of talking to each other that will interest the therapy. Thus psychotherapy is a one-way intimacy in the sense that the therapist may not openly share his or her own soul searching or personal pain with clients.

Then how does the therapist's truth-telling or lying reveal itself in therapy? The therapist's interventions are based on hard data, observed in the interactive space between the couple or family. In this context, the "truth" is as good as the observed data. In saying to a couple, "It seems to me that you, Josh, make the pronouncements, and you, Sally, listen and ask questions," a therapist is simply reporting to the couple what is seen and heard. "Keep talking," the practitioner may say, "and pay attention to this and see if it's true for you." Or the clinician could ask a question: "Does this pattern happen at home, or am I observing something unique in this situation?" The therapist is the camera. His or her "truth" is what is there.

In this context, lying by the therapist can take the form of interventions *not* based on phenomenological data. If the therapist says, "You two don't know what a couple is," he or she may be responding to some kind of personal emotional displeasure and not to what is happening within the couple. To that extent, the therapist is lying. On the other hand, if the therapist states, "You have trouble listening to each other" and substantiates this statement with concrete examples, the therapist is coming as close as possible to the truth of the actual, immediate situation. Based on the knowledge that listening well is a necessary skill for couples, the therapist reports what is actually seen and heard, and what the couple can receive and chew on, and possibly change.

The drama of the earlier statement, "You two don't know what a couple is," puts the couple on the defensive, focuses them on the person of the therapist, and mobilizes hearty resistance. Even though the therapist may think this thought while sitting with a young, immature couple, it is the therapist's responsibility to select the truth that is digestible by the couple, that which is simple and concrete and that implies a tangible, remedial skill to improve their situation.

Both the dramatic statement and the more concrete observation may have truth in them, but the dramatic one is much too hard a truth to digest, much less swallow, even if it can be substantiated.

The therapist chooses something small, "wraps it in chocolate," and delivers it for manageable consumption in an ego-syntonic learning experience. In this sense, the therapist's tactical knowledge, awareness of proper dosage, and a general sense of delivering statements of good form may be called *manipulations*. Every time we say something well and have an impact, every time we generate enthusiasm for change, we manipulate. It is our job, not a dirty word.

Manipulation becomes a dirty word when we cut through clients' resistance, do not speak directly to their awareness, and produce behavioral results that, while expedient, they did not actively participate in. This, then, may be a form of deceit, a form of lying—even a kind of betrayal—in the sense that the therapist does not honor the clients' wishes and experience.

What about the lying of an individual client within the couple or that of an individual subsystem of the family? How is that phenomenon understood? What is the therapist's role in these matters of deceptive behavior in couples and families? The therapist does not hand out truth-telling contracts to sign. There is no oath taken under penalty of perjury. Nor is it the therapist's role to determine what is distorted or lied about and to correct it by revealing "how it really is." The therapist's role is to help members of the couple or family to talk well together and to create a *process* by which individuals do not become mired in their communications and so learn how to overcome hurdles.

Repeated successful experiences of talking and working out problems reinforce trust. When truth-telling is successfully achieved, again and again, the couple or family is progressively prepared for the more difficult and painful revealing of heretofore hidden truths. So the therapist's task is to build a strong and smooth process within which thoughts and feelings can be shared safely without undue fear of catastrophic results.

We must remember that not telling the truth is an effective counterweight in an autocratic system where power is misused or abused. Children will lie to parents who do not honor truth-telling, who punish if it is not the "right" truth—a truth they do not want to hear, one that threatens their own narcissistically based values, images, and perceptions. Some wives lie to survive battering. Some husbands lie because they may not trust their wives' intentions or motives.

The therapist lives in a soup of little lies, big lies, distortions, ordinary truths, and ugly truths. In everyday practice, these matters are there all the time. We take the client system as it exists and, most of the time, we do not pronounce judgments. We do not advertise ourselves as priests or rabbis, but as problem solvers. We assume that there are reasons why people lie and we do not assume that truth-telling is categorically good in relationships that are less than intimate. It is the good process we support; not *what* should be confessed or revealed.

The therapist has the reward of helping to achieve, and share in, deeply satisfying resolutions in couples and families. The price the therapist pays is that he or she alone may carry the variety of difficult stories, truths, and lies that cannot be shared during the process of therapy. The sharing must take place within the boundaries of the couple or family. The stories do not belong to the therapist and are not his or hers to reveal outside of those boundaries.

Beware of the uncompromising "truth teller." He or she is either stupid, naive, or mercilessly cruel. "Truth" is used in all sorts of ways, for different purposes, and with different motives. Truth can hurt as well as heal.

How to Tell the Truth

The sharing of information takes place between two or more people. First, you must ask yourself, what are my motives for saying what I need to say? What do I want to accomplish by having said this? Before saying anything at all, you need to look at the other and ask yourself, "How well supported is this person to receive my truth?" In terms of your relationship, you may want to ask yourself, "How will it affect our relationship?" Aside from yourself, you want to be concerned for the other person and with your relationship—the "third entity" that makes you a couple. Here are some basic "how to's":

- Tell the truth gently and kindly while keeping an eye on the other's vulnerability.
- Tell the truth without an iota of righteousness or flippancy.

- Tell the truth when the other is grounded and not on the run between things.
- Tell the truth in a climate of contactfulness while being well connected with the other.
- Tell the truth compassionately (the way you would have it told to you).
- Tell the truth out of the clarity of your true motives and the clarity of *what the truth is* for you at that moment.

The truth is the "air" breathed by the relationship, keeping it alive and vibrant. As its quantity and quality are affected, so is the health of the couple or family system. It is also important to remember that there is no one truth; there is only "my truth" and "your truth," which, through open dialogue, patience, and understanding, become "our truth."

Conclusion

I have included this chapter on truth and lying in intimate systems because, given the myriad events and changes forced on the system in the course of life, our personal truths often become imprisoned in the realm of those "unbearable awarenesses and too-difficult actions" described in Chapter Six. This is especially evident when a system suffers the death of one of its members. Such a traumatic event evokes some of the most painfully unspeakable "truths" of the human condition—anguish, fear, loss, guilt, anger, and grief. Because their effects on couples and families are momentous, working with these experiences in couple and family therapy can lead to some of the most profound personal and interpersonal truths of our existence.

Notes to Chapter Ten

1. For a philosophical examination of lying and truthfulness as related to such existential topics as "bad faith" and "authenticity," see J.-P. Sartre (1957), *Being and nothingness: An essay on phenomenological ontology* (H. E. Barnes, Trans.) (New York: Philosophical Library). In distinguishing between "bad faith" and plain lying, Sartre states:

> We shall willingly grant that bad faith is a lie to oneself, on condition that we distinguish the lie to oneself from lying in general. Lying is a negative attitude, we will agree to that. But this negation does not bear on consciousness itself; it aims only at the transcendent. The essence of the lie implies in fact that the liar actually is in complete possession of the truth which he is hiding. A man does not lie about what he is ignorant of; he does not lie when he spreads an error of which he himself is the dupe; he does not lie when he is mistaken. The ideal description of the liar would be a cynical consciousness, affirming truth within himself, denying it in his words, and denying that negation as such [p. 48]. . . .
>
> The situation cannot be the same for bad faith if this, as we have said, is indeed a lie to oneself. To be sure, the one who practices bad faith is hiding a displeasing truth or presenting a pleasing untruth. Bad faith then has in appearance the structure of falsehood. Only what changes everything is the fact that in bad faith it is from myself that I am hiding the truth. Thus the duality of the deceiver and the deceived does not exist here [p. 49].

See also S. Bok (1989), *Lying: Moral choice in public and private office* (New York: Vintage Books); M. Heidegger (1977), "On the essence of truth," in *Basic Writings* (New York: HarperCollins); J.-P. Sartre (1992), *Truth and existence* (Chicago: University of Chicago Press).

2. Besides being a terribly traumatic, wonderfully embarrassing, and very amusing story (lo, these many years later!), it also strongly relates to the experience of being objectified and made shameful by "The Look" of the Other as explored by Sartre in his famous "being-caught-peeping-through-the-keyhole" example. See J.-P. Sartre (1957), *Being and nothingness: An essay on phenomenological ontology* (H. E. Barnes, Trans.) (New York: Philosophical Library).
3. An entire book could be devoted to answering this one question: "What happens when one lies to an intimate?" While there are deeper philosophical, psychological, and spiritual consequences of this all-too-human behavior—far too many to do justice to in the scope of the present work—my thoughts turn to the ideas of deceiving not only the Other, but oneself as well; of separation and alienation; of, as Buber called it, *self-contradiction*. See M. Buber (1958), *I and Thou* (R. G. Smith, Trans.) (New York: Charles Scribner's Sons). The following passage is from Buber's *I and Thou:*

What is self-contradiction!
If a man does not represent the *a priori* of relation in his living with the world, if he does not work out and realize the inborn *Thou* on what meets it, then it strikes inwards. It develops on the unnatural, impossible object of the *I*, that is, it develops where there is no place at all for it to develop. Thus confrontation of what is over against him takes place within himself, and this cannot be relation, or presence, or streaming interaction, but only self-contradiction. The man may seek to explain it as a relation, perhaps as a religious relation, in order to wrench himself from the horror of the inner double-ganger; but he is bound to discover again and again the deception in the explanation. Here is the verge of life, flight of an unfulfilled life to the senseless semblance of fulfillment, and its groping in a maze and losing itself ever more profoundly [pp. 69–70, original emphasis].

And, for a short examination of being false to oneself, see W. F. Fischer (1985), "Self-deception: An empirical-phenomenological inquiry into its essential meanings," in A. Giorgi (Ed.), *Phenomenology and psychological research* (Pittsburgh, PA: Duquesne University Press).
4. Author unknown, although it is probably safe to assume that the saying was coined by someone with paranoid tendencies: the author certainly knew what he or she was talking about in saying it.
5. Epictetus (1937), "The golden sayings of Epictetus" (Trans. H. Crossley), in C. W. Eliot (Ed.), *The Harvard classics* (New York: Collier).

11

Loss, Grief, and the Use of Ritual

That which we lose we mourn, but must rejoice
That we ever had.
—C. J. Wells

"I don't even want to think about it—that my father is dead—that his body is cold—that his spirit is gone forever. Part of me feels numb, unthinking, removed, unknowing, unbelieving."

These were my thoughts on the way to my father's funeral.

As Judith Viorst would say, life is full of *necessary losses*—birth, going away to school, illness, separation, death.[1] Death wears many faces, but its unchanging expression is always one of loss: loss of work, loss of pride, loss of love, loss of esteem, loss of security, loss of one's native soil. It is a tearing asunder.

These experiences of loss take place within the basic structures of our society—in couples, friendships, families, and work teams. The human spirit is nourished in relationships and it suffers its pains and losses there as well.

Loss and bereavement are a part of the total human drama. Every loss, great and small, is woven into the seamless fabric of our relationships, our attachments, and our evasions. The way we color our world is factored into each loss. Loss follows no rules or logic. People leave suddenly or die unexpectedly. They become ill and lose their zest for life. People become disenchanted with others for whom they had once held immense admiration. People cut each other off out of greed, spite, shame, or simply to avoid suffering.

So it is with families as well. The energy that glues families together and keeps them alive is the same force triggered when conflict arises, when invested feelings are trampled on, when rejection is experienced, and when loss occurs. Loss not only causes pain and sadness; it can also be accompanied by feelings of relief, rage, vengefulness, and guilt.

In one family, two brothers are set up as rivals for their parents' love. The family is seductive and charming in the outer world, but they do not deliver the much-needed love and appreciation to each other. So the boys set out on separate paths to prove themselves. One rebels by becoming a small-time thief, peddler, and occasional cocaine dealer. He is tough and brave, and he brags about his exploits. The other son decides to prove his goodness by showing his mother that he can do better than his father did. He sacrifices his youth by working his way through school. He achieves prominence in his field and sends his parents his published works.

The brothers become increasingly alienated. Each harbors a hope that they might become friends when Mom and Dad pass away but, in the end, the system prevails. The parents leave a will in which the "good" son gets everything and the "bad" one does not inherit a penny. The victor gives the loser a token payment, but the resulting victory and sense of betrayal are so great that the separation of the brothers is guaranteed. The two men part forever, because to see each other's faces is to renew the pain and anger and hunger of a lifetime.

That is how losses are woven into the fabric of one particular family. The intensity of old loves and longings is later matched by the shadows of bitterness and hatred.

To live a full life requires investment in work, in contact with others, in loving, intimate relationships. This means that we invest our energy, our affirmation, in these activities and persons. We internalize them—that is, we bring the activity or person into our being. In loving relationships, we bring our loved ones into our souls, our hearts, and when we are rejected or betrayed, or when they die, our hearts are "broken."

In experiencing the death of a loved one, the person is torn out of our hearts. The event is disorienting. Eleanor, whose husband of thirty years died suddenly, describes her experience this way: "Nothing seemed connected. I went on 'automatic pilot'—as my son calls it—doing what habit dictates from long experience, requiring no thought or concentration because all of the conscious awareness is elsewhere—in memory and in the sheer nausea, which is the physical response."

A man whose wife died of cancer wrote this about his experience:

> Marcia was my affirmation of life. I wanted to live, to enjoy my life and life-giving processes. I wanted to extend myself into the world. I ate and drank with pleasure; I took the "good parts" of life into me . . . When Marcia died, I had nothing to anchor me, nothing to remind me that I am wanted in the world, no one to touch me to remind me that I exist, that I have a history; no one to smell my skin and make love to me . . . no one to talk about the ordinary events of daily life. Not having her concrete image before me, I tried to conjure her up in my imagination, but the inner images lasted for only a few seconds. I became listless and quiet. I felt as if the life affirmation that I gave to her was buried with her deep in the black, moist soil of fall . . . It was easy to cry when it rained. I cried myself to sleep, holding on to my folding knees which were pulled up to my chest. I felt like a small child abandoned in the forest. I could not stand looking at or tasting food. I would waken at four

> in the morning feeling fully alert and ready to start the day. But what to do? In the beginning, I simply wanted to be alone, but as the weeks passed, I began talking to my friends about the ache of my loss.

Offering Support Through Witnessing and Through Rituals

When confronted with the unbearable pain of loss, it is tempting to deny it. Or we can become lost in the darkness and hopelessness of the pain. We want to see the pain, yet we want to run from it. The dying person alternates between the same two processes. There is also anger, hurt, regret, guilt. What does a therapist do? Affirmation and support often come from simply *being there* as a human being—fully witnessing the events and feeling and showing compassion, yet maintaining one's boundaries.

Eleanor, who felt suicidal after her husband's death, said the following about her therapist, Sonia Nevis: "The struggle was not accomplished alone. Sonia said to me early the most important of all messages, 'Yes, you want to die, but give it a couple of years and then decide!' She was not frightened by me, or else she weighed my struggle and gambled on the ultimate answer . . . There was a ritualistic quality of time I spent with her—inviolate time, not therapy—just time to be. There is absolutely no substitute, none whatsoever, for a safe place where tears and anger are not 'crazy' and where the obsessive thinking can be externalized."

To be a witness for someone, in this context, means to

- Stay with their process and listen
- Not push for outcomes
- Show respect for what is there
- See the usefulness and even the beauty of the way others express their mourning and sense of loss
- Allow oneself to be a firm ground on which the other stands

The therapist's presence and witnessing allow the family to see its own process, to see themselves rather than to flee from themselves, to be aware of their pain and sense of helplessness.

The Harrisons: Struggling with Grief

The Harrison family came to their first therapy session in crisis, anticipating an overwhelming loss. They shuffled into the consulting room. Max, the oldest child, was thin and somber, while his brother, Frank, the middle child, was muscular and vigorous. Both boys looked inconsolable. Behind them were their parents, a young-looking, middle-aged couple, with a third child: a bright-eyed girl named Bella. Max was eighteen, Frank was sixteen, and Bella had just turned ten. The parents were Alger, forty-five, and Ellen, forty-two.

As the family settled in and started talking, the following emerged: Max had been diagnosed months ago as having leukemia. His life expectancy was approximately three years. The parents complained that Max was not taking his medicine and felt helpless. The two younger children nodded as the parents spoke. Max remained impassive.

The therapist talked to the family for a few minutes, then oriented them as to how the session would proceed. They would be asked to talk to each other so that the therapist could learn more about them.

The family talked back and forth actively. The central theme was that of complaining to Max that he was making things difficult for everybody because he refused to take his medication. While everybody complained, Max said nothing.

Therapist: *I'd like to interrupt to tell you what I'm seeing. I'm seeing all of you insisting again and again that Max take his medicine. Again and again—caring a lot. And you, Max, just stay true to your position—you just don't take the medicine. I see you doing this repeatedly. Do you know you do that?*

Ellen: *Well, of course I know we do that. We just want him to take care of himself!*

Alger: *I didn't realize we did it as much as you say . . . but it would be better if he took better care of himself . . .*

Bella: *But the doctor says he should take it.*

Frank: *We worry that he's gonna get sicker. (He pauses, looks down at his hands in silence, and then, his voice softening somewhat, speaks again) But a person should be able to do what he wants to do. (He looks up at his mother as if checking if she might soften her position.)*

Max: *That's right! I wanna be left alone! (He turns to the therapist) Sure, you're right. That's exactly what they do! They bug me and I know that!*

Therapist: *I'm glad that you all seem to know how you're handling this and, mostly, I hear that you're satisfied with the way you're handling it, with the possible exception of you, Frank. (Each family member nods yes as the therapist scans the group.)*

The family continued their discussion for the rest of the hour. Basically, Max was being pushed by all but Frank to comply with the doctor's orders. At one point, Bella cried softly and her father stroked her hair as the others spoke. Before the session ended, the therapist spoke again:

Therapist: *All of you found a way to respond to this crisis that somehow fits each of you. What I would like to suggest to you is that you pay attention to how you continue to feel about being this way with Max. If you become dissatisfied, call me and we can schedule another appointment.*

The session ended here.

About a year later, Alger, the father, called for an appointment. On the phone he said, "I think we're no longer handling Max's illness satisfactorily." Even in the waiting room, they seemed different from a year previously. They were quieter. Max was visibly ill; his skin was pale and pasty, his cheeks collapsed.

Therapist: *To begin, I want to hear from all of you.*

Alger: *Things are different now. I think you guessed that they were going to be.*

Therapist: *Yes, I did guess that.*

Ellen: *(Looking very sad) It's been a hard year.*

Frank: *There is really not much to say.*

Therapist: *I appreciate that. Thanks for just telling me.*

Max: *You know they're having a hard time.*

Therapist: *And I guess that makes it hard for you, Max.*

Bella sits silently appearing as if she has merged with her mother's depression.

Therapist: *It's okay, Bella, if you don't say anything. Let me tell you all again what I'd like us to do: talk to each other about what's important to you and, again, let me watch you. I'll tell you when I see something that will be useful to you. Please ask me for help if you feel you need it or if you feel stuck in any way. Is that okay with all of you?*

The therapist once again relies heavily on what is actually experienced in the family. Many possibilities exist and may arise during this session. The emphasis may turn to any topic: the system may, for example, want to explore how they experience their loss as a system; how they shape their grief; or how they may want to mobilize their energy to articulate frustration, anger, dismay, conflict, or pain. The emphasis and direction will become apparent after a phenomenological examination of the system's process. The therapist later may organize a common theme, not out of his own sentimentality or grief (which, since he is human, are both present) but out of the material exchanged between members of the family. The articulated theme lends meaning to their existence, a meaning they may experience as a welcome form of support. Later, themes can be shaped and converted into experiments that hold the potential ground for a ritual.

The Harrisons, one by one, nod yes and begin talking with each other. The therapist watches for about fifteen minutes. Because their energy stays low, it is difficult at first to distinguish what is important from what is not.

Therapist: *I want you all to know that, as I'm sitting here, I'm feeling heavy and sad.*

Alger: *Sure you are, but it's the word* sad *that's hard for me to say.*

Ellen: *(With some anger) We're* not *gonna give up! Remember there's that therapy in Minnesota we're going to look into.*

Max: *That's what I'm talking about, Doctor. That's what makes it hard for me. I've got leukemia—give up already!*

Frank: *(Softly) Mom, that's what I've been trying to tell you. Give it up already.*

Alger begins to cry and Bella goes to him. He reaches out and embraces her.

Bella: *I also want to cry.*

Ellen: *There is nothing else to do but to cry, is there?*

Outside is an autumn day, and while the rain gently drizzles down from the gray sky, there is a stillness in the room.

Max: *(Quietly) I'd rather have you cry, Mom, than be mad at me.*

As if by prearrangement, they all move closer together. The therapist sits with the family in silence until the end of the hour, and that is how the session ended.

Another year had passed when Ellen called to report that Max had died six months earlier. She said she was not sure exactly what they needed, but they needed something. An appointment was set for the following week.

After hanging up, the therapist fell into a quiet sadness. A young life gone. A family with a hole in it. Absentmindedly, he walked toward the stereo and reached for Fauré's "Requiem." The music flowed with exhilarating beauty. As he listened to the music, he thought, "Perhaps I can play something from this or some other music to support their experience. But, of course, I don't even know what they need . . . This is what I need right now. This is for me."

The next week, the Harrison family filed into the room, each person lost in thought.

Therapist: *I've been thinking about you all since I heard about Max's death. Would you each talk to me and tell me how you're doing?*

Ellen: *(A little edgy) Everybody wants to know how I am. What am I supposed to say? Why do you ask something like that?*

Therapist: *Because I want to talk to you and I don't have anything better to ask.*

(Ellen nods in understanding.)

Alger: *I guess we're okay. What can I say? We don't talk to each other very much. I was so happy that Ellen called you. I was too scared to suggest it, thinking Ellen wouldn't like it.*

Therapist: *Thanks for telling me that.*

Frank: *Yeah, we're not allowed to talk about Max. I don't even like to be in the house anymore. The house is like a morgue.*

Therapist: *Thanks for telling me that, Frank.*

Bella: *I wish everything could be like it used to be.*

Therapist: *I can see how you'd want that, Bella. (To everyone) Now I'd like for all of you to turn to each other and talk about the things you've been saying to me. Let me watch and listen to you, and I'll tell you as soon as I see something emerge that can be useful to you. Remember that if any of you get stuck and need help, ask me for it. Now I'll just lean back and see if I can notice how you're not doing so well.*

The family talks for about fifteen minutes with little energy, often changing the subject.

Therapist: *Let me interrupt and tell you what I see. I see how you could use some help. It looks like it's real hard to say anything, and no one is helping anyone else to say things more fully. You each look like you're on your own.*

Alger: *Yes, that's exactly how I feel—all alone. I didn't realize until just now that I'm also leaving everyone else alone. It didn't use to be like this.*

Ellen: *Things are never going to be the same again.*

Alger: *(Turning to her) That's true, but I don't want to be alone anymore, and I don't want to leave you alone.*

Ellen: *I don't know how to be with you since this . . .*

Alger: *"This" is that our son died and I don't want to cry alone anymore.*

(Ellen looks silently at her husband, her face hardened and tired.)

Frank: *I want to be able to talk about Max.*

Bella: *I miss Max.*

Therapist: *I can guess how hard it is for all of you to talk to each other and to touch each other because it makes you feel your sadness even more. But the truth is that you are very sad—you're full of tears. It's helpful sometimes to have a specific time and way to be sad with each other so that you don't feel sad all the time. Does that make sense? (Each member nods.) Does anybody have any ideas? (The family is silent.) Do you want ideas from me?*

Bella: *Yes, tell us.*

Therapist: *Well, one idea I have is that on Max's birthday . . .*

Bella: *His birthday is next week!*

Therapist: *Thank you, Bella. Max's birthday might be a good time to be sad together. Everybody could say exactly how they miss Max and what they would give him for a birthday present if he were here. How does that sound?*

Frank: *I like that.*

(The others appear interested as well.)

Therapist: *Let's do it now as if it's his birthday today. Would you be willing to try?*

(There is a long pause. Then they shift their chairs and look around, but not at each other or at the therapist. Then the silence is broken . . .)

Frank: *I want to try it. "Happy birthday, Max!" It's your birthday, you know, don't you? You're twenty now. And I know how much you love basketball, so I got you a real professional ball . . . I can just imagine your smiling face and how you love to jump high into the air to lob that ball right in. Happy B-b-b . . . (he can't get the word out). I miss you a lot . . . I even miss you shoving me around when your buddies come over and you're fooling around.*

Ellen: *(Wiping her eyes) That was lovely, sweetheart.*

Everyone in the room is weeping or on the verge of tears.

Bella: *(Her voice is still that of a child, sweet and innocent) Guess what I got for your birthday, big Max. You really liked Jenny over on Berkshire Street. She's gonna come over and watch TV with us like she did once last year, remember?*

Ellen: *Poor Max, you'll never get to really fall in love, and you'll never get to go away to college or Europe. And you'll never get to tease or hug or wrestle with your brother and sister. What can I give you now my poor, sweet darling? I suppose I can give you a promise that your sweet soul is still living inside me, inside all of us. I still remember how I carried you in my belly and how lively you were inside me . . . as if it was only yesterday. I hope that on this birthday your soul is in peace . . . (Alger sits close to his wife, holding on to one of her hands tightly.)*

Another silence follows, but the energy in the room is different. The listlessness and scatteredness have shifted into a focused, softly held sentimentality along with a bit of joy. It is as if Max has sat himself down in the middle of the room and pulled everyone together.

Alger: *And I'm giving you those skis you always wanted, so you and I can go skiing together. Happy birthday, son. May your spirit come back to us every birthday, so we can remember you together every year and love you once again. And between birthdays we can let go of you and leave you in peace . . . yes, leave you in peace. (He moves his gaze from the imaginary spirit in the middle of the room and looks at the therapist with his soft, moist eyes.) Is that what you meant for us to do?*

Therapist: *Yes, exactly, that was wonderful. I suggest you do that again next week on Max's birthday. I think you'll like being sad together like you were today.*

(A long silence ensues and then the therapist continues.)

Therapist: *As you turned your eyes away from Max in confusion and a sense of emptiness, you also turned away from each other. You not only lost Max, you lost each other and the comfort and warmth that you had created as a family.*

Alger: *Yes, Max lives in all of us, and he would want us to be a family again, not only by celebrating his birthday but celebrating each other.*

Therapist: *Exactly. If you could turn to each other now and just look into each other's eyes, what feelings might come to you that you might share? Please try to look at each other.*

Bella: *Mom, Dad, Frank, I love you.*

(As if in rehearsed unison, they respond with "I love you" to Bella and then they weep softly together.)

Alger: *(Looking warmly at Ellen) I've missed you, Ellen . . .*

Ellen: *And I've missed you and Frank and Bella, too. (She extends her open arms to Bella, who comes and hugs her.)*

Alger: *(Standing and approaching Frank) I've neglected you too long. I've been so preoccupied and withdrawn, son.*

Frank: *(Hugging his father) It's okay, Dad, I've been in bad shape myself.*

The family continues talking among themselves, sharing feelings, and crying intermittently. The therapist is sitting alone. He is aware that in helping them mourn, he has helped revitalize their family unit. He is quietly pleased. He reminisces internally about the losses in his own life—and his gains.

Conclusion

There are many ways to work with a couple or family experiencing grief and loss. The sessions with the Harrison family are only one example of the power of the therapist's presence with, and witnessing of, a family's struggle to come to grips with shared pain. As in all Gestalt work with couples and families, the foundation is the phenomenological data presented by the couple or family as a system. In working with loss and grief, there are several ways the therapist's presence can take shape.

You can join the family in the grieving process or can stay with their awkward experience of not knowing how to grieve and search with them for *their* best way of expressing themselves. It is important not to have a preformed model for grief work, but to help the family find one that fits them.

At times, you may need to rally the family to promote cohesiveness and unity and to combat their impulse to run away.

You can help the family recreate itself in its new form and can help them attend to their process of grieving rather than rushing through it to a premature completion.

Finally, you can assist the family in creating a ritual or rituals that will support their repeated urges to grieve and remember. These rituals, found in most cultures and dating back to ancient times, help the family avoid getting stuck in the perpetual darkness of their loss and make it easier for them to return to the normal routines of daily life.

Religious rituals that give a family an opportunity to commemorate the death of a member are powerful events for both the family and the larger community. This way, the community has a chance to support them during their period of sorrow. The family is aided by friends and relatives who attend memorial services, send letters of condolence, and, in some instances, provide food and company during the formal period of mourning.

The work we do in therapy has no prescribed ritual but allow the family and therapist to create a ritual that fits a particular family's situation. Our work takes into consideration the individual needs of the members, their temperaments, and their particular set of resistances to contact around a given or anticipated loss. The family's timing is also considered. As we saw earlier, for example, the Harrisons needed to struggle with the crisis by themselves before they were receptive to a second intervention by the therapist.

The ritual created by the Harrisons united them, made them feel more cohesive as a family, and continued to console them for years. As each family member offered a "birthday gift" to Max, he or she selected that essence, that powerful and sweet aspect of his or her special connectedness to Max. Each acted or spoke in accordance with his or her own relationship to him.

There is no right or wrong process for mourning. Scholars recognize some aspects of mourning, such as denial, acceptance, rage, and sadness, but these are merely concepts floating in the "soup" of actual experiences in a given family.[2] They may arrange themselves in a given order or not. When we add the additional factors of the particular sequence for a given family's development and the ages of the parents and children, these concepts may or may not be useful.

The formal religious prayer for the dead offers a respect for the awesome event in its relation to God and to one's community. The family ritual stimulates each person to give a kind of personal and consistently changing eulogy to the missed sibling, child, or parent. The combined effect of these rituals allows the family to speak in one harmonious voice even as they contribute differing textures, metaphors, and meanings in their individual voices.

But what about the therapist's own voice? How does it fit here? To the very end, it is a voice that softly evokes, reminds, acknowledges, empowers, comforts, and witnesses. Rarely does it claim its own wisdom or heroism for a solo performance. The therapist's voice is not cantorial as it recedes and is superseded by the choir of the family.

It is perhaps fitting as we near the end of this book that we do so with the experience of death, that most painful and powerful mystery of human existence. Mystics believe that death is merely a change in form, a passing on to something else beyond our known reality. In this thought there lies a truth: that there is a form to dying just as there is to living, that there can be a "good form" even in death as there is in life. Perhaps it takes the experience of death, either of one's own self or of another, to reveal this truth. We began this book by "searching for good form" as if this ideal state was somewhere "out there," as if it could be magically found if only we looked long enough, hard enough, and with all the right instruments. On one level, this is true, and we used the image of flowing gestalten gracefully rising and falling like waves lapping against the shore as one possible instrument with which to find this good form.

But, on a deeper level, the aesthetic of good form already exists and merely needs to be uncovered by the therapist, its life and beauty revealed by the act of awareness itself. We conclude our discussion by meditating on how the awareness of process leads to the revelation of good form.

Notes to Chapter Eleven

1. J. Viorst (1986), *Necessary losses* (New York: Simon & Schuster).
2. E. Kübler-Ross (1969), *On death and dying* (New York: Macmillan). Also see "Marie Creelman at 77" (1986, Spring), *News* (Center for the Study of Intimate Systems, Gestalt Institute of Cleveland, *6*(1), 1-2; "Loss and growth: An interview with Eleanor Warner" (1981, Spring), *News* (Center for the Study of Intimate Systems, Gestalt Institute of Cleveland), *1*(2), 1-3; J. Zinker (1966), *Rosa Lee: Motivation and the crisis of dying* (Painesville, OH: Lake Erie Press).

12

Conclusion: The Aesthetics of the Gestalt Approach

Though we travel the world over to find the beautiful, we must carry it with us or we find it not.

—Ralph Waldo Emerson

The Gestalt approach, because of its unique psychological heritage, lends itself to the exploration of an aesthetic model more than any other school of thought.[1]

Gestalt Values: Toward an Aesthetic Vision

Gestalt psychology grew out of the experimental and phenomenological investigation of visual perception, and we must acknowledge this distinctive influence. The original Gestalt psychologists focused on principles of *seeing*—in how humans organize their visual field, the kinds of factors that influence

Note: This chapter was coauthored by Joseph Zinker and Paul Shane.

perception, and so on. For example, they were interested in foreground-background, lines, shapes, contours, proximity, depth, points, colors, planes, motion, and spaces. The idea of form—especially the notion of *Gestaltqualitäten* or the qualities of the form—was central.[2] In short, Gestalt psychology was a psychological theory and methodology tailor-made for the study of aesthetics.

Though Gestalt psychologists turned their attention to the organization of psychological and geographical space, they did make occasional references to the problem of aesthetic perception.[3] Thus, as noted earlier, it would come as no surprise to a Gestalt psychologist to learn that the term *aesthetic* derives from a Greek word meaning "to perceive."

Developing an aesthetic vision of human interaction and therapeutic intervention in a Gestalt context begins not with abstraction such as goodness or beauty but with values. The appreciation of values, like the appreciation of the perception and organization of visual phenomena, was of great interest to the early Gestalt psychologists, Köhler in particular.[4]

To sketch a working theory of the aesthetics of human interaction within Gestalt therapy, we must first define our values by asking questions such as these: Why did we ourselves choose the Gestalt approach in preference to the many other therapies? What is it in us that resonates with Gestalt therapy? *What do we expect to happen* in the therapy session? What guides us when doing Gestalt therapy? What does it mean to be a Gestalt therapist? When we think of values in Gestalt theory and practice, we look for statements of what matters most to us, what is precious to us, what we hold dear, what is significant to us in our thinking, in our work, and in our relationships to each other. The answers to these questions lead us to the value system embedded in our structured personal ground.

The historical progression of Gestalt values is akin to the unfolding of a flower. In the beginning, all the ideas were condensed in the delicate bud of Fritz Perls and Paul Goodman's early writings. Over time, as the bud became a flower, each notion developed its own vivid color, detail, and beauty—and continues developing. This development can be categorized into four sets of values that have emerged over the last several decades: folk values, content values, process values, and system values.

1. *Folk values.* Folk values are categorical imperatives—the introjected slogans that came out of Perls's dramatic demonstrations and some of his later writings. These became the "headlines" of the personal growth movement and subculture of the 1960s. These values are generally monolithic and disconnected from the flow of Gestalt theory in its most substantial form. Here are some of the slogans expressing Gestalt concepts:

> "Stay in the here and now."
> "Lose your head and come to your senses."
> "I do my thing and you do your thing . . . "
> "Live *in* the moment, not *for* the moment."
> "I and thou, what and how, here and now."

These sayings are not untruths. They contain elliptical references to deep truths and played an important role during our learning process in the 1960s—a time of rebellion against the staid, overly intellectual, academic teachings of orthodox psychoanalysis and other disciplines. But their condensed power gradually waned through overuse (and misuse), and people soon forgot that they were created in reaction against the fragmentation of human thought, feeling, and action. Perls, Hefferline, and Goodman stressed the totality of human experience and rejected this fragmentation. The following "opposites" are among categories they characterized as "false dichotomies" of experiencing:[5]

- Self and external world
- Organism and environment
- Conscious and unconscious
- Body and mind
- Infantile and mature
- Biological and cultural
- Poetry and prose
- Spontaneous and deliberate

- Personal and social
- Love and aggression
- Illness and health

Perls, Hefferline, and Goodman emphasized the notion of the context or field in human relationships. Here is how they described their "contextual" method: "The only useful method of argument is to bring into the picture the total context of the problem, including the conditions of experiencing it, the social milieu, and the personal 'defenses of the observer.'"[6] They were aware of Lewin's field theory and selected a key quotation to substantiate their view of the therapeutic encounter: "It is particularly necessary that one who proposes to study whole phenomena should guard against the tendency to make the wholes as all-embracing as possible. The real task is to investigate the structural properties of a given whole, ascertain the relations of subsidiary wholes, and determine the boundaries of the system with which one is dealing. It is no more true in psychology than in physics that 'everything depends on everything else.'"[7] Perls, Hefferline, and Goodman use this passage in a special way. They urge that we not consider all social values and implications and related systems in a given therapy situation, but focus on the patient's and therapist's encounter around the patient's world and its potential for *organismic self-regulation*. They warn therapists not to impose their theory of illness and health on the patient, but to attend to the person's own process of experiencing, thus "drawing boundaries" around those phenomena: "It is obviously desirable to have a therapy that establishes a norm as little as possible, and tries to get as much as possible from the structure of the actual situation, here and now."[8] Perls, Hefferline, and Goodman's field in therapy consisted of delineated boundaries around the phenomenology of the patient as well as the encounter between therapist and patient. This was the field within which the work of psychotherapy existed; as such, it was the standard of aesthetic beauty for individual therapy. Enlarging it to include couples, families, or social groups—and to apply the principles of the formation and destruction of gestalten to those systems—was not even on the horizon in the

1950s, when Gestalt theory was first formally elaborated. After all, Perls himself was still just a hop, skip, and jump away from his own earlier work as a psychoanalyst.[9]

2. *Content values.* Content, as it is commonly defined in psychotherapy, is the stuff of the person's life: the "presenting complaint," the "issue," the "problem." We distinguish this regular content—the "what" of the person's life—from meaningful content—what the person experiences and chooses with awareness to do in life and in therapy.

As you watch a small system—a couple or a family—you see and hear an incredible amount of complex material. You may be attracted to what they are talking about; this is what is commonly known as content. Content is seductive—it draws you in because it often arises from conflict and disagreement; it is polarized and polemical; it is magnetized by one's countertransference issues. In polemical disagreement, the opposing sides are bent on winning. If they are merely polarized (but not polemicized), there is still disagreement but they are willing to make some effort to resolve the problem. As you continue watching the system, you may notice that, independently of content, there is process. For example, you may notice that their talk has a circular quality: they go around, get stuck, and repeat themselves. If you keep an open mind about how they talk, where they sit, who is the "troublemaker," who is the "good one," and so forth, the data can be truly overwhelming. But if you focus on the content—the material that divides them—you may fall into the following common errors.

1. You find one side more attractive than the other (a countertransference effect).
2. You may want to solve the problem by encouraging them to find a compromise. The weakness of this intervention is that they do not really learn anything about *where* they become stuck in their process, and so similar conflicts will arise in future, content-laden situations.
3. You may want to teach them to talk differently and could offer an intervention something like, "Say I want . . . " instead of "You should . . . "

Interruptions in the system's process tend to occur repetitively regardless of what problem is on the table. We are far less interested in the logistics of a life decision, for example, than in how the person arrives at the decision and what they experience in that process. We are interested in how choices are made, but this is more a process value than one of content.

Everyday content is seductive because it is so engaging, but it is a trap: awareness appears to be generated—issues being explored, opinions rendered, wants and needs articulated—but there is no energy to move it beyond endless discussion. There is a lot of verbal motion, but no movement toward a clear figure. Since there is no contact, there is no sense of completion, and only inevitable frustration is achieved. As long as the system does not invest its energy in making something happen, the effort—as minimal as it may be—is wasted. Meaningful content by our definition is the purposive and relevant aspect of process—what the person is doing in the moment and how he or she is doing it.

3. *Process values.* Process is action that continues and progresses. Process implies a living, organic, spontaneous movement. Process is curvilinear, patterned, in constant flux, uncontrived, unplanned, pure—propelled by energy created by two or more persons. Process thinking is devoid of obsession with, or preoccupation about, content and the push to create particular outcomes. *To be one with one's process is to be fully alive.*

Attending to the process of the therapy session almost always supersedes the content of what the patient is talking about. Here are some statements from Perls, Hefferline, and Goodman that imply the valuing of process in the Gestalt approach:

> The patient . . . finds and makes himself.
> The self is the contact boundary at work.
> The self is the synthetic unity . . . [it] is the artist of life.
> Working with the awareness of resistance means working with the person's creative energy.
> All contact is creative adjustment of the organism and environment.[10]

In the Gestalt view, human nature is a *process*—as opposed to categorical conceptions like "Human beings are rational animals." This value is a developmental one—we are in a constant state of *becoming,* our nature is *potentiality.* Our essence is not predetermined. Essence is process. We are a process in constant motion; our boundaries are never the same. What Perls, Hefferline, and Goodman valued most about this process model was the directed awareness of it, the concentration that takes place between therapist and client. This was the exciting place, the battleground, the encounter where one could see and hear the other fully, ask questions, and deliver observations of what is obvious to the therapist but unfelt and unseen by the patient.

Let us look at an example. You are watching a couple argue about how to run their business. She wants plans in advance—thirty days minimum. He, on the other hand, likes to wait and get more information before making a decision. This is their content.

Now for their process. The argument—their polemic—begins to heat up and you observe the phenomenology of their interaction. She raises her voice and he becomes increasingly tense and even more entrenched in his position. It is evident that in the Interactive Cycle of Experience, they are located somewhere in the energy/movement part and stuck between energy and contact. Here is the first intervention you might make:

Therapist: *I've been watching you talk now for ten minutes. You talk well and stay with the issue, but there is something else going on. Barbara, as your voice rises and you get more frustrated, you, Bill, get stiffer and more rigid both physically and intellectually. Have you ever noticed this?*

Now you have found a pattern almost devoid of content but very real and easily seen again and again. You have made a pattern out of chaos—a pattern with phenomenological validity and reliability. The couple may question the usefulness of your observation regarding their stuckness and reply, "Not really, but what good does knowing this do for us?" Here is one answer:

Therapist: *You see, if we get curious about how you repeatedly get stuck in the process of your arguments, you'll be able to get unstuck no matter if you disagree about the business or vacation plans or what time to have dinner. If either one of you learns to change your behavior—for example, either by relaxing your voice, Barbara, or by sitting back in your chair without tensing up, Bill, you will do much better no matter what topic you deal with.*

So, they "want to try it," but since this is completely new for them, you need to coach them a little.

Therapist: *Bill, this time would you be willing to sit back and try and not stiffen up no matter how angry Barbara's voice gets? And you, Barbara, would you try playing with your voice a little when Bill starts getting really tense and immobile in his position?*

Then they try it and—miracle of miracles!—their *content* changes and they begin to sound more conciliatory with one another. A metaphor can be used to describe the intervention in aesthetic terms:

Therapist: *It's like you're dancing together but you both want to lead. I say, forget about who's leading and both of you just get into the rhythm, the beat. You don't even know what the dance is yet—a fox-trot or a tango or whatever.*

But it is not a question of whether the intervention is artistic as much as it is about their artistry as a couple. Her angry voice and his tenseness are an aesthetic expression of "not good enough." The therapist attempts to make it gracefully functional.

4. *System values.* The Gestalt approach values the notion of systems and fields because these create the framework for a holistic, dynamic, and comprehensive understanding of human events and interactions. Fundamental to our view is the idea that most characteristics of psychological systems are virtually identical to those of psychological fields and of psychological gestalten. Perls, while he used the language of field theory and frequently spoke of the "organism-environment relationship," was actually impatient with any theory if it did not imply a

human struggle, an action. If he were alive today, Perls would be critical of systems theory because it would feel too abstract to him. His emphasis was consistently on the active nature of being and becoming.[11] To cite just one example, here is a typical comment Perls, Hefferline, and Goodman once made about the field orientation of Gestalt psychologists: "They often seem to be saying . . . that everything is relevant in the field of the whole except the humanly interesting factors."[12] The fact is that Perls, Hefferline, and Goodman, because of their own intellectual bias, failed to realize that everything is relevant in the field of human experiences and that everything in the field is potentially beautiful. Although they were aware of the work of Lewin and other theoreticians, they were primarily focused on the individual and not the environment. They felt the individual was submerging the personal self under the expectations of society and that society was up to no good. And perhaps they had a point, because in the late 1930s the world exploded in global war, and one of the most cultured nations on earth used its highly developed technology to slaughter millions of people. Society *was* up to no good, since conformity to the dictates of the state mattered more than the welfare of individual human beings. During and after World War II, the existential philosophers, theologians, and psychologists began formulating ontological statements—statements about the meaning of individual development. Husserl's phenomenology became popular because it offered a system for studying subjectively experienced phenomena of single persons.

In certain respects, the intellectual atmosphere of the late 1940s through the 1960s supported the liberation of the individual. Within this context, Perls, Hefferline, and Goodman focused on individuals and their boundaries. Only after this wave of individualism was over did we as practitioners become aware, once again, of social units as support systems for personal and interactional growth. After all, Western social systems did not require total submergence of individual needs to the needs of the group, as we see in the East. In the West, it became possible for people to actualize themselves in marriage or family, circle of friends, or job. Within this context, systems theory achieved a new meaning and status. Boundary phenomena were extended from the intrapsychic, to the interpersonal, to the group, to the larger world of corporations, nations, and the cosmos. On the interpersonal or familial level, for example, encouraging a patient to show anger to a parent may result in alienation of the parent and rigidifying of the patient's adaptive stance. Inviting the parent in and allowing him or her to respond to the patient's anger offers the possibility of arriving at a creative solution that ameliorates the larger interactional stuckness of both persons.

Systems values are deeply compatible with Gestalt theory, applying principles of the whole and its parts to larger units. Thus, we must look at whole cities to understand their deterioration, for they are different from the sum of their parts. It is sheer foolishness to correct slum conditions by building new housing, because the solutions overlook the total social fabric of a metropolis: its couples and families, their education, their socioeconomic stratification, the city's parks and museums, its welfare system, its economy, and so on. Yet, as Lewin pointed out, there is a danger in considering everything relevant in a given field. For one thing, it makes investigation of a given human phenomenon too complex and far too methodologically clumsy to investigate. Lewin knew a great deal about this problem because he actually researched various social phenomena for many years.

With respect to values, the problem of seeing human interactions through a system perspective is more serious. When we look at all the factors in a given situation, we are in danger of becoming complacently relativistic in our evaluation. If we get rid of causes and effects, whom can we hold responsible for a given tragedy? What do we do with the legal notion of culpability in a crime? For a therapist, this dilemma is enormous. Are we going to be complacent when a rapist or wife beater tells us about his exploits because we "understand the complexity" of such events? What about the gang member who kills another—is he just a "victim of society"? As therapists, we must struggle with issues of maintaining social order. We cannot hide in the ivory towers of our offices and behave like religious confessors. And so, with all the sense of compassion and enormous regret, we must report murder, rape, beatings, and other violations of human rights to authorities. Why with regret? Because we know that jail sentences do not solve psychological illness or social problems. Punitive measures are at best a means for protecting potential victims from repeated crimes.

So the potential relativism of systems thinking does not protect us from the painful responsibility of deciding what we will not tolerate in a family in our community, in our lives, or in a given therapy session. A systems orientation offers a set of values for understanding the structure of primary groups, various social institutions, political events, natural disasters, ecological problems, and international relations. Systems thinking can help us understand complex problems and sidestep polemic or simplistic solutions. When we see the world comprehensively, we can use effective strategies to help influence it. Thus, if we report a rapist to the police, we do not give away our choice to talk to his family, to influence the thinking of the probation officer, to make contact with the victim, to go to court—in short, to help influence a comprehensive program in society's handling of our patient. Every time we take action in this way, we make a small dent not only in a single family's life, but in a sector of the social structure in which we live. This attitude reflects the Gestalt practitioner's rekindling of concern for *community* as well as the existential freedom and responsibility for taking choiceful action. We cannot, of course, presume that all therapists, Gestalt therapists included, have this concern, but we believe that most do, especially those who work in an institutional setting that is a vector of many of these social forces.

In spite of his interest in the boundary, Perls focused mostly on the individual's capacity to function at the boundary with an abstract world rather than describing the interactive quality of a relationship. What is often missing is the active quality of the world as it responds to the person, couple, or family. Perls at least implies this attitude when talking about a good analyst being more than just a tabula rasa or an interpreter of a transference phenomenon—and instead a different person who allows the patient to do better this time around, in *this* relationship.

After the advent of systems theory, many of us in Gestalt

therapy who became interested in this interactive process began rethinking the concept of resistances as being *individual* experiences. For example, in retroflection, Perls, Hefferline, and Goodman said that "when a person retroflects behavior, he does to himself what originally he did or tried to do to other persons or objects."[13] The question then became, Why did the person stop trying to get for himself from the environment? What happened in the environment? After some reflection, it was evident that *resistances are created and continuously maintained by two or more persons.* For example, in the case of retroflective couples and families, "people do not reach out to each other either in warmth or in anger, in curiosity or in attempts to influence one another. Such resistance is maintained when nobody protests or insists on reaching out."[14] The "retroflectors" do not ask to be comforted and the "retroflectees" do not offer to help while seeing the discomfort of the others; "all accept the assumption that boundaries must be over-respected, that intrusiveness is forbidden."[15] Slowly, it dawned on many Gestalt psychologists that it is not always good to mind our own business—that the folk value of "I do my thing and you do your thing" was just an introject. There is a point at which self-autonomy as a value ceases to be healthy self-responsibility and becomes mere callousness or licentiousness.

Over the years, as we began to work more with couples, groups, families and corporations, we were forced to enlarge the arena of the explicit and implicit meanings of interactions at the boundary. First, we began to develop a more coherent process model out of Perls's individual concepts of sensation, awareness, excitement, movement, and contact. We created a cycle in which one phenomenon follows another in a kind of chain, moving from vague sensory experience to the formation of a gestalt, to the excitement that asks for satisfaction, then to the movement that reaches out, and finally to the contact that satisfies. As our work progressed, we adapted a series of values and principles from systems theory and incorporated them into our Gestalt approach. This notion of moving from sensation to awareness to completion and satisfaction became our first and fundamental aesthetic value.

Cardinal Values and Principles of Gestalt Therapy

These "cardinal" values, as we like to call them, developed over time; through trial-and-error experience, they have grown to twenty-two values, along with corresponding intervention principles. These values and principles tend to overlap in function, and so we have categorized them into six subgroups. The categories of our Gestalt value system are Balance, Change, Development, Self-Awareness, Holism, and Form.

Values of Balance

1. VALUE: *Balanced relationships.*
   PRINCIPLE: *Our life's work as human beings is to become both dependent and autonomous. We teach self-support and also model mutual support—the balanced rhythm of fusion in the couple or family and individual differentiation from it.*

Life occurs in the middle range of being, doing, and having.[16] We develop out of fusion with our parents into differentiated adults who then, in turn, seek fusion with another, and then differentiation in relationship. This is the rhythm of being and becoming in relationship with others. To remain in fusion is infantile; to be isolated in autonomy is schizoid. In the Gestalt approach we are extremely sensitive to the natural rhythm of human interaction. When working with families, we are very cognizant of the degree of protection given to children by adults. For example, in the case of the Madiar family, the parents were in danger of sheltering their two children too much and so stunting the much-needed development of independence.

2. VALUE: *The importance of the sharing of power in the couple or family.*
   PRINCIPLE: *Understand and observe the differential of power in small systems. Strong discrepancies in power can result in abusive behavior.*

The power in the family system should clearly be in the hands of the adults until the children reach the development stages calling for fuller differentiation. Families are not "democratic" but should be "benign dictatorships" until the children come of age. We look for complementarity in the use of power in couples and in the adult subsystems of families. Power carries obligation and responsibility and must not be used as an excuse for irresponsible or abusive behaviors. This is also true in large systems such as the politician's "landslide victory," leading to the temptation of justifying abusive actions on "a mandate from the people."

3. VALUE: *Clear boundaries in both the couple or family and in the therapist.*
PRINCIPLE: *Never take sides or lose your boundary. Balance one intervention with another; model and work for good boundary definition and management.*

Where do "I" end and "you" begin when we are a couple? What is mine, what is yours, and what is ours? A boundary includes and excludes at the same time, thus creating meaning. Boundaries make living clear and conscious. Lack of awareness, problems in fusion and differentiation, and resistances such as introjection, retroflection, and projection can obscure boundaries, confuse meanings, and hobble interpersonal relations.

A criterion of good couple and family functioning is the ability to form, destroy, and re-form clearly delineated roles and subgroupings. This process is graceful in healthy, functioning couples and families. It is "good form."

The therapist lives his or her own boundary as a witness present to the couple or family. There is no room for small talk or distractions once the therapy session gets underway, since the main task is to help the system become aware of its process by making bold, creative, well-articulated interventions and withdrawals, to allow their process to continue.

Values of Change

4. VALUE: *Self-actualization through organismic self-regulation.*
PRINCIPLE: *A vision of the couple or family as striving for a wholeness, integration, fluidity, and spontaneity of functioning. The system strives for balance between stasis and forward movement.*

Organismic self-regulation has been the cornerstone of the Gestalt approach ever since Perls wrote his first work, *Ego, Hunger, and Aggression,* in the 1940s. As a value, it guides us in how we view the interactions within the couple or family. We tend less to think in terms of the *individual* organism (except when viewing it as a subsystem) and more in terms of the *relational* organism. Take for example the short case study we provided on John and Nelly Mathienson. Their dyadic organism is striving for self-regulation in terms of sexual needs-satisfaction. As separate individuals they are both healthy, orgasmic adults but together their rhythms of self-regulation differed. Helping John and Nelly adapt to one another—he by voicing his fantasies and needs and she by stimulating her awareness earlier—brought their combined sexual rhythm as a couple into better synchrony.

5. VALUE: *Learning through doing.*
PRINCIPLE: *Learning through doing works better than rational discussion only. We teach, encourage, and support experimentation with novel, fresh behavior, moving the couple or family beyond its present, stagnant, limited functioning.*

Experiential action is highly valued in Gestalt work with couples and families (as it is with individual therapy). In our approach, the experiment is used as a primary tool for heightening awareness of not only what is but *what can be.* Talking is fine, as in the use of fantasy exercises, but actual doing is much better because it mobilizes energy, leads to contact with others, and allows the practice of new behaviors—the so-called "safe emergency" of the therapy environment—which opens up new learning. The experiment is a creative act on the part of both the therapist and the couple or family—the former by devising it and the latter in executing it. To develop and engage in an experiment is part of the aesthetic process of Gestalt therapy in that it supports and unifies what is figural by contrasting experiential behaviors. It is in this sense that Gestalt therapy has been called a "phenomenological behaviorism."

6. VALUE: *Change through awareness.*
PRINCIPLE: *Change takes place through awareness and active choice making and is more fully integrated and longer lasting than change that bypasses awareness and choice.*

Gestalt therapy differs from all other schools of therapy in possessing a formal theory and model of awareness. Using awareness as a fundamental tool for change is of the utmost value. This is because we, probably more than the adherents of other approaches, view meaningful change as being solely dependent on the heightening of experiential awareness; the degree of change realized is equal to the degree of increased awareness. We teach through the active enrichment of the couple or family system's awareness and not through bypassing awareness. We are teachers, not magicians or gurus. We encourage active participation of the couple's or family's learning process (asking questions, arguing, discussing, and so on) in engaging the therapists' interventions, ideas, and images. We discourage the introjection of interventions.

7. VALUE: *Paradoxical change.*
PRINCIPLE: *Support resistance while joining the couple or family. The more you support what is, the more change will occur.*

Change can also be achieved, paradoxically, by supporting the "isness" of the couple or family system. Since each system possesses inherent styles of resistance, we respect this resistance as a healthy expression of the couple or family attempting to protect itself and achieve harmonious functioning as a collective unit. Raising awareness of how the couple or family is competent in what it does validates them as individuals and as a group. This affirmation naturally leads the system's awareness to the negative side of their behaviors—how they are "stuck" in their predicament—and their way out of it as well. It is for these reasons that we are critical of other psychotherapies that bypass or confront resistances to achieve short-term, functional change. This is also why we conceptualize the role of the therapist as a witness rather than a change agent.

8. VALUE: *Process over content.*
PRINCIPLE: *In diagnosing places of stuckness, how a couple or family expresses itself is almost always more important than what is being discussed.*

In the Gestalt view, content is literally a "dead" issue, as opposed to process, which is about living energy, the drama and dynamics of interaction. It does not matter if a problem of content could be magically solved in the course of the therapy hour, because another issue will magically appear. Problems are like the mythical Hydra; solve one and two more take its place; life is like that. And when you come right down to it, the content of life is all pretty dull stuff: rides to school, shopping for food, paying bills, when to have sex, how to get that promotion, mowing the lawn, fixing a gutter, and so on. There is nothing aesthetic about whether or not a couple should take out a second mortgage or where to go on a family vacation.

The beauty or "ugliness" of the system is in *how* it transacts its business over these issues. If we return to the example of the business couple—Barbara and Bill—we are reminded that their process was far more intriguing than the amount of time they needed to make joint decisions. Thirty days or fifteen days, it does not really matter. What was interesting to the therapist and to the couple was how when Barbara became loud, Bill tensed up physically and became more hardened in his position. This change in awareness allows them to begin to experiment with how they process their content and gives them endless opportunities for creative change in the future.

Values of Development

9. VALUE: *The rule that there are exceptions to every rule.*
   PRINCIPLE: *You need to understand and appreciate development and what is developmentally appropriate in your interventions. While they can be most useful, all rules are potentially stupid and dangerous (including this one).*

It is said that "there is nothing less common than common sense." And there is no substitute for sound judgment. Interventions must be stage-appropriate to the couple or family, and this entails consideration of developmental history as well as the development of their process in the here and now. When in doubt, stay in the here-and-now process of what is.

10. VALUE: *Equality in experiential development (or "What's good for the goose is good for the gander").*
    PRINCIPLE: *We believe that therapists, like clients, are in a state of constant change and development and that they need the nourishment of exposure to their own therapy as well as a full life in a world much larger than their own craft.*

In the end, we believe that there is no such thing as a "therapist," only a more experienced patient. Many of our colleagues may argue that one does not need to have experienced a great personal misfortune to help someone with a profound loss or with a terminal illness. Yet there is a difference between helping someone on a journey and being prepared to fully participate in it in a way that is inspiring to all those involved. It is one thing to help someone to adjust to a situation and another to be a *moving* presence, a presence that stimulates spiritual transcendence rather than mere survival.

The innate ability of the therapist to be an evocative presence comes from the horizontal and vertical depth of his or her "apperceptive mass," the life-well of personal experience. This is why the breadth of our own personal experiences—our private therapy, our loves and sorrows, travels, education, passions, and memories—is so important to us as individuals and as professionals.

Values of Self-Awareness

11. VALUE: *The therapist's tendency to "color" the couple or family.*

    PRINCIPLE: *As a therapist, you must constantly track your own moods, desires, conflicts, needs, and changing ideologies, because the couple or family in your presence will be affected in one way or another, consciously or unconsciously.*

Personal boundaries are difficult to manage and model. The therapist is only human, and being present means being there with one's strengths as well as weaknesses. In Gestalt theory, we believe that we tend to affect the couple or family through personal encounter in the moment, and more by who we are than what we do. Indeed, who we are and what values we hold guide what we do. And how we do what we do is guided by the immediate process unfolding before us.

12. VALUE: *Professional humility.*

    PRINCIPLE: *Respect the systemic integrity of the couple or family. No matter how dysfunctional they appear, they do have the capacity to change on their own.*

Finally, a couple or family does most of its living and processing outside of our office. Our influence, as powerful as it may appear at times, is really quite limited. We, as therapists, are at most like boulders in a river: the water streams past us and we can only affect its current a little bit, here and there. A witness witnesses; being present is being there. What more can we or others expect from ourselves?

Values of Holism

13. VALUE: *Systems theory—the whole influences all the individual parts and is larger than their sum.*
    PRINCIPLE: *We conceive of the couple and family as related to a systems context of the extended family, the community, the larger world. We make an effort to respond to the person/system out of an understanding or experience of this larger context.*

Related to this value is the fact no one is ever truly and absolutely alone. A hermit on a mountaintop is in relation to somebody somewhere . . . even if only in memory. A street schizophrenic has contact with others—people he or she begs from, the police, a social worker, volunteers in a shelter. Humans are gregarious creatures and are always related to other people—if not to a single Other or a family, then at least to "strangers" in the greater community and social system. Human relatedness is a question of degree.

14. VALUE: *That "No man or woman is an island."*
    PRINCIPLE: *Every intervention must carry as ground the pattern of the couple or family's outside world. You must seek to understand the "soup" in which they float in their daily life. (Imagine that all the characters in the patient's life are standing behind him or her like an ever-present "Greek chorus.")*

Besides considering the greater social context, we think of the "family" as all relatives extending back at least two generations, including any "transient" members who might be related even if only superficially at any given time. We also tend to include the influence of relations who are physically distant or deceased. Examples of these include working with the surviving widow or widower or the relationship between one family member and a deceased parent, grandparent or, as we saw in "Samuel's Dream," even a great-grandfather. Unfinished past relationships linger like ghosts, shadowy, indistinct, yet still troubling, and we exorcise them by working with the couple or family in the here and now.

15. VALUE: *The "third-person" entity of the relationship.*
PRINCIPLE: *In couple therapy, interventions must be both systemic and complementary. Interventions with one person and not the other—positive or negative—will not be beneficial to the system.*

This value and principle acknowledge that every couple is composed of three individuals—a "you," a "me," and a "we." Gestalt couple therapy, being process and system oriented, tends to study the relational space occurring between two people. In couples work, we pay special attention to the interactions of both partners as a unit and balance all observations and interventions in terms of the "we-ness" of the couple. This is the case even in individual work with a lone partner, as we saw in the example of Gabriel and his absent spouse, Sue.

16. VALUE: *The collective voice of the couple or family.*
PRINCIPLE: *Attend to the unique voice (in the psyche and system) as well as to the pattern of voices.*

You can hear the aesthetic quality of a couple or family members as they interact with one another, just as you would in listening to a musical performance. Opera often comes to mind. Harmony and cacophony, rising and falling, ebb and flow, the tone, volume, and give-and-take rhythm of conversation tell us much about the individuals together and as a system. Energy, boundaries, dominance, resistances, and many other characteristics are conveyed in the couple or family's vocal patterns.

Values of Form

17. VALUE: *Completed gestalten.*
PRINCIPLE: *We focus on how the couple's or family's very strength creates disowned parts that need to be uncovered and reintegrated into their inner life. We always start from their strengths, not their weaknesses.*

The Harrison family's strength was that it banded together around their son, Max, in his process of dying. But after he was gone, they found themselves at a loss in their personal grief and alienated from one another. What was missing was the familial sharing of grief. As a result, the gestalt of Max's absence remained incomplete, the loss of his presence lingered on. In watching the Harrisons, the image of a Greek tragedy comes to mind: a beautiful son taken by the gods and the house of the family falls under the weight of its own grief. The only difference here is that Max was not the tragic hero . . . it was the family system itself. Its tragic flaw? its inability to come together and mourn with one another. Even something as simple as the experiment of a little birthday ritual was enough to begin uniting the family toward "completing the circle" of the unfinished gestalten.

A family's strength is often paradoxically its own weakness and vice versa. This is why we start with an appreciation of its strength—its goodness—followed by an observation of the negative side or disadvantage caused by that strength. In Platonic thought, a Form is necessary in order to hold a dialogue, a discussion, in the search for truth. In therapy with couples and families, change occurs by heightening awareness through contact, and while contact can take many forms, it is mainly achieved within dialogue—the encounter of I-Thou. Our three-step intervention strategy is a dialectical process culminating in the synthesis of an experiment. Our interventions are intended to heighten awareness and learning by first supporting what is, then contrasting it with what is not, and finally integrating both sides into a new gestalt, a new what is.

18. VALUE: *Good form.*
PRINCIPLE: *We let the couple or family be, and we let them go. (And regardless of how they are being and where they are going, we support the good form that is "just good enough.")*

Every couple or family, much like an individual painting, has a form that can be experienced, evaluated, appreciated, and critiqued. The aesthetic judgment of a painting—in this case, let us say a painting the viewer does not like—is just that: a judgment based on a particular value system. A value system is merely a unique stance in the world, a place to see from. A painting itself is neither right nor wrong; every work of art is "just different." On the other hand, neither is the critic wrong in subscribing to a particular set of preferred values. If we consider the case of the Houghton family, we see that their form as a system was stuck in blaming behaviors. Their interactive pattern was based on assumptions and interpretations. This can be considered a kind of good form—they feel strongly about one another and are striving for contact—but is it good enough? What was missing from the system was the basic curiosity about one another that leads to more information, more understanding, greater tolerance, and mutual satisfaction. Have they been transformed into the perfect family? No, but their form was incrementally improved and for the time being is "just good enough." The therapist relieved pressure and anxiety, thus allowing the family to capitalize on its small improvement and so prepare itself for more work in the future.

19. VALUE: *The importance of the whole therapeutic relationship as an integrated entity and aesthetic event.*
PRINCIPLE: *We stress the process of therapy (and intervention) and its quality of movement. We value seeing beauty, as well as ugliness, and the aesthetic validity of the client-system's struggle with its symptoms and pathology.*

20. VALUE: *The developmental integrity of Gestalt therapy.*
PRINCIPLE: *We seek the simple beauty found in therapeutic interventions having themes, developments, and resolutions. Every therapy encounter is potentially a work of art.*

21. VALUE: *The integrity of the couple or family as they are right now.*
PRINCIPLE: *We accept the person/system where they are, join them, and encounter them with a sense of appreciation for their existing competence.*

We view not only the couple or family's process but the entire system of therapy, including the aesthetic form of the therapist's presence and interventions, as an aesthetic event. The client-system, as individuals and as a whole, struggles with its problems, while the therapist is there working at their boundary as a benevolent, supportive, and involved witness. As in the earliest days of our personal Gestalt therapy experience, we help our clients leave the consultation room feeling "friendlier" with the very source of their bothersome, painful experiences. We help them recognize that their symptoms and behaviors, even their resistances, are creative efforts that have goodness, aesthetic validity, and purpose. We strive to help them leave each therapy session with the sense that they as persons are affirmed as "good."

Much of what we do as "artists" is based on framing phenomenological data about the system's process in terms of a metaphor or a theme. This gives the couple or family a greater perspective on how they are with one another and their problems.

22. VALUE: *The phenomenology of the here and now.*
PRINCIPLE: *We look for patterns in both the psyche and the larger system. The most useful observations are based on actual phenomenological/process observations.*

Gestalt couple and family therapy values *what is*—the actual, the immediate, and the tangible. We are not interested in speculation, interpretation, or categorization for their own sakes. On the other hand, this does not necessarily mean that we eschew all basic tools of our business such as personality tests, genograms, the DSM-IV, and other diagnostic instruments. In the Gestalt approach, for example, we tend to "diagnose and classify" system phenomena in terms of contact-resistance and boundary patterns. Such tools are important for clinical determinations and provide good background information, but they remain just that: background and only secondary in purpose. For instance, identifying the Madiar family as a "retroflected system" is logical based on their history and current behavior and is quite useful. But what will they be like in the next session? Or a month from now? Every therapy is a new meeting, and so what remains figural for us at all times are the phenomenological aspects of the immediate interactive encounter with and among the couple or family members. These aspects include dimensions of time, space, change, awareness, sensation, polarized specialization, energy, choreography of movement and location, beauty, balance, harmony, complementarity, rhythm, contrast, quality of contact, nature of withdrawal, capacity to let go and start over again, humor, and a sense of the philosophical.

From our point of view, each session with a couple or family is a new encounter with "what is" and so is much like taking a new trip to the art museum to see a different work by the same artist.

Conclusion

These are the core values of our Gestalt approach to couple and family therapy. Notice how each value supports and guides a technical skill or caveat. Perhaps the inclusion of each principle is superfluous because when you are clear about your values, then you can act clearly in the world. In other words, techniques, if relied on exclusively, eventually become blinders limiting your vision and growth. When you have sought out and assimilated integral values, you naturally have a "style": a distinctive stance of being-in-the-world. Technique is no longer needed, because you possess something far more powerful and profound—a philosophical approach—making personal creativity endless.

Gestalt values give us a particular way of intervening in couple and family systems, but they should not be taken as categorical imperatives. Here we must be careful to slowly and consciously "chew over" our values because, if "swallowed whole," then in just a few years' time, our statements of value and principle degenerate into merely a new set of slogans. Gestalt therapy, like other therapies, has had enough slogans in its history. Finally, one last advantage to possessing values means that one can make *choices for action* based on rules of conduct, while knowing that these rules are not monolithic but living and breathing things, changing with the changing times.

We express our values by acting in the world.[17] We must

act. Even when we choose not to act, our very inactivity expresses a value (boredom, indifference, tacit agreement, nonattachment, passive protest, and so on). Besides, when we restrain action we must retroflect, often hurting ourselves when turning the expressive energy against ourselves. The question is, How can we "act well" in the world?

When the children of Israel were traveling from Egypt during the biblical days of Exodus, God kept trying to help them through Moses. In rereading the Book of Exodus, one finds that very often the Israelites did not listen to God and thoughtlessly did what they pleased. Finally, when Moses presented the Book of the Covenant to the people, they replied, "All that the Lord has said, we will heed and do."[18] The command was to act in accordance with God's order and *only later to understand.* God behaved the way we do with young children, carrying the awareness function for them. They were his "children." We say "Don't hit Johnny" to a two-year-old because the young child does not have adequate awareness and inner control to make that choice personally. When one becomes an adult, one puts away childish things and begins to carry awareness for oneself and, in that sense, one becomes one's own "god"—meaning, I become a person as I become fully aware. As that happens, I substitute my own ontological commands for God's categorical imperatives. I say, "I will do this because it feels right to me." In the words of Sonia Nevis, "It is our fate to destroy. Destructuring is necessary for something new to occur, for growth to take place. Therefore, we often feel good when we partake in destructuring. However, that it 'feels good' is not a sufficient condition for actions. 'Feeling good' is a child's criterion—we are adults when our actions flow from complex awareness. For example, it may feel good to discontinue a relationship, but in that particular case this act may be deemed 'immoral' when taking everything into consideration. . . . It may feel good to stab someone in a fit of jealousy, but it isn't moral."[19] The comfort of acting according to a higher authority's categorical imperatives is that at the moment of choice we may not need to struggle as much. Nevertheless, when we consider all possible outcomes, all final actions are in a sense arbitrary. It is impossible to act righteously without denying a piece of reality. *There are no pure moral acts.* If a person chooses to be "free" and leaves his or her spouse, it is also a choice of abandoning another and the choice to see one's children less frequently. If a woman chooses an abortion for the sake of health, she also chooses to destroy a potential life; if she chooses to have the child, she may also choose to suffer from poor health and possibly to place the child in the world without a fair prospect of adequate supports for growth. If a group chooses to free all the animals from a laboratory, it also chooses to destroy scientific study and the devoted work of other people.

Our theory encourages us to complete a gestalt and thus to resolve something within us so we feel complete. But again, the voice of Sonia Nevis: "The weakness in our Gestalt theory is that it presents an ideal picture of no disturbances in the field. But disturbances in the field—out there—are profound . . . [and at times] the best we can do is to reduce the inner disturbances because there is no way to reduce the outer disturbances."[20] We cannot control the environment all the time. As best as we can, we must use our richest awareness, because all human behavior has its polar possibility embedded within it. We listen to both (or all) voices in our heads, and then we act. The more complex our awareness is, the more complex our potential actions become. Informed actions allow us to know many sides of a given issue. This kind of singular outcome has been called "acting with regret." Acting with regret means to choose to do something while recognizing that it must also have a range of consequences, some of them bad for oneself, for another, for one's family, or for the world. *Because of the nature of polarities, you can never, never not do harm. Therefore, our decision is always made with regret at best; the choice is the best possible act.* And so we cannot avoid hurting others, and we must learn to carry the disapproval and pain of others with us. This makes it imperative that we make our choices with the highest standards of responsibility. And we can learn to do that with some semblance of humility, courage, and compassion.

Perhaps never more so than today are our responsibility, courage, and compassion needed, since it now increasingly falls to the therapist to help heal disturbed, broken, and changing families. In this age of disintegrating families, a growing divorce rate, and the dynamic restructuring of newly formed family entities, we need to honor and cherish old-fashioned and beautiful notions of *taking care of our children* and *supporting respect within couples*. We need to remind ourselves repeatedly that this is an age of incredible stress on our children, who by the age of kindergarten are prodded by their overworked and overburdened parents to show enormous self-support and high performance levels. This is the age when our children can no longer afford not to understand computers and high technology. It means that adults must practice both discipline and compassion to nurture the younger generation for preparation of life in the twenty-first century. This book repeatedly shows concern for and attention to how a couple and then a family can nurture basic values of mutual caretaking and respect in their struggles from one life stage to another. The therapist is not only a healer but a grandparently figure who bestows blessings on a generation of young parents whose own parents did not have either the skills or the time to prepare them for the complexities of modern life.

Notes to Chapter Twelve

1. I am grateful to my close friend and colleague Donna Rumenik for our many conversations about the centrality of values, both Gestalt and personal, in therapy. Our conversations led to the "Development of the Therapist" workshops we conducted for many years that focused on therapists becoming more aware of their own values underlying their work. Rumenik encouraged me to present in a larger forum the importance of Gestalt values, which led in turn to my opening address at the 1986 Gestalt Journal conference. She has read, re-read, challenged, and supported my writings in this area over many years. This section was adapted from J. Zinker (1986), "Gestalt values: Maturing of Gestalt therapy," keynote address at the 8th annual Conference on the Theory and Practice of Gestalt Therapy, May 1986, Provincetown, Mass.
2. The idea of an aesthetic appreciation of visual phenomena is inherent in Gestalt psychology. According to W. Köhler (1947), *Gestalt psychology: An introduction to new concepts in modern psychology,* (New York: Liveright, pp. 176–177, original emphasis),

"Simple," "complicated," "regular," "harmonious," are words which invariably refer to products of organization. When we call something "symmetrical," this something is certainly a segregated object. Similarly, "slender," "round," "angular," "clumsy," "graceful" are specific properties of things or extended events. From these instances there is only one step to such more particular shape-qualities as are given in characteristic appearance of a circle, a triangle, a pear, an oak tree, and so forth. These qualities, too, occur only as attributes of specific entities . . . . Ehrenfels, taking the case of shape as the most important and obvious among his qualities, used the name *"Gestaltqualitäten"* for all of them . . . . The general definition of this term applies to the specific properties of a melody, for instance, to its "major" and "minor" character, just as it does to the "angularity" of a figure. Movements as visual facts have *Gestaltqualitäten* which are temporal and spatial at the same time. As examples may serve forms of dancing and the characteristic movements of animals such as "jumping" or "creeping."

3. See K. Koffka (1935), *Principles of Gestalt psychology* (New York: Harcourt Brace).
4. Köhler was a cultured man who had a great appreciation for art, especially music, and one of his earliest books was devoted to values in life. See W. Köhler (1966), *The place of value in a world of fact* (New York: Liveright, originally published 1938).
5. F. S. Perls, R. Hefferline, & P. Goodman (1951), *Gestalt therapy: Excitement and growth in the human personality* (Ne York: Julian Press).
6. Perls, Hefferline, & Goodman (1951, pp. 2 -287).
7. Perls, Hefferline, & Goodman (1951, p. 32.
8. Perls, Hefferline, & Goodman (1951, p. 329).
9. According to Isadore From, who began therapy with Perls in 1946, Perls was still at that time using the psychoanalytic touch. See E. Rosenfeld (1981), "An oral history of gestalt therapy, part two: A conversation with Isadore From," in J. Wysong & E. Rosenfeld (Eds.), *An oral history of Gestalt therapy* (Highland, N.Y.: Gestalt Journal, p. 27).
10. The first quotation applies to the context of psychotherapy. These quotations are taken from Perls, Hefferline, & Goodman (1951, pp. 275–276, 294).
11. Perls was intellectually (and personally) irritated with Abraham Maslow because he felt this *active* quality of becoming was missing from Maslow's theories. Maslow's Platonic ideals were not dynamic enough to satisfy Perls.

12. Perls, Hefferline, & Goodman (1951, p. 271).
13. Perls, Hefferline, & Goodman (1951, p. 171).
14. S. Nevis & E. Warner (1983), "Conversing about Gestalt couple and family therapy," *Gestalt Journal, 6*(2), 9.
15. Nevis & Warner (1983, p. 9).
16. The following section was adapted from J. Zinker (1993), "Polemics, systems, and the nature of interventions," address to the seventh British Gestalt Conference, Cambridge University, England.
17. The concept of ethical regret was developed by Sonia Nevis and Edwin Nevis. For a fuller discussion, see E. Nevis (1987), *Organizational consulting: A Gestalt approach* (New York: Gestalt Institute of Cleveland Press).
18. Here is the full passage: "Taking the book of the Covenant, he [Moses] read it aloud to the people, who answered, 'All that the Lord has said, we will heed and do.' Then he took the blood and sprinkled it upon the people, saying, 'This is the blood of the covenant which the Lord has made with you in accordance with all these words of his" (Exodus 2:7–8).
19. Personal communication.
20. Personal communication.

Appendix: Profiles of the Major Schools of Family Therapy

Behavioral Family Therapy[1]

Forerunners	Watson, Skinner, Bandura, Grindler
Philosophy	Empiricism
Model	Behaviorism; content oriented.
Major influences	Behavior modification, learning theory, operant conditioning, contingency management.

Note: I developed this chart by gathering and interpreting information from A. S. Gurman & D. P. Kniskern (1991), *Handbook of family therapy* (Vols. 1 & 2) (New York: Brunner/Mazel). I do not claim comprehensive knowledge of all these schools of thought and so, in the event of any possible misinterpretation, I ask for the reader's understanding and forgiveness.

View of function	Achieving goals; all members of equal influence.
View of dysfunction	Members have difficulty recognizing deviant behaviors; lack of clearly defined family rules; deficiency in emotional communication.
View of awareness	No formal theory of awareness.
View of change	Behaviorally defined and supported by education and conditional reinforcement.

Bowen Therapy[2]

Forerunners	Medicine, physics.
Philosophy	Natural philosophy, empiricism, evolutionism.
Model	Medical, natural systems, process oriented.
Major influences	Biology, evolutionism, systems theory.
View of function	"Life moves toward life" in a natural process leading to maturation and self-regulation.
View of dysfunction	Lack of self-regulation from "immaturity."
View of awareness	No formal theory of awareness.
View of change	Self-regeneration through differentiation, self-regulation, and self-responsibility; therapist's presence as agent of change.

Brief Therapy (MRI)[3]

Forerunners	Bateson, Erickson, Foerster.
Philosophy	Constructivism.
Model	Cybernetic, nonnormative, process and content oriented.
Major influences	Cybernetics, communication theory.
View of function	Efficient handling of difficulties.
View of dysfunction	Problems occur from the *mishandling* of difficulties.

View of awareness	Secondary; no formal theory of awareness.
View of change	Induced by intervening in the problem-causing "solutions" used by the client(s) to solve the presenting problem.

Contextual Therapy[4]

Forerunners	Freud, Ferenczi, Klein, Fairbairn, Winnicott, Guntrip, Sullivan, Buber, Weiner, Bateson, Boszormenyi-Nagy.
Philosophy	Dialectical, dialogic, philosophical anthropology.
Model	Relational, process oriented.
Major influences	Cybernetics, object relations, interpersonal psychiatry, communications theory.
View of function	Balanced distribution of family resources and relational options.
View of dysfunction	Imbalanced distribution of resources, stagnation through "destructive entitlement," detrimental relationship configurations, split and/or invisible loyalties, collusion, exploitation, parentification.
View of awareness	"Relational accountability" is primary; no formal theory of awareness.
View of change	Insight is one component of the healing process; change depends on deepening the "relational reality" of the group.

Ericksonian Family Therapy[5]

Forerunners	Freud, hypnosis.
Philosophy	Eclecticism and pragmatism.
Model	Ecosystemic.
Major influences	Hypnotherapy, content oriented.
View of function	Growth and development through creative problem solving that allow for the flexible stimulation of individual resources.

View of dysfunction	Unconsciousness of personal resources, lack of communication, symptoms as communications.
View of awareness	Secondary; insight is bypassed in favor of learning through action; no formal theory of awareness.
View of change	Achieving goals that increase flexibility and self-expression to further family evolution.

Focal Family Therapy[6]

Forerunners	Freud, Klein, Bion, Winnicott.
Philosophy	Empiricism.
Model	Systemic; process and content oriented.
Major influences	Psychoanalysis, hospital psychiatry, object relations, group/family therapy.
View of function	A seven-level hierarchy of functioning based on interaction, meaning, affect, communication, boundaries, alliances, stability, and competence.
View of dysfunction	Past trauma indicated by interactions marked by repetition, irrelevance, vicious circles, compulsion, urgency, and presenting problems (symptoms).
View of awareness	Of equal importance with change in behavioral patterns; no formal theory of awareness.
View of change	Resolution of family trauma and reconstruction of the family culture.

Functional Family Therapy[7]

Forerunners	(?)
Philosophy	Empiricism and (apparently) relativism.
Model	Systems theory and behaviorism; relational; process and content oriented.
Major influences	Palo Alto Group.

View of function	Efficient relational processes lead directly to purposeful and consistent relational outcomes; mediation between distance and intimacy in relationships.
View of dysfunction	"Problems" and "symptoms" (so-labeled by cultural consensus) are indicative of a relational functionality.
View of awareness	Mixed; no formal theory of awareness.
View of change	Change occurs after a change in how family members view themselves and others.

Integrative Family Therapy[8]

Forerunners	Auerswald, Bateson, Erickson, Minuchin, Piaget, Satir.
Philosophy	Eclecticism.
Model	Systemic; organismic; process and content oriented.
Major influences	Systems theory
View of function	The conscious ability to exercise a range of behaviors instead of repetitive, automatic responses; strong sense of competence, well-being, and self-esteem.
View of dysfunction	System marked by automatic behaviors, rituals, no novelty, blocked to new information, closed boundaries; relational flow is marked by blockage, unwillingness, inaccessibility.
View of awareness	Essential and multileveled in keeping with an integrated, systemic approach; no formal theory of awareness.
View of change	Change occurs after automatic and familiar behaviors become strange.

Milan Systemic Approach[9]

Forerunners	Freud, Jackson, Haley, Watzlawick, Bateson.

Philosophy	Ecosystemic epistemology.
Model	Systemic; contextual; process and content oriented.
Major influences	Second-order cybernetics ("the cybernetics of cybernetics"); constructivism.
View of function	What works for the individuals involved.
View of dysfunction	The problem is the meaning unit created by the distress and all members involved in supporting that meaning comprise the treatment unit.
View of awareness	Mixed: change depends on new relational connections and meanings, not insights; no formal theory of awareness.
View of change	Change levels of meaning to a higher-order context to change worldview and behavior.

Strategic Family Therapy[10]

Forerunners	Erickson.
Philosophy	Pragmatism (?)
Model	Direct, planned intervention; content oriented.
Major influences	Laing, Haley, Madanes.
View of function	To control the negative, encourage the positive, and solve shared problems.
View of dysfunction	All problems stem from a dilemma between love versus violence.
View of awareness	Problem solving favored over insight or awareness; no formal theory of awareness.
View of change	Change occurs when the family learns to overcome its crisis and move on to the next stage of its development.

Structural Family Therapy[11]

Forerunners	Freud, Sullivan.

Philosophy	Constructivism.
Model	Biosociocultural systemic; process and content oriented.
Major influences	Montalvo, Haley, Minuchin, Koestler, Prigogine.
View of function	The family effectively handling stressors in fulfilling its function of nurturing the growth of its members.
View of dysfunction	The family cannot fulfill the function of nurturing the growth of its members.
View of awareness	Mixed: implicitly addressed by techniques such as "enactment" and structural changes; on the other hand, resistance is either circumvented or confronted. No formal theory of awareness.
View of change	Almost the therapist's sole responsibility to "make it happen."

Symbolic-Experiential Family Therapy[12]

Forerunners	Freud, Rank, Klein, Aichorn
Philosophy	(?)
Model	Process oriented.
Major influences	Child psychiatry, play therapy.
View of function	Structural integrity; clearly defined boundaries; flexible subsystems; emotional process supports expression and love.
View of dysfunction	Disorganized boundaries; nonfunctional subsystems; emotional process supports inauthenticity and conflict.
View of awareness	Immediate experience and affect valued; insight is seen as a by-product; cognitive realization of change is secondary; no formal theory of awareness.
View of change	New relationships and behaviors precipitate change.

Notes to Appendix

1. I. R. H. Fallon (1991), "Behavioral family therapy," in A. S. Gurman & D. P. Kniskern (Eds.), *Handbook of family therapy* (Vol. 2) (New York: Brunner/Mazel, pp. 65–85).
2. E. H. Friedman (1991), "Bowen theory and therapy," in A. S. Gurman & D. P. Kniskern (Eds.), *Handbook of family therapy* (Vol. 2) (New York: Brunner/Mazel, pp. 134–170).
3. L. Segal (1991), "Brief therapy: The MRI approach," in A. S. Gurman & D. P. Kniskern (Eds.), *Handbook of family therapy* (Vol. 2) (New York: Brunner/Mazel, pp. 171–199).
4. I. Boszormenyi-Nagy, J. Grunebaum, & D. Ulrich (1991), "Contextual therapy," in A. S. Gurman & D. P. Kniskern (Eds.), *Handbook of family therapy* (Vol. 2) (New York: Brunner/Mazel, pp. 200–238).
5. S. R. Lankton, C. H. Lankton, & W. J. Matthews (1991), "Ericksonian family therapy," in A. S. Gurman & D. P. Kniskern (Eds.), *Handbook of family therapy* (Vol. 2) (New York: Brunner/Mazel, pp. 239–283).
6. A. Bentovin & W. Kinston (1991), "Focal family therapy: Joining systems theory with psychodynamic understanding," in A. S. Gurman & D. P. Kniskern (Eds.), *Handbook of family therapy* (Vol. 2) (New York: Brunner/Mazel, pp. 284–324).
7. C. Barton & J. F. Alexander (1991), "Functional family therapy," in A. S. Gurman & D. P. Kniskern (Eds.), *Handbook of family therapy* (Vol. 1) (New York: Brunner/Mazel, pp. 403–443).
8. B. S. Duhl & F. J. Duhl (1991), "Integrative family therapy," in A. S. Gurman & D. P. Kniskern (Eds.), *Handbook of family therapy* (Vol. 1) (New York: Brunner/Mazel, pp. 483–513).
9. D. Campbell, R. Draper, & E. Crutchley (1991), "The Milan systemic approach to family therapy," in A. S. Gurman & D. P. Kniskern (Eds.), *Handbook of family therapy* (Vol. 2) (New York: Brunner/Mazel, pp. 325–362).
10. C. Madanes (1991), "Strategic family therapy," in A. S. Gurman & D. P. Kniskern (Eds.), *Handbook of family therapy* (Vol. 2) (New York: Brunner/Mazel, pp. 396–416).
11. J. Colapinto (1991), "Structural family therapy," in A. S. Gurman & D. P. Kniskern (Eds.), *Handbook of family therapy* (Vol. 2) (New York: Brunner/Mazel, pp. 417–443).
12. L. G. Roberto (1991), "Symbolic-experiential family therapy," in A. S. Gurman & D. P. Kniskern (Eds.), *Handbook of family therapy* (Vol. 2) (New York: Brunner/Mazel, pp. 444–476).

Index

W

Z